Recasting Welfare Capitalism

Mark I. Vail

Recasting Welfare Capitalism

Economic Adjustment in Contemporary France and Germany

TEMPLE UNIVERSITY PRESS
Philadelphia

Mark I. Vail is Assistant Professor in the Department of Political Science at Tulane University. He is a contributor to *The State after Statism,* edited by Jonah D. Levy, and has published work in *Comparative Politics, European Journal of Political Research,* and *West European Politics,* among other venues.

TEMPLE UNIVERSITY PRESS
Philadelphia PA 19122
www.temple.edu/tempress

Published 2010
Printed in the United States of America

Library of Congress Cataloging-in-Publication Data

Vail, Mark I.
Recasting welfare capitalism : economic adjustment in contemporary France and Germany / Mark I. Vail.

p. cm.
Includes bibliographical references and index.
ISBN 978-1-59213-967-5 (cloth : alk. paper)
1. Welfare state—France. 2. Capitalism—France. 3. Welfare state—Germany. 4. Capitalism—Germany. I. Title.

HN425.5.V35 2009
330.12'60943—dc22 2009013154

031411-P

In memory of Bernadette Popovitch

Contents

List of Tables

Preface

How and why capitalism changes is among the most important and most difficult questions in comparative politics. As the Heisenberg uncertainty principle teaches us in the study of particle physics, it is often difficult to measure the position and momentum of particles with equal precision. Similarly, in comparative political economy, many have chosen to emphasize either the "position" or the "momentum" of advanced capitalist countries, thereby capturing important aspects of political-economic dynamics while neglecting others. Structural approaches, whether Marxist, sociological, or institutional, tend to highlight capitalism's enduring class or institutional foundations. Except with respect to rare and cataclysmic moments such as revolution or depression, however, such approaches fail to capture the subtle mechanisms through which capitalism changes, or else they assume unproblematically that capitalism will continue to evolve in ways that are consistent with broad historical trajectories, characterized by vague monikers such as "late" or "advanced." Other, more "voluntarist" approaches tend to emphasize change and the role of human volition, whether of groups or of individuals, more than underlying structures. Such perspectives are good at capturing the process of change but often gloss over the organizational and institutional predicates that provide capitalist economies with long-term stability.

This book grew out of my dissatisfaction with both tendencies. It provides a synthetic analysis of change in the welfare states and broader political economies of two advanced industrial countries over a period of several decades. For reasons both disciplinary and ideological, studies of these two domains of capitalism have remained largely separate; this book aims to help bridge that gap. It also works to remedy some of the relatively thin treatments of politics that are prevalent in contemporary comparative political economy. It sees politics not merely as a foundational bargain (between, say, employers and the working class or workers and social-democratic parties) or as an institutionally congealed underpinning for relatively static national features, but, rather, as a fluid—but identifiable and traceable—driver of political and economic change. In this way, it represents an attempt to reconnect analytically the institutional structures of capitalism to the evolving political relationships that govern its adjustment.

Unfortunately, there has been more recent change in advanced capitalist societies than in the analytical tools used to study them. In the mid-1960s, Andrew Shonfield's magisterial *Modern Capitalism* eloquently conveyed the diversity of postwar capitalist systems and inspired a rich series of scholarly studies of that variation and explanations for its endurance. Since the 1970s, major strands of comparative political economy—from studies of corporatism in the 1970s and 1980s, to the proliferation of studies of the state in the 1980s and 1990s, to the more recent and influential "Varieties of Capitalism" approach inaugurated by Peter Hall and David Soskice, to the "worlds-of-welfare" school initiated by Gøsta Esping-Andersen—have continued along similar lines. As a result, we have a rich array of studies of variation in certain aspects of capitalist economies and advanced welfare states but relatively few accounts that explore how and why broad models of *welfare capitalism* change as they do. Work that does explore such drivers of change has often reverted to tropes about "globalization" (often invoked but rarely defined) or "politics" (used as a catchall category). Though this book is far from a comprehensive response to these concerns, it suggests a fruitful path for, and an initial step or two toward, developing one.

Like the welfare-capitalist systems that it describes, this book has developed in two distinct stages, during each of which I have incurred more debt to more people than I can adequately convey. The first stage involved the research for and writing of the dissertation that provided the foundation for the book while I was at the University of California, Berkeley. Without my dissertation committee—Jonah Levy, Gerald Feldman, Margaret Weir, J. Nicholas Ziegler, and John Zysman—I could not have gotten this project off the ground. Margaret and Nick provided patient support and engaged critically with the work in ways that improved it immeasurably. My dissertation chair, Jonah Levy, has been both a continuing source of support and the very model of an energetic and conscientious scholar. It is to him that I owe my greatest intellectual (as well as an important personal) debt.

At Berkeley, I also benefited from intellectual and personal guidance from friends and colleagues, many of whom continue to offer their support. Wade Jacoby and Pepper Culpepper offered important views on the German case;

John Cioffi educated me on the complexities of German finance; and Julie Lynch helped me to keep things in perspective during some difficult periods. Robert Adcock, Nick Biziouras, Ben Bowyer, Anamika Chakravorty, Iris Davis, Bill Hurst, Alison Kaufman, Naomi Levy, Sally Roever, Nadav Shelef, Sara Watson, Sarah and Kevin Wiliarty, and Daniel Ziblatt have provided the kind of friendship that makes the profession so rewarding. Outside Berkeley, Chris Howell became a mentor and has continued to offer incisive and supportive criticism of my work, encouraging me to persevere and providing an exceptional model of engaged scholarship.

I received support from a number of institutions and programs while conducting research for this book. The Alexander von Humboldt Foundation provided me with outstanding financial and institutional support in the form of a Bundeskanzler Fellowship in 2000 and 2001, and a Chateaubriand Fellowship from the French Embassy to the United States supported me during the following year in Paris. In Berlin, the Wissenschaftszentrum Berlin für Sozialforschung (WZB) equipped me with an elegant office and excellent logistical support, and David Soskice offered helpful feedback on my work. In Paris, the Centre de Sociologie des Organisations graciously allowed me to use its facilities. I also benefited from Anton Hemerijck's hospitality and insight during a visit to the Netherlands on the occasion of a collaborative project and from Bruno Palier's important guidance throughout my work in France.

I also forged a number of important friendships (both in Europe and at home) through which I received the moral support that helped me complete the early stage of my work. Philippe, Laurent, Jean-Claude, and Bernadette Popovitch and Edwige Le Brettevillois have long been my second family, through whom I gained priceless, firsthand access to French political and social life seen through native eyes. Eliza Garrison and Ryan Minor helped to turn a fascinating year in Berlin into a truly memorable experience. Robert Fannion, who has been a close friend and colleague since we met at the WZB in 2000, continues to provide me with helpful feedback on my work. Other friends, of less recent vintage, were no less important: Denise and Brent Glass, Kerry and Craig Herrmann, Cathy Rearick, and Julie Stewart were there when I needed a shoulder or an ear or assistance with some thorny problem in the dissertation.

The second phase of this book's development involved three eventful years at Tulane University in New Orleans, during which I began the painful but rewarding process of converting my dissertation into a book. I arrived at Tulane in July 2005, a proverbial "freshly minted" Ph.D. eager to begin his scholarly career. Even before I could teach my first class, however, the city was hit by Hurricane Katrina, that hybrid catastrophe born of equal parts malevolent weather, stunning governmental incompetence, and depressing human indifference. After evacuating, watching in horror as my newly adopted city filled with water, and then evacuating again with my parents ahead of Hurricane Rita three weeks later, I struggled to keep my eye on the scholarly ball as I fought to rebuild my home and secure the insurance proceeds that, despite the fact that we were entitled to them, so many New Orleans residents were being denied. This set of events, which could not help but change me personally in important ways, also provided powerful testaments to the importance of research on social protection and state capacity. The ongoing international economic crisis provides yet another powerful reminder of the importance of these issues.

It is a gross understatement to say that the support of others was crucial during this time. Bill and Alma Davis gave my parents and me a home during the first two weeks after the second storm. The Minda de Gunzburg Center for European Studies (CES) at Harvard University provided an outstanding intellectual home at a time when I had none; Linda Bamber offered shelter, friendship, and the insight and counsel of a senior faculty member; Patricia Craig and Abby Collins at the CES helped me to navigate Harvard's institutional landscape; and Peter Hall patiently read the entire manuscript and provided me with invaluable feedback. I can never thank them enough for helping me to keep my career on track and my sanity intact.

After I returned to Tulane when it reopened in January 2006, I forged relationships with friends and colleagues who continue to make life in this wonderful city wonderful. I am grateful to my chair, Tony Pereira, and my senior colleagues in the Department of Political Science for their guidance. I am also indebted to Brian and Christy Brox, Chris Fettweis, J. Celeste Lay, Aaron Schneider, and Dana Zartner, all of whom have offered an admixture of supportive friendship and helpful advice, and to Jo-Ellen Miller for her cheerful administrative assistance. The friendships of Judy Ruch and Tony and Donna Cook are additional reminders of the kinds of unique personal connections that this imperfect but beautiful city fosters.

This book also owes much to the support provided by Tulane University. A Committee on Research Summer Grant, a Provost's Award for Faculty–Student Engagement, and a Phase II Research Enhancement Fund Award from the university helped me to complete follow-up research. The H. Sophie Newcomb Memorial College Institute also provided financial assistance, in the form of a Faculty Research Summer Grant; I thank Janice Mulvihill, Rebecca Mark, and the Newcomb Fellows Grant Committee in particular for this support. I am also grateful to George Bernstein and Anne McCall in the School of Liberal Arts for their help, to Xingzhou Liu for research assistance, and to Eric Wedig for providing the kind of library assistance that most scholars can only dream about.

During my field research in Europe over the past two years, I have benefited from the support of a number of people and institutions. In the summer of 2007, I spent two months at the Max-Planck-Institut für Gesellschaftsforschung in

Cologne, which is a model community of engaged scholars. Marius Busemeyer, Martin Höpner, Philipp Klages, Armin Schäfer, Wolfgang Streeck, and Raymund Werle—as well as Jürgen Lautwein in the institute's administrative office and Elke Bürger and Susanne Hilbring in the (outstanding) library—provided me with assistance and unparalleled hospitality. Achim and Andrea Goerres have become friends in the course of my work in Germany; I thank them in particular for hosting me on the occasion of my talk at the University of Cologne in July 2008. In Paris, I am indebted to the Centre d'Etudes Européennes at Sciences Po for an affiliation during the summer of 2008; to Olivier Borraz and Cornelia Woll for collegial support and suggestions; and to Nicolas Véron for providing me with invaluable contacts and advice.

During the long process of bringing this book to publication, my acquiring editor, Alex Holzman; my production editor, Joan Vidal; and the entire staff at Temple University Press have been wonderful from beginning to end. Publishing the book with them has been one of my best professional decisions.

I also extend special thanks to my parents, Gwyn and Dennis Vail, for their unwavering support. Throughout my scholarly career, they have provided me with friendship and cheered me on even when they may have doubted the wisdom of particular decisions. My father also helped me to edit the manuscript, and there are few better editors than he. The good of what I have become as a scholar and human being is in no small measure their doing; the flaws and limitations are my own.

Finally, I thank Charlotte Maheu, whose love and support have changed my life and helped to restore my faith in myself and my species. Although Charlotte, like so many others, was ill-treated by Katrina, she has never let it erode the warmth, sensitivity, energy, and optimism that make her unique. Among the many ways that Charlotte has contributed to my life, she has also provided incisive criticism of my work. I am inexpressibly grateful to her for everything that she has done, but most important of all, for being the person that she is. Thank you, Charlotte.

Abbreviations

AAH	*Allocation pour adulte handicapé*
AGIRC	Association Générale des Institutions de Retraite des Cadres
ANPE	Agence Nationale pour l'Emploi
APA	*Allocation personnalisée d'autonomie*
API	*Allocation de parent isolé*
ARRCO	Association des Régimes de Retraites Complémentaires
ASS	*Allocation de solidarité spécifique*
AUD	*Allocation unique dégressive*
BA	Bundesanstalt/Bundesagentur für Arbeit
BDA	Bundesvereinigung der Deutschen Arbeitgeberverbände
BDI	Bundesverband Deutscher Internisten
BPA	Berufsverband der Praktischen Ärzte und Ärzte für Allgemeinmedizin Deutschlands
BSHG	*Bundessozialhilfegesetz*
CDU	Christlich Demokratische Union Deutschlands
CFDT	Confédération Française Démocratique du Travail
CFTC	Confédération Française des Travailleurs Chrétiens
CGC	Confédération Générale des Cadres
CGP	Commissariat Général du Plan

CGPME	Confédération Générale des Petites et Moyennes Entreprises
CGT	Confédération Générale du Travail
CIASI	Comité Interministériel pour l'Aménagement des Structures Industrielles
CMU	*Couverture maladie universelle*
CNAMTS	Caisse Nationale d'Assurance-Maladie des Travailleurs Salariés
CNAVTS	Caisse Nationale d'Assurance-Vieillesse des Travailleurs Salariés
CNPF	Confédération Nationale du Patronat Français
CPE	*Contrat première embauche*
CSG	*Contribution sociale généralisée*
CSMF	Confédération des Syndicats Médicaux Français
CSU	Christlich Soziale Union
DARES	Direction de l'Animation de la Recherche, des Études, et des Statistiques
DATAR	Délégation à l'Aménagement du Territoire et à l'Action Régionale
DGB	Deutscher Gewerkschaftsbund
DM	Deutsche Mark
EDF–GDF	Electricité de France–Gaz de France
EMS	European Monetary System
EMU	European Economic and Monetary Union
ENA	Ecole Nationale d'Administration
ETC	Employment and training company
EU	European Union
FDP	Freie Demokratische Partei
FFr	French franc
FMF	Fédération des Médecins de France
FNE	Fonds National d'Emploi
FNS	Fonds National de Solidarité
FO	Force Ouvrière
GDR	German Democratic Republic
GRL	*Garantie de ressources licenciement*
IGF	*Impôt sur la grande fortune*
JUMP	*Sofortprogramm zum Abbau der Jugendarbeitslosigkeit*

KBV	Kassenärztlichen Bundesvereinigung
KfW	Kreditanstalt für Wiederaufbau
MEDEF	Mouvement des Entreprises de France
MG France	Fédération Française des Médecins Généralistes
NAIRU	Non-accelerating-inflation rate of unemployment
NAV	Verband der Niedergelassenen Ärzte Deutschlands
OECD	Organization for Economic Cooperation and Development
OPEC	Organization of the Petroleum Exporting Countries
ÖTV	Gewerkschaft Öffentliche Dienste, Transport und Verkehr
PAP	*Projet d'action personnalisé*
PARE	*Plan d'aide et de retour à l'emploi*
PCF	Parti Communiste Français
PDS	Partei des Demokratischen Sozialismus
PPAE	*Projet personnalisé d'accès à l'emploi*
PS	Parti Socialiste
PSD	*Prestation spécifique dépendance*
RATP	Régie Autonome des Transports Parisiens
RDS	*Remboursement de la dette sociale*
RMA	*Revenu minimum d'activité*
RMI	*Revenu minimum d'insertion*
RSA	*Revenu de solidarité active*
SED	Sozialistische Einheitspartei Deutschlands
SME	Small and medium-sized enterprise
SMIC	*Salaire minimum interprofessionnel de croissance*
SMIG	*Salaire minimum interprofessionnel garanti*
SML	Syndicat de la Médicine Libérale
SNCF	Société Nationale des Chemins de Fer Français
SPD	Sozialdemokratische Partei Deutschlands
SUD	Solidaires, Unitaires et Démocratiques
UDF	Union pour la Démocratie Française
UIMM	Union des Industries et Métiers de la Métallurgie
UNCAM	Union Nationale des Caisses d'Assurance-Maladie
UNEDIC	Union Nationale pour l'Emploi dans l'Industrie et le Commerce
VAT	Value-added tax
WASG	Arbeit und Soziale Gerechtigkeit—Die Wahlalternative

Introduction

Recasting Welfare Capitalism in an Age of Austerity

This book examines how national models of welfare capitalism evolve when they move from prosperous times to periods of economic austerity. The end of the postwar boom has presented policymakers in Western Europe and the United States with unprecedented challenges, including rising rates of unemployment, sluggish economic growth, declining rates of productivity, and growing fiscal and demographic pressures on the welfare state. Faced with the unenviable task of presiding over a period of economic austerity while struggling to hold on to power and preserve social peace, public officials across the advanced industrial world have cast about for ways to preserve central components of their postwar arrangements while adjusting them to growing competitive pressures, all with fewer political and economic resources at their disposal. This process of readjustment—similar in some respects to what Paul Pierson has called "recalibration"—has entailed significant reform of a wide array of policies and institutions, from labor markets, to systems of taxation, to policies of social protection.[1] No advanced industrial country has been exempt from this process of reform or from the political and social challenges arising from it.

This book investigates the dynamics of adjustment of national models of welfare capitalism through an analysis of French and German social- and economic-policy reform since the 1970s. It seeks to explain two basic facets of how advanced industrial societies transform when they shift from a climate of prosperity to one of austerity. First, it shows that the process of adjustment involves interrelated and mutually constitutive changes in social and economic policies. Prevailing approaches in the welfare-state and comparative-political-economy literatures tend to focus on particular policy areas at the expense of others that are equally instrumental for the process of economic adjustment. As a result, they leave us few tools for developing a systematic understanding of how political economies as broad institutional entities adjust to long-term changes in economic context.[2] This book, by contrast, analyzes how liberalization and adjustment to austerity transform systems of *welfare capitalism,* including both the welfare state and the broader political economy.

Equally important, it shows that the advent of economic austerity redefines the political processes through which reform takes place. As climates of prosperity give way to slowing growth and rising unemployment, the policy incentives facing and political resources available to key actors change. Over time, the political relationships that govern adjustment are renegotiated, often in unpredictable ways. This shift in political opportunities and incentives is driven in part by the discrediting of older models in the wake of their failure to manage the process of adjustment. As this erosion of credibility undermines the legitimacy and effective authority of actors that had been dominant under the older models, it creates pressures for new kinds of bargains that allow greater influence by actors that had previously been weak or marginalized. In the process, new coalitions emerge to drive the process of reform, often in ways that are quite different from what either the formal distributions of political authority in national political economies or past practice would lead us to expect.

By highlighting such shifts in both the substance of policy and the style of politics under austerity, this book offers a significant set of revisions to the postwar literature on "national models" of capitalism. The seminal work in this tradition was Andrew Shonfield's *Modern Capitalism,* which described how Britain, France, Germany, Italy, and the United States devised novel political-economic institutions that replaced the penury and destruction of the war with prosperity and economic renewal.[3] Shonfield and, later, scholars such as Peter Hall and John Zysman identified distinct national institutional configurations, which yielded enduring national patterns of political interaction and policy trajectories in advanced industrial countries.[4] In France, for example, a highly centralized and powerful state gave rise to an insular process of economic planning, the exclusion of weak and fragmented trade unions, and the neglect of shopkeepers and small business. French economic policy was governed by a "conspiracy in the public interest" between the state and powerful business groups that acted as the engine of rapid industrialization.[5] In Germany, by contrast, regular negotiations between a "semi-sovereign" state and powerful producer groups supported a consensual, gradual policymaking process in which the state was a first among equals.[6] In both countries, the character of politics was thus seen to flow predictably from formal constellations of political authority, even if the "new institutionalism" of the 1970s and 1980s placed increasing emphasis on informal relationships and political contingency.[7]

Though the work of Shonfield and his heirs provided critical insights into the varied character of national models of capitalism during the postwar boom, it has proved less well suited to understanding the climate of economic austerity since the mid-1970s. When growth rates were high and unemployment was low, the exercise of public authority was generally seen to be consistent with the public good. As the advanced industrial world stagnated in the 1970s, however, the very institutional configurations that had been credited with postwar success were blamed for failure. As a result, and as the near-revolution of May 1968 in France showed, marginalized political actors with little recourse to official levers of power could exert significant influence, though often in unconventional ways. Over time, such shifts in authority redefine prevailing relationships between governments and interest groups and transform national political dynamics as a result.

Models in Motion: Rethinking the Politics of Economic Austerity

To be sure, the concern with how countries adjust to austerity is hardly new. Since at least the time of John Maynard Keynes, and more recently in books such as Peter Gourevitch's *Politics in Hard Times,*[8] scholars of comparative political economy have examined how policy challenges shift with economic circumstances. Though inspired by work such as Gourevitch's, this book adopts a different perspective on the political effects of economic austerity. The central focus of work like Gourevitch's is how given economic interests, represented in constellations of social and economic actors, respond to discrete economic shocks. Though such structural perspectives show well how such shocks reshape policy regimes, they are less useful for identifying the evolving relationships among key political actors *within* a given policy regime or for showing how these changes redefine policy trajectories. By adopting an approach that is less structural and more political, this book captures many of the diachronic, cumulative changes in political dynamics that such earlier work fails to identify.[9]

Other recent work in comparative politics and political economy likewise requires modification if it is to illuminate interconnected shifts in policy and politics. Paul Pierson's work and the rich literature on welfare reform that he has inspired have shed light on one aspect of that process: how and to what extent welfare states change in the wake of mounting fiscal and economic pressures. Such work is emblematic of much of the work in comparative politics in that it provides an excellent analysis of change in particular policy domains but neglects how such changes relate to reforms in other areas of the political economy. In part, this fact derives from the stubborn separation of welfare-state scholarship from work in comparative political economy. Even work such as Gøsta Esping-Andersen's seminal *Three Worlds of Welfare Capitalism,*[10] which purports to situate social policy within a broader policy and institutional context, focuses largely on welfare states and industrial relations while ignoring other dimensions of economic policy. There have so far been few systematic analyses of the broad character of contemporary change in national models of capitalism across policy areas and of how that complex process of reform relates to qualitative, systemic changes in the politics of economic adjustment.

Such limitations are reflected in much of the recent literature on comparative politics and comparative political economy. Since the 1980s, scholars have generated two broad answers to the question of how national models of capitalism have adjusted to the climate of economic austerity, each of which is problematic in several important respects. The first position is that globalization, variously defined, is eroding nationally distinctive political-economic features as countries converge on a liberal, Anglo-American economic model with a limited welfare state and a constrained role for public authorities.[11] Though perhaps less dominant now than a decade ago, such images of rampant globalization driving convergence on a model of market-based adjustment remain influential. One has only to look at the Anglo-American press or the work of prominent neoclassical economists to encounter the argument that economic pressures from the global economy are undermining non-market arrangements such as collective-bargaining rights and generous welfare states.[12] Though contemporary capitalist economies have clearly changed a great deal since the 1970s and 1980s, this book shows that such change has not involved convergence on a neoliberal model. Instead, it has entailed historically rooted and nationally distinctive patterns of adjustment whose dynamics have been continually renegotiated.

The second prevailing set of arguments, which is both more credible empirically and more influential among many social scientists, contends that little has changed. Though advanced industrial countries have been confronted with a series of daunting economic challenges, many scholars have argued that national models of capitalism have displayed remarkable levels of policy and institutional stability. Since Shonfield revolutionized our understanding of how capitalist economies vary, a rich tradition of scholarship has provided compelling reasons why such diversity is likely to endure. The most recent and best-known formulation of this framework is the Varieties of Capitalism approach inaugurated by Peter Hall and David Soskice. Hall and Soskice define their project as creating "a new framework for understanding the institutional similarities and differences among the developed economies" and as "a firm-centered political economy that regards companies as the crucial actors in a capitalist economy." Though they may change in limited respects, Hall and Soskice argue, capitalist political economies are likely to experience long-term stability in their policies and institutional arrangements due to "institutional complementarities" and "equilibria in many strategic interactions of the political economy."[13] This kind of work represents a major advance in our understanding of the institutional structures and enduring diversity of advanced political economies. It also provides a parsimonious theoretical framework for refuting of the notion of convergence on an Anglo-American model of hegemonic markets, a limited welfare state, and a constrained scope for public authorities.[14]

That said, the Varieties of Capitalism approach tends to throw the political baby out with the neoliberal bathwater. By emphasizing stability and self-reinforcing institutional structures as the sources of nationally specific models of capitalism, it underestimates the capacity of politics to renegotiate the contours of political-economic institutions and redefine trajectories of economic change.[15] Furthermore, by focusing largely on firms and on the institutional contexts in which they are embedded, the approach neglects social policy, which is equally instrumental in shaping trajectories and dynamics of economic adjustment to austerity.[16] This book shows that existing institutional arrangements provide sources of nationally distinct patterns of adjustment, involving both the welfare state and the broader political economy. Such contexts are not merely sources of inertia or "institutional complementarities" that explain the enduring diversity of national arrangements. They also generate distinctive dynamics and trajectories of change, which are both shaped by inherited arrangements and renegotiated through the political process.

Like the Varieties of Capitalism approach, recent work on path dependence focuses on political and institutional stability at the expense of change. Paul Pierson, for example, argues that long-term stability in political economies is attributable to "self-reinforcing or positive feedback processes," which create a "status quo bias" within political and economic institutions. Though perspectives such as Pierson's recognize the possibility of political-economic change, their central concern with stability and continuity provides few analytical tools with which to identify the substance or dynamics of such shifts in policies and institutions.[17]

Recent work on the welfare state likewise overemphasizes the long-term resilience of national arrangements. Following the lead of Esping-Andersen's influential *Three Worlds of Welfare Capitalism,* during the past two decades, welfare-state scholars have developed typologies of advanced welfare states that describe these distinctive national arrangements and provide theoretical justifications as to why they are likely to endure. By showing that postwar social policies gave rise to powerful constituencies willing to mobilize to defend them against reform, Pierson's earlier work on welfare reform shows the political mechanisms for the stability of distinctive welfare states that scholars such as Esping-Andersen identify.[18] Though important for understanding why national welfare states have neither disappeared nor been reduced to a residual Anglo-American minimum, prevailing typologies of advanced welfare states, as well as Piersonian explanations for policy and institutional inertia, leave us with few tools to understand the significant reforms that many advanced welfare states, in point of fact, have undertaken since the 1990s.

Existing analyses of national models of welfare capitalism are not only overly static; many are also relatively myopic, focusing on developments in particular policy and institutional areas without explicating how they relate to shifts in other domains. Though focusing on a different institutional arena, scholarship on the welfare state, like the Varieties of Capitalism literature, excludes important policy and institutional arenas from its analysis of economic adjustment. By contrast, this book argues that the process of political-economic adjustment can best be understood as the development of systems of *welfare capitalism,* involving interrelated changes in both the welfare state and the broader political economy. Accordingly, a focus on either the welfare state or economic policy alone provides at best a partial understanding of the dynamics of economic adjustment.

From Crisis to Renewal: Reconceptualizing French and German Political-Economic Adjustment

In perhaps no two countries has the discrepancy between the prevailing image of stasis and the actual degree of change been greater than in France and Germany. Though their image as sclerotic and politically dysfunctional regimes of "welfare without work,"[19] marked by overly generous social benefits and stubbornly high unemployment, has been shaken somewhat by Europe's economic recovery in the mid-2000s, such portrayals have nonetheless proved resilient. When they do recognize patterns of reform and economic recovery in the two countries, many adherents of such perspectives dismiss them as temporary and conjunctural rather than part of a meaningful, sustained record of reform.[20]

A first set of perspectives attributes this ostensible failure of adjustment primarily to the perversities of the two countries' "Bismarckian" welfare states, named after the prototypical employment-based system of social benefits created under the nineteenth-century German chancellor. Because these systems finance benefits primarily through payroll taxes rather than through general taxation, they tend to lead to high non-wage labor costs, which increase unemployment by making it more expensive for firms to hire. Rising joblessness produces pressures for higher social expenditures and increased payroll-tax rates, which in turn exacerbate labor-market rigidities.

A second set of arguments identifies the sources of the alleged French and German sclerosis in institutional impediments to policy change within the two countries' economic institutions and political systems. In the German case, scholars emphasize an array of constitutional "veto points," or "places in the [legislative] process . . . where bottlenecks are likely to occur"[21]—in particular, federal and corporatist divisions of authority that yield a "restricted capacity for active economic steering."[22] Drawing from Peter Katzenstein's influential study of German politics,[23] such treatments contend that fragmented political power limits both the scale and the scope of reform, even in the (rare) presence of reform-minded governments. These limitations on state authority, combined with parochial social partners who perpetuate self-serving policies that are inimical to economic growth and adjustment, are blamed for Germany's political sclerosis and economic decline in the post-reunification era.[24] France's "poor capacity for reform" is explained by the absence of regularized bargaining between the state and social partners and the legacies of unions' and employers' historically antagonistic relations with an imperious state.[25] Such dysfunctional relationships, along with the political risks associated with welfare reform, are said to yield ambitious state initiatives that are often diluted or abandoned in response to ungovernable social protest or other forms of resistance by alienated interest groups.[26] France and Germany thus share characterizations of "difficult, blocked" public debates and governments that are unable either to enlist support for policy change or to impose reform in its absence.[27]

This book shows that these images of sclerotic, dysfunctional political economies are profoundly misleading and represent a fundamental misunderstanding of how—and the extent to which—the two political economies have evolved. Though often derided as "frozen welfare states,"[28] France and Germany have actually continued, and in many ways accelerated, the processes of political-economic change that began during the postwar boom, in terms of the substance of social and economic policy, the characteristic modes of policymaking, and the social and political coalitions that underlie them. In the process, the "national models" described by Shonfield and by scholars such as Peter Hall and John Zysman in the 1980s have been left far behind, giving way to a fundamentally different set of political-economic arrangements.

During the 1950s and 1960s, France and Germany were seen as exemplars of successful postwar recovery. Having inherited discredited social and political systems and devastated economies from the war and its aftermath, the two countries completely transformed their social, economic, and political arrangements within the space of a decade and a half. Their revamped political and economic institutions underpinned a period of unprecedented prosperity and social peace. The terms employed by observers at the time reflected the nearly miraculous character of this recovery: the *trente glorieuses,* or "thirty glorious years," of French postwar growth, and the West German *Wirtschaftswunder,* or "Economic Miracle," enshrined France and Germany as leading examples of vibrant capitalist economies and stable democracies. By the early 1960s, as two of the world's largest exporters, France and Germany had become testaments to the capacity of enlightened public policy to reconcile the imperatives of economic growth and representative politics.[29]

These processes of political and economic renewal were driven by a period of institutional and policy innovations that were suited to the two countries' challenges. The postwar French model was driven by a powerful and exclusionary state whose central goal was rapidly transforming the country from a sleepy agrarian society into a vibrant industrial economy. Under the Fourth French Republic, between 1946 and 1958, France instituted a model of dirigiste, or state-led, development that rapidly transformed the Malthusian, risk-averse models of the nineteenth and early twentieth centuries.[30] As French elites rebuilt their economy from the top down, they reformed their social-protection system, eventually expanding coverage to foster political stability and social peace. Changes in Germany were even more dramatic. Upon the ashes of the Third Reich, German governments developed a model of high-quality production and bank-centered finance that laid the foundations for a period of vibrant growth and renewal, transforming a barter economy in 1945 into the world's largest exporter by the early 1960s.[31] These arrangements were supported by a generous welfare state that promoted political incorporation, even as it shored up the legitimacy of the fledgling German democracy. They were also supported by a neocorporatist model of social partnership, which shared authority for social and economic policy among the state and other social and economic actors, enabling governments to reconcile the imperatives of rapid economic change, social peace, and political stability.[32]

During the 1970s, in the wake of the Organization of the Petroleum Exporting Countries (OPEC) oil shocks, stagnating growth rates and rising unemployment placed these arrangements under strain, undermining both economic performance and governments' political credibility. France's and Germany's fall from grace was all the more dramatic—and all the more worrying for the two countries' elites—because their postwar transformations had once seemed so complete and irreversible.[33] The advent of mass unemployment, deindustrialization, and increasing social unrest not only called into question the economic viability of the postwar French and German models of capitalism; it also eroded the legitimacy of the political and social arrangements that underlay them. This book tells the story of the twin process of political-economic transformation inaugurated by this advent of austerity in France and Germany and provides important insights into how advanced industrial countries evolve when confronting such shifts in social and economic climate.

If the 1970s were characterized by intensifying pressures on France's and Germany's postwar models, the 1980s and early 1990s witnessed their utter transformation. Following an ill-fated experiment with reflationary Keynesianism in the early 1980s, France completely dismantled the postwar dirigiste model and liberalized and privatized the economy with an alacrity that even Margaret Thatcher and Ronald Reagan could not match. After this complete reorientation of economic policy, France expanded antipoverty benefits and active-labor-market instruments to facilitate the process of adjustment and then embarked on a period of ambitious, if politically contentious, welfare reform. Following reunification in 1990, Germany integrated the devastated former East Germany into the West German Social Market Economy, expanding the welfare state and transferring institutions of industrial relations and vocational training to the East to help millions of untrained and impoverished workers adapt to the exigencies of capitalism. As in France, this seismic process of economic restructuring was supported by a process of welfare-state expansion and followed by a period of reform. In neither country, however, has welfare reform involved the dismantling of the welfare state. Instead, both France and Germany have rationalized their systems of social protection and prioritized labor-market activation even as they have preserved—and in some cases, expanded—the social safety net. In the process, they have preserved the distinctiveness of their social and economic models even as they have adjusted them to the challenges of economic austerity.

The Argument: Political-Economic Adjustment under Austerity

This book explains these transformations in the French and German models in two distinct but related arenas. First, it describes the changes in social and economic policies that have defined trajectories of economic adjustment. During the past three decades, France and Germany have revamped and reconfigured a series of policies and institutions in both the welfare state and the broader political economy, including the rationalization of social benefits, a reorientation of labor-market policies, substantial economic liberalization, and a bolstering of the social safety net.

This process of policy adjustment to economic austerity has proceeded in two distinct phases. Between the 1970s and the early 1990s, the first stage involved extensive economic liberalization supported by major expansions of the welfare state, a process that I call "socialized marketization." In France, this process began with the dismantling of the dirigiste system that had served the country so well during the "thirty glorious years" of postwar economic growth but that, by the 1970s, had become dysfunctional and maladaptive. Governments, first of the left and then of the right, not only abandoned the redistributive Keynesian agenda adopted by François Mitterrand in the early

1980s; they completely dismantled the postwar dirigiste model.[34] Though clearly liberal, the abandonment of dirigisme was not neoliberal in inspiration, however, as governments expanded the welfare state to buffer workers from the effects of liberalization and to help them to adapt to a more market-based economic system. In Germany, following reunification in 1990, authorities transformed Eastern Germany into a capitalist economy and integrated it with the West German Social Market Economy while undertaking a major expansion of social protection designed to preserve social peace and to sustain political support for a painful process of economic adjustment.

In the early to mid-1990s, French and German governments embarked on the second phase of policy adjustment, which I call "managed austerity," involving the reform and recalibration of the expanded network of social protection that had facilitated liberalization during the previous decade. In a wide range of policy areas, including labor-market policies, pensions, health care, and antipoverty programs, both countries have undertaken significant, and often politically difficult, initiatives. These reforms have aimed to bring welfare expenditures in line with social contributions, to shift from passive subsidization of the jobless to actively creating jobs, to make welfare programs more market-conforming, and to address growing demographic pressures on traditional social insurance. In labor-market policy, governments have expanded job-creation schemes, invested in new training and placement programs, reduced non-wage labor costs, and introduced conditions for unemployment benefits. In pensions and health care, reforms have reduced reliance on job-dampening payroll taxes and brought expenditures more in line with revenues. At the same time, governments have introduced measures to shelter those who have fallen through the cracks of the two countries' Bismarckian systems of social protection by expanding antipoverty benefits and shoring up compensation at the low end of the wage scale.

The book's second central argument relates to the *process,* as opposed to the *substance,* of reform. Across divergent national and policy contexts, adjustment to a climate of economic austerity involves changes in the political relationships and the dynamics of the bargaining processes through which reform is negotiated. In France and Germany, the politics of reform since the 1970s have not followed the traditional patterns of the postwar period—exclusionary statism in France and gradualist, consensual neocorporatism in Germany. Beginning during the first stage of liberalization but accelerating during the second, a "new politics of austerity" has developed, leading to major changes in the two countries' postwar political models. Economic austerity has altered the political dynamics of economic adjustment in two fundamental ways. First, it has discredited traditional political arrangements inherited from the postwar period of economic prosperity, which have failed to respond to contemporary economic challenges. As a result, new coalitions have emerged, providing renewed impetus and momentum to reform.

The second, related driver of the new politics of austerity relates not to the decline in economic performance per se, but to the failure of inherited political models to manage social and political unrest in its wake. In France and Germany, as elsewhere in Europe, the economic downturn of the 1970s and 1980s led to growing political protest that undermined the legitimacy of existing political arrangements and interfered with the capacity of political elites to see through reforms. As unemployment rates and public deficits soared and growth sputtered, governments were forced to confront a litany of policy demands, even as economic austerity, international economic pressures, and an erosion of legitimacy provided them with fewer means with which to do so. This growing mismatch between political resources and demands and an alarming incapacity to govern effectively have transformed relationships among the state and other political actors.

Over the past decade and a half, political and economic pressures for reform and the failure of inherited arrangements to fashion coherent responses to them have led to the emergence of new models of governance in France and Germany. Across a range of policy areas, from labor markets and social insurance to wage bargaining and immigration, French and German politics have begun to operate in new ways. This shift in the political dynamics helps to explain the surprising extent of reform in the two countries, and suggests that images of "frozen" political landscapes are largely based in outdated conceptions of the two countries' political systems. In France, traditional statism has given way to what I call "competitive interventionism," in which the state and social partners compete for dominance over the reform agenda and each significantly influences policy outcomes. In Germany, neocorporatist gradualism has yielded to "conflictual corporatism," in which an increasingly aggressive state has worked to force the social partners to adopt reforms in areas under their purview and often imposed reform in the absence of such agreement. This new pattern reflects significant changes in the postwar German model of consensual, gradualist adjustment as the state has become a leader rather than a follower of producer groups in defining trajectories of social and economic development.

These changes in the prevailing dynamics of policymaking have been driven by the emergence of new reform coalitions, which have replaced the traditional postwar alliances of business and the right, on the one hand, and unions and the left, on the other. Long defined by shared attitudes toward the market and the desirable balance between economic freedom and equity, these alliances have been replaced by coalitions of moderate unions, elements of the business community, and governments of the Social Democratic left or moderate right.

TABLE I.1 Post-1945 Models of French Policymaking

Period of Adjustment	Policymaking Model	Characteristics
Welfare-capitalist expansion and crisis of postwar model (late 1940s to 1983)	Classical dirigisme; Diverted dirigisme	State dominance of macroeconomic policy, industrial policy, and social policy; in 1970s, social and electoral concerns trump economic concerns
Socialized marketization (1983 to early 1990s)	De-dirigization	State-directed marketization and social-policy expansion
Managed austerity (late 1980s to present)	Competitive interventionism	Competing initiatives by the state and social partners; alternating episodes of state intervention and retreat; uneven trajectories of reform

Prompted by the failure of older arrangements to achieve economic renewal, these new constellations of actors have worked to promote labor-market adjustment even as they have sought to benefit politically by influencing the reform agenda and by portraying themselves as credible agents of reform. In both countries, these changes reflect shifts in the *operating dynamics* of existing institutions, without significant alterations in the formal political-institutional order. An important lesson of these developments is that enduring economic crisis creates new power relations and can drive the emergence of a new politics, even in the absence of major changes in a country's formal political institutions. I present a summary of these changes in Tables I.1 and I.2.

TABLE I.2 Post-1945 Models of German Policymaking

Period of Adjustment	Policymaking Model	Characteristics
Welfare-capitalist expansion (late 1940s to 1980s)	Neocorporatism/ consensual corporatism	Broad distribution of policymaking authority between state and social partners; consensual political and social relations and gradual adjustment
Socialized marketization (reunification to mid-1990s)	Expansionary corporatism	Expanded state spending to finance transformation of former East Germany into a market economy; other corporatist arrangements left unchanged
Managed austerity (mid-1990s to present)	Conflictual corporatism	Increasing insularity of policymaking; conflicts with social partners and political opposition; state bypasses established neocorporatist channels and procedures; uneven trajectories of reform

The Book in Brief

This book provides a new understanding of how advanced industrial societies adjust to austerity. Though important in historical perspective, such a task is particularly crucial today, when the entire advanced industrial world is confronting a series of daunting, and in some ways unprecedented, challenges to its political-economic arrangements. By shedding light on how national political economies adjust across a range of policy and institutional contexts, the book offers a more complete understanding of the nature of contemporary capitalism, a more precise identification of the policies and institutions that are critical to political-economic adjustment, and insight into the kinds of policies and institutional arrangements that are most likely to contribute to sustainable processes of adjustment.

Chapter 1 offers a theoretical analysis of the politics of economic austerity and shows that prevailing political dynamics have been redefined as French and German policymakers have turned to liberalization and welfare reform. It shows that the development of new political models and policymaking dynamics have involved the emergence of new reform coalitions in both France and Germany, as the advent of austerity has altered the political incentives facing key political actors. These shifts in incentives have been accompanied by changes in political opportunities, as the discrediting of older models and previously dominant actors (the state in France and the social partners in Germany) have enabled other actors to capitalize politically and exert greater influence over reform.

The book's empirical chapters analyze how France and Germany have responded to shifts in the prevailing political-economic context since World War II. Chapter 2 focuses on the postwar "golden age" of vibrant economic growth, an era of "welfare-capitalist expansion" during which the postwar French and German economic models and welfare states were created. In France, authorities fashioned a dirigiste model designed to modernize society and the economy from above while creating the most comprehensive welfare state the country had ever known. In Germany, the Social Market Economy, supported by bank-led development, an extensive welfare state, and neocorporatist bargaining structures, laid the foundation for an economic miracle of rapid, export-led growth and rising incomes.

Chapters 3 and 4 analyze the dramatic changes that the two countries underwent during the period of "socialized marketization" in the 1980s and early 1990s, when they undertook unprecedented projects of liberalization and marketization supported by welfare-state expansion. Chapter 3 describes French policymakers' abandonment of the postwar edifice of dirigiste development in the 1980s. In 1983, France abruptly abandoned its "redistributive Keynesian" platform of massive aid to industry and stepped-up industrial policies. In the ensuing decade, French authorities undertook a wholesale dismantling of the dirigiste edifice of voluntarist industrial policies, large "national champions," inflationary public spending, and "aggressive" devaluations. The government redeployed and extended the welfare state to cushion workers from economic dislocation and to preserve social peace even as it privatized, liberalized, and slashed the public sector.[35]

Chapter 4 analyzes the process of German reunification in the early and mid-1990s, which involved the monumental task of absorbing the formerly communist East and transforming it into a market economy. Reunification entailed both the social and economic integration of two complex and disparate societies and the fundamental transformation of a devastated communist system into a functioning capitalist economy, all within a few years. This process required the devotion of massive financial resources and a major expansion of the German social-protection system. The challenges of reunification also led the state to adopt a more central role in the policymaking process, auguring a further shift in this direction during the subsequent period of welfare reform in the 1990s and 2000s. In both France and Germany, then, the 1980s and early 1990s witnessed far-reaching processes of liberalization supported by expansions of the welfare state designed to support a transition to a more liberal economic order.

In Chapters 5, 6, and 7, the book turns to the contemporary period of "managed austerity," involving the rationalization of labor markets and social protection. Since the early to mid-1990s, both France and Germany have enacted reforms that have cut costs and sharpened incentives to work even as they have sought to maintain or even extend protection to disadvantaged groups while rewarding employment, investment, and economic innovation. In Chapter 5, the book analyzes reforms in labor-market policy, which have involved a shift from passive subsidization of the unemployed to active policies designed to reintegrate excluded groups while reducing unemployment and reliance on traditional jobless benefits. These reforms have attenuated, if not eliminated, many of the perversities of the two countries' "welfare-without-work" syndromes. As enhanced labor-market performance has become a central focus of policymaking, reforms in many other areas have been undertaken with a view to replacing the traditional strategy of reducing labor supply with the promotion of labor-market activation.

Chapter 6 turns to the second major component of recent French and German reform, involving changes in the two countries' social-insurance programs. The primary targets of such measures have been pensions and health care, which represent huge financial burdens and have come under increasing pressure from aging populations and declining social-contribution receipts. Since 1990, French and German governments have limited benefit and reimbursement rates, increased state authority over health-care budgets and administration, partially shifted funding from social contributions to general taxation, and increased contribution periods required for pension vesting. Particularly in Germany, governments have also extended the scope of market forces in health care by increasing patients' choice among health-care providers and forcing doctors to compete for resources based on their record of cost-containment.

In Chapter 7, the book turns to programs of income support designed to shelter workers from poverty while helping the labor force adjust to an era of more market-friendly welfare states and labor-market activation. In France, governments of both the left and the right have expanded the network of income-support policies, reflecting a sustained effort to fill gaps in the contributory, Bismarckian social-security system created during the late 1940s and 1950s. In Germany, by contrast, authorities have prioritized active labor-market policies, supplemental pensions, and education benefits while beginning to experiment with sectoral minimum-wage laws, an unprecedented development in a country where *Tarifautonomie,* or "wage independence," has long reserved wage setting to the social partners. Authorities in both countries have worked to ensure citizens' access to basic income even as they have encouraged them to seek out and accept the jobs that economic liberalization and active labor-market policies are helping to create.

The Conclusion provides an overview of the trajectories of French and German welfare-capitalist adjustment and assesses the book's contributions to the literatures on national models of capitalism, welfare reform, path dependence, and institutional change.[36] It argues that the dynamics of adjustment to economic austerity are shaped by both inherited political and economic institutions and politically negotiated bargains that are reconfigured during the process of reform. It also suggests that these bargains often develop in ways that are quite surprising in view of formal distributions of political authority and that the failures of earlier political models are frequently as important as the capacities of current ones in defining both the style and substance of reform. In France and Germany, as in other advanced industrial democracies, therefore, the dynamics of political and economic change are tightly linked, and neither can be properly understood without careful attention to the other. It is in this sense that the systems of "welfare capitalism" invoked in the book's title should be understood: as mutually constitutive, mutually supportive, and evolving components of political-economic order.

1

The Politics of Austerity in Advanced Industrial Democracies

Economic prosperity and political stability in postwar Western Europe developed in parallel with novel scholarly interpretations of the continent's success. In France and Germany, as elsewhere in Western Europe, rebuilding ravaged economies, beginning to heal deeply divided societies, and reconstructing discredited political systems required fundamental innovations across the full range of national political and economic institutions. This process of self-reinvention gave rise to what Andrew Shonfield called "Modern Capitalism," whose hallmarks were an enhanced role for public policy and nationally distinct constellations of public authority responsible for promoting economic development. During the heyday of the postwar golden age, national elites across Europe created legitimate, effective governing arrangements, which were testaments to the capacity of enlightened public policy to ensure prosperity and social peace. Shonfield aptly captured the optimistic spirit of the age: "It is hard for us to believe that the bleak and squalid system which we knew could, in so short a time, have adapted itself, without some covert process of total destruction and regeneration, to achieve so many desired objectives."[1] As reconstruction provided the foundations for a period of unprecedented economic growth, broad political consensus developed behind these new "national models" of

Portions of this chapter include revised versions of material presented in "The Myth of the Frozen Welfare State and the Dynamics of Contemporary French and German Social-Protection Reform," *French Politics* 2, no. 2 (August 2004): 151–183, by Palgrave-Macmillan Journals (available online at http://www.palgrave-journals.com/fp/journal/v2/n2/pdf/8200055a.pdf). Used by permission.

capitalism, involving distinctive roles for the state and producer groups and characteristic patterns of political bargaining.

Just as the postwar boom had legitimized postwar Europe's models of capitalism, the economic downturn during the 1970s began to discredit them. Stagnating economies, rising unemployment, and intensifying fiscal pressures shattered assumptions about possibilities for sustainable prosperity and tarnished the prestige of governing institutions. Within a decade, national authorities found themselves presiding over a period of economic decline rather than one of prosperity. Instead of distributing economic gains, elites were now forced to undertake the unenviable task of imposing losses and, in the process, were forced to rethink both the goals and the means of economic policy. The advent of stagflation was merely one alarming indication that the governments of the period were doing a poor job of managing economic adjustment. Over time, and with varying degrees of success, governments began to shift their focus to supply-side efforts to restart growth, reduce unemployment, and unleash the power of markets while preserving the core of the generous welfare states that had maintained social peace during the postwar boom.

This shift from prosperity to austerity in the 1970s and early 1980s did not merely involve changes in policies, however; nor did these shifts happen overnight. Instead, the change in strategy was a result of a gradual evolution in prevailing understandings of the relationship between political choice and economic outcomes. Peter Gourevitch aptly captures the logic of the mutually constitutive relationship between economic context and the dominant mode of politics:

> Policy requires politics. . . . In prosperous times it is easy to forget the importance of power in the making of policy. Social systems appear stable, and the economy works with sufficient regularity that its rules can be modeled as if they functioned without social referent. In difficult economic times this comfortable illusion disintegrates. Patterns unravel, economic models come into conflict, and policy prescriptions diverge.[2]

In his analysis of political responses to international economic crises, Gourevitch shows that the advent of economic austerity, or any enduring change in economic context, redefines the policy options available to authorities and the social and political coalitions that underpin them. Times of crisis can engender major alterations in policy orientation, such as the shift from nineteenth-century classical economic orthodoxy to Keynesianism during the Great Depression. In explaining how "hard times" transform politics, Gourevitch emphasizes structural factors, such as relationships among social groups and existing political institutions, in mediating the effects of economic pressures on policy outcomes.

Though inspired in part by work such as Gourevitch's, this book takes a different approach to explaining how national models of capitalism adjust to economic austerity. Gourevitch's primary concern is with how economic interests, represented in stable constellations of social and economic actors, respond to discrete economic shocks. Such structural, interest-based perspectives provide powerful tools for identifying successions of relatively stable political coalitions and for explaining cross-national variation over relatively long periods of time. They are less useful, however, for identifying the evolving relationships among key political actors *within* a given policy regime or for showing how these developments gradually redefine policy trajectories. Because they view political coalitions as relatively stable and link policy regimes with identifiable constellations of interests, they are also less helpful for explaining policy outcomes that may not correspond coherently to a prevailing policy regime, why bargaining patterns fluctuate within given economic contexts, or how particular groups might be led to support or to oppose different polices that are part of the same broad strategy of adjustment.

As a result, understanding changes in the substance of reform and in the mode of policymaking in advanced industrial democracies requires several significant extensions and modifications of perspectives such as Gourevitch's. This book shows that national responses to austerity involve complex, shifting networks of policy outcomes, which are driven by evolving relationships among key political actors rather than by stable coalitions defending identifiable, coherent sets of interests. Second, it broadens its policy focus to include both economic policy and changes in the welfare state, which are instrumental to adjustment in times of austerity and periods of prosperity alike and are intimately bound up with changes in the broader political economy. Third, it adopts a more dynamic understanding of coalitional politics and shows that shifts in political bargaining arise from changes in the incentives and opportunities facing key political actors and modifications in how actors *interpret* these interests. Echoing Mark Blyth's formulation, this book calls for resisting the temptation to treat "interests as given and crises as unambiguous."[3] Instead, it highlights the process by which certain ideas gain ascendance over others in times of crisis and the interaction of such ideational shifts with more formal distributions of political authority, sometimes significantly altering how that authority is exercised. To do so, it focuses on how "economic ideas provide agents with an interpretive framework" that "allow[s] agents to . . . propose a particular solution to a moment of crisis, and empower[s] agents to resolve that crisis by constructing new institutions in line with . . . new ideas."[4] Accordingly, it treats shifts in bargaining dynamics under austerity as arising from changes in the incentives and opportunities facing key political actors—and from the gradual redefinition of the narratives of the existing political-economic context and their roles within it.

In this way, the book departs from prevailing conceptions of how political authority drives policy outcomes, which tend to emphasize how varying constellations of power and formal authority define national political processes. Though it recognizes the importance of formal distributions of authority, this book shows that changing political dynamics flow also to an important extent from alterations in the *relational* and *interpretive* aspects of politics. More specifically, it contends that shifts in the dynamics of policymaking tend to occur against a background of enduring economic crisis and in the wake of earlier, failed attempts to manage adjustment, which discredit both inherited arrangements and the dominant actors within them. This cumulative loss of legitimacy presents other, less powerful actors with opportunities to exert greater political influence by presenting themselves as more credible agents for reform, exploiting gathering cynicism about the traditional political game. Together, these factors drive actors' reinterpretations of their economic interests and political strategies and, over time, lead to the emergence of new coalitions, bargaining dynamics, and policy trajectories.[5]

The book develops this theoretical perspective through an investigation of four decades of political-economic adjustment in France and Germany, tracing out shifts in both the substance of policy and the dynamics of politics. It argues that adjustment to austerity has entailed a fundamental reorientation of policy strategies in both the welfare state and the broader political economy and that reforms in both areas have been driven by significant changes in prevailing political relationships. The remainder of this chapter identifies the salient dynamics of this "politics of austerity" and shows how the advent of hard times since the 1970s has reconfigured politics and policy. It also suggests that understanding how France and Germany have adjusted to austerity allows us to develop broader insights into which kinds of policies and economic and political arrangements are likely to generate productive, equitable, and economically viable responses to difficult economic circumstances, as well as insights into the relationship between economic context and politics, across advanced industrial democracies.

The Limits of Prosperity and the Quest for Alternatives: Europe in an Age of Austerity

The contemporary era of austerity shows important differences relative to the postwar boom. Beginning in the late 1960s, as economic performance declined and rapid growth and full employment gave way to stubbornly high unemployment, sluggish growth, and growing economic exclusion, inherited policies and institutional arrangements were discredited. This reversal of fortune was wholly unanticipated by postwar governments, which had engineered one of the most dramatic and successful processes of innovation in European history.

After the war, economic devastation and the failures of interwar democracies provided an unprecedented need, and a unique opportunity, to revamp political and economic institutions. Beginning in the early 1950s, a long "period of unprecedented prosperity" legitimized Europe's reconstituted political economies, suggesting that "[an] increase [in] the available powers of control over the economic system" had provided a recipe for overcoming the kinds of economic disruptions that had defined the interwar period.[6] Though the countries of Western Europe embraced Keynesian demand management with varying degrees of enthusiasm, they all shared a commitment to Keynes's broader insight: that economic growth can be sustained by coherent, deliberate approaches to policy, and that economic development need not be surrendered to the vagaries of the business cycle or the "natural" development of capitalism. Accordingly, "The rules of co-ordination and macroeconomic structure reinforced each other, both resting on a system of production that generated a high rate of productivity growth and continued wage growth."[7]

France's and Germany's breathtaking postwar success, with consistently impressive rates of economic growth, low levels of unemployment,[8] and vibrant export sectors, rendered their subsequent fall from grace all the more traumatic. The advent of austerity in the 1970s hit hard in several ways. First, the economic climate faced by both firms and workers deteriorated significantly. For firms, profit levels and rates of investment plummeted as productivity rates steadily declined without concomitant reductions in wage bills.[9] At the same time, wages did not keep pace with inflation, which was an even greater concern for the growing number facing the prospect of having no job at all. As widespread layoffs and declining corporate profits fueled increases in unemployment, earlier assumptions of an enduring climate of full employment faded.[10] For both labor and capital, it became clear that what had first seemed to be a temporary pause in growth had become a structural crisis that would require fundamentally different ways of managing economic change.

As observers soberly realized the enduring nature of the downturn, the arrangements that had been credited with Europe's postwar recovery began to attract blame for its decline. Austerity undermined the legitimacy of European political-economic models on multiple levels. First, slowed growth and rising rates of inflation and unemployment tarnished the prestige of governments, making the very idea of managing the economy seem, at best, ineffective, and at worst, a form of unpardonable meddling. If not dead, Keynesianism was clearly on life support, leading observers to question the legitimacy of state intervention in the economy, "which [was] viewed with tremendous suspicion, as prone to inefficiency, corruption, and rent seeking."[11] Austerity shook observers' faith in many of the cornerstones of the postwar European economic order, such as industrial policies and the generous welfare states that distinguished France and Germany from the more market-based model of the United States.

As it discredited the postwar European economic order, austerity presented elites with a daunting set of political challenges. The postwar Keynesian consensus, based on an implicit exchange of wage moderation and labor peace for government support for economic growth, progressive taxation, and generous social policies, had acted as a bulwark of political and social stability for nearly three decades. When Europe's models of capitalism could no longer deliver the consistent economic performance on which this compromise rested, growing social and political unrest forced governments to alter their political strategy. One of the earliest and most alarming indications of such pressures came with the revolt of May–June 1968 in France, when workers and students shut down the country for weeks. Though clearly more extreme, this near-revolution was different only in degree from other episodes of social unrest during this period, ranging from the assassination of prominent government and industry leaders by left-wing extremists in Germany and Italy during the 1970s to the Winter of Discontent in Britain in 1978, when waves of strikes by public-sector workers left corpses unburied, garbage uncollected, and hospitals shuttered. The emergence of a literature on a "crisis of governability" at the time both reflected and reinforced growing apprehensions that poor economic performance was contributing to a wider social and political crisis.[12] The apparent failures of contemporary capitalism thus were not merely questions of economics; they also seemed to question the viability of Europe's postwar social and political order.

Both of these factors—the decline in Europe's economic performance and the alarming incapacity of elected officials to govern in its wake—defined a new political-economic context whose contours observers then could only dimly perceive. Over time, this enduring climate of austerity would reshape expectations of future economic realities, redefining basic assumptions about how the economy worked, actors' perceptions of their interests, and the political relationships to which such perceptions gave rise. As Paul Pierson has shown, reforming the welfare state, one of the centerpieces of the new policy agenda, involves a different kind of politics from that of postwar welfare expansion. Instead of distributing gains and "claiming credit" for presiding over a process of welfare expansion, elites were increasingly forced to undertake the more difficult and politically risky task of imposing cuts in benefits. But this book shows that the prevailing policy challenges go far beyond the welfare state, and the associated political challenges are not limited to "avoid[ing] blame" for the imposition of concentrated costs for the sake of "diffuse, long-term, and uncertain benefits."[13] Instead, the process of adjustment under austerity involves a much broader set of political and economic challenges than reforming the welfare state, including sustaining economic growth, promoting employment, maintaining economic competitiveness and productivity, and keeping fiscal arrangements in relative balance, all while preserving social and political stability.

Across a wide range of policy areas, governments have thus had to do more with less, confronting a daunting array of economic challenges with fewer political and economic resources at their disposal. This change in political-economic context has led in turn to fundamental shifts in both the substance of policy-making and the process of politics. This book employs a theoretical framework that enables us to identify the critical components of this twofold process, cross-nationally and cross-temporally. In France and Germany, the dynamics of adjustment have been shaped by powerful legacies from the past, but they have also been subject to an ongoing process of renegotiation and shifts in political bargaining. The political strategies available to both governments and interest groups have been defined in part by available institutional levers of power, but they have also been changed by the legacies of historical relationships between state and society and shifting perceptions of legitimacy and political and economic interests. These factors have created new political relationships and bargaining dynamics that a focus on formal distributions of authority alone simply cannot explain.

Theoretical Stakes and the Intellectual Landscape

Though the post-1970s economic downturn has been a major theme of contemporary scholarship, there have been few systematic attempts to explore how this change in economic context has transformed the politics and the policies of national models of welfare capitalism.[14] In developing such an approach, this book draws on and extends the insights of a number of bodies of scholarship, which provide an important but incomplete set of tools for understanding how national models of capitalism adjust. Some of the most promising recent work in comparative political economy in this respect can be found in the burgeoning literature on institutional change. As Wolfgang Streeck and Kathleen Thelen have shown, scholars of comparative political economy and comparative capitalism have tended to focus much more on why national arrangements endure than on how they change. Though this emphasis on stability has allowed scholars to refute claims of neoliberal convergence, it has also come at the cost of both underestimating the extent of institutional change and under-theorizing the processes that drive it. Streeck and Thelen aim to explore "*a wide but not infinite variety* of modes of institutional change," to identify "incremental change with transformative results," and to explore how "institutions can be transformed in subtle but very significant ways through a variety of specific mechanisms."[15] In contrast to the Varieties of Capitalism approach, which sees political economies as systems of coordination characterized by long-term institutional stability, this work sees institutions as undergoing "an evolutionary process that unfolds in an incremental manner and without major disruptions over long periods of time and resulting in profound change."[16] Recent shifts in policies and politics in France and Germany share elements with Thelen's concept of "institutional conversion," or "the adoption of new goals or the incorporation of new groups into the coalitions on which institutions are founded [that] can drive change in the functions these institutions serve or the role they perform."[17] They also echo what she and Streeck, borrowing from Eric Schickler, call institutional "layering," or "successive rounds of institutional reform," characterized by "differential growth" and "amendments, additions, or revisions to an existing set of institutions."[18]

This work offers several promising avenues for advancing our theoretical understanding of how capitalist economies evolve and how the politics of adjustment change over time. First, it shifts our attention from the broad stability of capitalist political economies since World War II to elements within them that have changed quite dramatically during the past three decades. As a result, it shows that long-term continuity within political-economic arrangements can mask important changes that are taking place beneath the surface. Second and relatedly, it loosens the relatively structured, formalistic understanding of the link between the structure of institutions and their operation by recognizing the possibility of informal, but nonetheless real, changes in political relationships within a broad context of formal institutional stability. As Jacob Hacker points out, "An institution's effects can occur without fundamental shifts in formal institutional structures."[19] This attention to both formal and informal effects is quite helpful for identifying changes in political relationships that develop in the interstices *between* formal institutions. At the same time, however, the focus of this work is on changes in particular policies and institutions rather than in the broader political dynamics that shape outcomes across a range of policy areas. In part, this limitation derives from a continued focus among historical institutionalists on "the formal rules, compliance procedures, and standard operating practices that structure the relationship between individuals in various units of the polity and economy" and from a view of economic adjustment as shaped by stable "regimes" governing the relationships between "rule makers" and "rule takers."[20]

Though recent scholarship on institutional change provides a helpful shift in focus, we must therefore look elsewhere for the tools required for understanding the relationships among policy outcomes, formal and informal institutions, and political dynamics. Though rare in work on the advanced industrial world, analyses of informal politics and institutions that suggest promising avenues in this respect have become common in work on less developed countries, where the relationship between formal rules and political dynamics is understood to be looser.[21] In their work on Latin America, for example, Gretchen Helmke and Steve Levitsky define informal institutions as consisting of "socially shared rules, usually unwritten, that are created, communicated, and enforced outside officially sanctioned channels."[22] Scholars in this tradition explore a variety of contexts in which informal understandings and arrangements shape outcomes as much as or more than do formal laws and regulations. From patterns of electoral competition, to party organization, to the regulation of social order, this literature shows that informal politics can strengthen or undermine the force of formal legal arrangements.

Such work hints at some ways in which we can gain intellectual leverage over the shifting political strategies and bargaining dynamics that have defined French and German economic adjustment. In contrast to the bulk of historical institutional work, it creates analytical space for considering how shifting informal alliances and coalitions can develop within a context of broad formal institutional stability. Helmke and Levitsky argue that "the prevalence of informal institutions . . . suggests a need to broaden the scope of institutional analysis in comparative politics."[23] This conception brings us closer to an understanding of how shifting economic contexts and related incentives reshape relationships between the state and social groups.[24] It also helps us to identify possible mechanisms for the kinds of institutional change with which scholars like Streeck, Thelen, and Hacker are concerned.

An important component of this book's theoretical approach involves an emphasis on how modes of governance and politics change with shifting economic contexts, a concern that is central to the work of the Regulation School. Regulationist scholars argue that capitalist economies and the institutional arrangements that underpin them vary from one stage of development to the next,[25] leading to changes in governments' adjustment strategies and shifts in their relationships with interest groups. Chris Howell, a leading Regulationist scholar, aptly formulates the core insight of the approach: "Broadly speaking, a particular pattern of accumulation may be said to correspond to a set of institutions that are necessary for that accumulation to take place"[26] By treating capitalism as a dynamic set of socially embedded institutions, such work offers important tools for understanding the relationship between economic and political change. It also reminds us that formal institutional capacities and the political relationships on which they are based may operate differently in different economic circumstances.[27] That said, Regulationist scholarship tends to adopt a somewhat functionalist understanding of the structure of political institutions and the dynamics of politics, which it sees as predictable outgrowths of underlying economic factors. As a result, this body of work is better equipped to illuminate the changing relationship between economic context and politics than to explain the mechanisms by which political change occurs.

To capture the relationship between bargaining dynamics and policy trajectories, we must go beyond the observation that economic context and both formal and informal institutional capacities matter. We must also be able to say something about *how* they matter and through which *mechanisms* they influence policy and politics. This in turn requires that we think carefully about how actors' perceptions of their own and others' interests change over time and how these ideational shifts redefine policy priorities, perceptions of common political ground, and actors' willingness to join or abandon particular political coalitions.

Scholarship that adopts a more "interpretive" approach to the study of comparative politics provides important tools for doing so. Like the work of Mark Blyth invoked earlier, Pepper Culpepper's concept of "joint belief shifts," or situations "when . . . central strategic actors within the system are persuaded, collectively, that their old cognitive maps are wrong and that they need to devise new ones," suggests the need to view political relationships as evolving, dynamic patterns of interaction rather than merely as formally structured differentials of power.[28] "Beliefs" and "ideas" are notoriously slippery concepts, of course, and scholars of comparative politics have rightly dealt with them with some degree of trepidation.[29] Nonetheless, they are essential parts of the story of economic adjustment and must be tackled if we are to develop powerful explanations of how and why such adjustment occurs.

Each of these perspectives provides important tools for understanding contemporary political-economic adjustment in France and Germany. To be sure, formal institutional arrangements, such as the administrative capacities of the state and the prerogatives of unions and employers' associations, are important explanatory variables in such an account. To understand how those capacities translate into influence over reform agendas and policy outcomes, however, we must recognize that the relationship between the formal *distribution* of political authority and the manner of its *exercise* is less straightforward than many scholars have assumed. Changes in economic context can have profound effects on political dynamics, a possibility to which recent work on institutional change and the approach of the Regulation School can make us receptive. That said, we must go beyond the observation that context matters to develop a more systematic understanding of factors other than the formal capacities of countries' political and economic institutions. This in turn requires that we think carefully about how the legacies of past politics and new economic challenges come together to reshape governments' and producer groups' understanding of their interests, modify their legitimacy and credibility as agents of reform, and redefine political coalitions.

The Changing Politics of French and German Welfare-Capitalist Adjustment

Over the past three decades, structural shifts in the economy and qualitative transformations in politics have changed the content of a wide array of social and economic policies in France and Germany, including patterns of state intervention, the structure of labor markets, and the character of economic regulation. French and German reforms have been part of a broader European struggle to liberalize the economy and to sustain economic growth and employment in the face of a much less hospitable economic environment. As governments have struggled to reform existing arrangements, they have acted according to an evolving set of political rules and assumptions. As I describe later, these changes in the dynamics of reform have been at least as dramatic—though less recognized—than the policy changes over which governments have presided.

In France and Germany, adjustment to austerity has taken place in two distinct phases, though the length of each stage and the associated policy changes have been heterogeneous across the two countries. The first phase, roughly from the late 1970s to the late 1980s, involved the liberalization of the macroeconomy and the abandonment of traditional policy instruments—such as sectoral industrial policies—in favor of a prioritization of supply-side policies designed to encourage investment and business profitability. During this process, governments liberalized their economies and extended the reach of market forces, which replaced government intervention as the focus of economic policy. Though clearly *liberal,* this first stage of adjustment to austerity was not *neoliberal* in inspiration, however, as authorities redeployed and extended the welfare state to cushion workers from economic dislocation and to preserve social peace even as they privatized, liberalized, and reduced the reach of the public sector. In a way that is consistent with Karl Polanyi's "double movement," French and German policymakers understood that a robust welfare state was not only consistent with economic liberalization and marketization; it would also greatly facilitate the transition to a more liberal economic order.[30] Far from acting as an impediment to liberalization, then, and contra the dark predictions of many neoclassical economists,[31] an expanded welfare state has provided essential support for the process of economic liberalization across the advanced industrial world, acting as a *means* of reform, not an alternative to it.

This pattern of what I call socialized marketization, involving linked processes of welfare-state expansion and economic liberalization, facilitated some of the most dramatic social and economic changes in the postwar period. In France during the early 1980s, authorities not only abandoned the leftist redistributive Keynesian agenda adopted by Socialist President François Mitterrand in 1981; they also dismantled the entire dirigiste edifice, involving centralized economic planning, "aggressive" devaluations designed to alleviate competitive pressures on exports, ambitious industrial policies, and the promotion of large "national champions" as the country's international economic vanguard.[32] During the 1980s and early 1990s, this system was replaced by an emphasis on "competitive disinflation" (meaning the effort to shore up the franc and boost competitiveness by keeping inflation levels below those of France's trading partners), the promotion of small and medium-sized enterprises, and an expansion of market forces to encourage French firms to become more competitive. Even as they liberalized and marketized the economy, French authorities expanded the welfare state, placing particular emphasis on programs such as early retirement and new forms of income support designed to preserve the legitimacy of reform.

In Germany, the challenges of this first phase of adjustment to austerity were even more daunting. Though German economic performance had begun to decline in the 1980s, with rising unemployment and declining rates of economic growth, the shock of reunification created a full-blown social and economic crisis. Despite initial optimism, it quickly became clear that absorbing the devastated economy of the former East Germany, along with the integration of 17 million impoverished workers ill-prepared for the competitive pressures of Western capitalism, was going to be a long, brutal, and expensive process. It would not only involve the large-scale privatization and liberalization of what was left of the Eastern economy; it would also require a massive expansion of the welfare state to preserve social peace and political stability.[33]

In both France and Germany, moreover, this phase of socialized marketization sowed the seeds of the new politics that would define the second stage of adjustment to austerity. In France, pressures on governments to compensate the losers from adjustment not only led to the expansion of the social-protection system; they also increased the influence of the social partners, who exercised significant, though often latent, authority. Although the state was still the leading force for reform during the 1980s, both employers and trade unions were becoming more assertive in trying to shape the policy agenda as governments shifted from presiding over economic expansion to the more difficult and politically contentious process of imposing costs on recalcitrant constituencies. In Germany, the shock of reunification thrust a strange kind of greatness on an unwitting—and largely unprepared—German government. The monumental task of integrating East and West Germany while preserving the Social Market Economy was ill-suited to the postwar German model of gradual change mediated through consensual politics. Increasingly, the German state was forced to step in to manage the enormous social and economic tasks that reunification involved, inaugurating further increases in government activism in the late 1990s.

The second phase of adjustment, to which I refer as one of managed austerity, has involved a continuation of the processes of liberalization begun during the 1980s and early 1990s, combined with reforms of the networks of social protection whose expansion had been critical to adjustment during the preceding period. As I describe in Chapters 5–7, adjustment during this period has been much more dramatic than most scholars have recognized. Far from sclerotic countries mired in an insoluble dilemma of welfare without work,[34] France and Germany have actually been among the most aggressive and innovative reformers of social protection in Europe. This second phase of adjustment has centered on labor markets, social insurance (particularly pensions and health care), and policies of income support. French and German governments have shifted the focus of labor-market policy from passive subsidization of the unemployed to activation and job creation, rationalized pension and health benefits by bringing them more in line with contributions while introducing market mechanisms to control costs, limited non-wage labor costs by shifting the onus of financing away from social contributions to general taxation, and expanded the social safety net available to vulnerable economic groups. Rather than merely cutting benefits, French and German authorities have recalibrated and redeployed their welfare states to sustain the core of their social protection systems while adjusting them to the pressures of marketization and economic austerity. A new kind of social-protection system—with employment and competitiveness as core concerns—has emerged to replace the traditional, Bismarckian welfare states created during the 1950s and early 1960s.

The two-stage pattern of adjustment followed by France and Germany shows a broader logic that has characterized adjustment in many advanced industrial democracies.[35] The initial phase of adjustment, involving economic liberalization and the expansion of markets supported by welfare-state expansion, creates the economic foundation and political stability required for continued economic growth. Though reports of the demise of the state in the wake of "globalization" have been greatly exaggerated, the state *has* been forced to assume different tasks. The new economic order has made older approaches to economic policy—such as extensive nationalizations and heavy-handed industrial policies—very expensive, if not completely infeasible. As a result, remaining economically competitive and ensuring economic growth now require different ways to address important social and economic concerns. In a way that Jonah Levy has elegantly described, economic liberalization has thus involved the redeployment rather than dismantling of the state: "Many of the characteristic policies described by Shonfield are no longer practicable. . . . While old forms of state intervention may be discredited and cleared away, new interventions often emerge to take their place."[36] As new challenges have emerged, public authorities have been forced to redeploy the financial and political resources of the state to preserve economic growth and social peace.

There are other reasons that this broad process of economic stabilization and marketization tends to precede the subsequent phase of welfare reform and revamping of social protection. First, governments often need a robust welfare state to make large-scale liberalization socially and economically feasible. Second and relatedly, policymakers cannot attack all sources of economic support simultaneously without seriously jeopardizing the stability of their economies and their hold on power. In a way that Paul Pierson has described with respect to welfare reform,[37] imposing costs on mobilized constituencies requires maintaining legitimacy and convincing voters (or at least enough of them) that governments are acting in the public interest. Third, the task of the second phase of economic adjustment—revamping social protection and making welfare more supportive of economic growth and employment—requires a functioning economy. Only an economy that has begun seriously to confront the challenges of liberalization can produce the resources and jobs that can make substantive welfare reform politically viable and economically feasible. Doing otherwise would be counterproductive—like trying to remodel a house while re-laying its foundation.

The new politics of the age of austerity have led to some surprising policy outcomes that would have been quite unlikely under older political arrangements. During the postwar boom, the French dirigiste system had accomplished so much precisely because it had included so few. The "conspiracy in the public interest" between big business and the state had excluded unions, small business, and other social groups, dismissing them as parochial, self-serving constituencies prone to interfere with economic modernization.[38] In Germany, the neocorporatist model of consensual adjustment was likewise suited to Germany's unique postwar challenges. If the French imperative was rapid industrialization, Germany's was achieving economic reconstruction and modernization while sustaining support for a young and fragile democracy in a country where history had provided ample reason to distrust unilateral state action. Sharing both the responsibility and the credit for economic prosperity enabled Germany to achieve prosperity while investing a wide array of economic actors with a sort of collective legitimacy and responsibility. As one postwar German economist aptly put it, the system used "as much competition as possible, and as much planning as necessary."[39]

Though stunningly successful during the 1950s and 1960s, France's and Germany's postwar policymaking models proved less adept at adjusting to austerity. As the economic climate darkened during the 1970s, it became increasingly clear to observers and policymakers that old ways of conducting politics were no longer effective. Just as economic success had been a source of political legitimacy during the postwar boom, mounting unemployment and sluggish growth steadily discredited established political models. In France, the concentration of authority in the central state, which had been so effective at imposing modernization on a reluctant country, now focused blame on policymakers who had spurned potential allies during the postwar boom. Such insularity led a growing number of observers to blame the state for the country's economic woes. A failed effort to garner allies among economic and social actors during the 1980s merely highlighted the state's inability to build coalitions for reform and left it alone to face voters' ire at rising unemployment and generalizing economic insecurity.[40] In Germany, likewise, a slowing economy and the social partners' inability or unwillingness to engineer needed reforms discredited both them and the policymaking model in which they were the pre-eminent actors. Unions and employers—who had been so instrumental in driving the postwar German *Wirtschaftswunder*—reacted by digging in their heels and defending their prerogatives, thereby becoming impediments to reform rather than forces for adjustment. Over time, this parochial strategy discredited the entire neocorporatist system, leading to a "crisis of hyper-stability, or stagnation, due to an ingrained over-commitment to old institutions and historical entitlements."[41]

Even as they discredited inherited policymaking models, mounting economic problems created pressures on existing bargaining frameworks and opportunities for marginalized actors to exert greater influence. In France, the social partners had long been excluded from most areas of economic policymaking. Though such an approach worked well in a context of widespread prosperity, the advent of economic austerity encouraged both unions and employers to become more assertive in promoting policies that would enable them to defend their increasingly beleaguered economic positions. The near-revolution of May 1968 was perhaps the most dramatic indication of the potentially disruptive capacity of formally weak actors, but a series of episodes during the ensuing two decades, such as small shopkeepers' protests in the 1970s and an increasingly aggressive employers' confederation in the 1980s,[42] presaged a more fundamental shift in bargaining dynamics in the 1990s. In Germany, the crisis of reunification accelerated an analogous shift in policymaking dynamics whose roots could be found in the beginning of economic decline in the late 1980s. Rising unemployment, mounting budget deficits, and an erosion of export competitiveness all showed that the vaunted neocorporatist system was failing to respond effectively to the new economic context. The social partners' inaction, coupled with mounting pressures on governments, led the latter to adopt a more aggressive policymaking stance, often circumventing the social partners or unilaterally imposing reforms.

In both France and Germany, the economic downturn of the past three decades, the legacies of inherited political models and past conflicts among key actors, and shifting incentives and interpretations of their own and other actors' interests have led to significant changes in bargaining dynamics. In France, dirigisme has been replaced by what I call competitive interventionism, involving competition between the state and social partners over the reform agenda. Though these changes began to emerge in the 1980s, they have accelerated during the past decade and a half, with the absorption of the dismantling of dirigisme and the shift away from macroeconomic liberalization to the reform of labor markets and social protection as the central policy focus. The changes in bargaining dynamics have been equally dramatic in Germany. There, the neocorporatist model, based on a cozy political consensus among producer groups and relatively quiescent state, has given way to a pattern of conflictual corporatism, involving a more aggressive state and declining influence by unions and employers' associations.[43]

In both countries, then, the advent of austerity has redefined the political incentives facing the state and social partners, their respective visions of the future, and the constellation of political and economic interests in which they operate. Over time, and partially as a result, it has also altered their interpretations of their own and other actors' interests. This shift has led marginal actors to conclude that they stand to benefit politically and economically from policy activism rather than by defending established arrangements. At the same time, previously dominant actors—the French state and German social partners—can no longer credibly claim that their defense of inherited arrangements serves the public weal, and they have come to understand that political payoffs are increasingly tied to their being perceived as responsible economic stewards and agents of reform. This shift in incentives and interpretations, driven by the failure of earlier attempts at adjustment, has provided renewed impetus to reform and led to a reconfiguration of bargaining institutions and practices.

Looking Ahead: Lessons of the French and German Experience

The French and German experience offers important lessons about the dynamics of adjustment in an age of economic austerity. Long derided as sclerotic and incapable of reform, France and Germany have undertaken major changes in both the welfare state and the broader political economy. Austerity has led to a two-stage process of policy adjustment involving successive waves, first, of economic liberalization supported by welfare-state expansion, and later of reform of labor markets and systems of social protection. As during the postwar boom, this process of adjustment has entailed mutually constitutive changes in the welfare state and the broader political economy—in the system of *welfare capitalism* invoked in this book's title. Looking at either the welfare state alone, as does much of the worlds of welfare literature that focuses on social spending as an index of reform—or at firms in relative isolation, as in the Varieties of Capitalism literature—will provide at best a partial and even misleading picture of both the substance and the dynamics of reform.[44]

This book also shows that the policy outcomes that define capitalism's response to austerity are driven by new political dynamics, which arise from the new economic context. Austerity provides mechanisms for converting institutional weaknesses under prosperity into sources of influence even as it transforms institutional strengths into political weaknesses. The shifts in incentives and interpretations that produce these changes affect national models differently in ways that are partially defined by both distributions of formal authority and the legacies of past political conflicts. They also redefine their desire and ability to seek new allies and reshape coalitions in support of or in opposition to reform.

As I emphasize throughout this book, these new coalitions and bargaining dynamics have not made reform inevitable in France and Germany, but they have made it possible. It is difficult to see how the scope and scale of contemporary French and German labor-market and social-protection reform could have been accomplished under the old political models. In France, a state-led process of modernization from above could not have secured the allies and political legitimacy that reform requires, any more than a system dominated by a relatively passive German state and parochial social partners could have overcome the inertia that had transformed postwar neocorporatism into a sclerotic, reform-averse system. The reforms described here have thus been as much a story of political change as one of policy reform. To invoke Gourevitch, new policies require new politics, and the past two decades have involved fundamental—and interconnected—changes in both.

In the next chapter, I begin my analysis of French and German adjustment with a discussion of the postwar golden age of welfare-capitalist expansion, characterized by rapid economic growth and expanding welfare states. During this period, the two countries were transformed from economic wastelands with discredited political systems into exemplars of successful, democratic capitalism. Like those that emerged during the subsequent eras of socialized marketization and managed austerity, the systems that emerged in the 1950s and 1960s were the products of complex processes of political negotiation and institutional transformation whose outcomes were far from inevitable. To be sure, the challenges of postwar reconstruction favored certain solutions over others, but there were a number of courses that the two countries could have taken. Their choices of paths, informed by historical precedent and political innovation, would in turn help to define the contexts within which later adjustment strategies would develop.

2

The Rise and Fall of the Postwar Golden Age and the Development of French and German Welfare Capitalism

In 1945, France and Germany were unlikely candidates for the political and economic successes that would mark their next three decades. The events of the interwar period and the war itself had left a legacy of completely discredited political elites and institutions, shattered economies, fractured societies, and, particularly in Germany, an unprecedented scale of physical destruction, even for a country well familiar with the ravages of war. In France, the disgrace of Vichy collaboration had seemingly furnished a negative answer to the old question, born during the Revolution, whether a stable democracy could ever firmly take root there. With the liberation, those who had suffered at the hands of the regime carried out an anti-collaborationist purge of political, social, and business elites marked by thousands of executions, many carried out in summary fashion.[1] The economic situation was scarcely more encouraging. Stifled during the late nineteenth century and early twentieth century, during the war the French economy had suffered extensive shortages exacerbated by the Germans' large-scale expropriation of resources. If the French situation was one of chaos, recrimination, and deprivation, Germany's was one of complete devastation. Most major cities had been bombed into rubble; millions of soldiers and civilians had been killed in the war and the Holocaust; countless survivors were starving in the streets; and millions of destitute refugees from formerly German territory to the east continued to stream into the country. The war had left the country occupied and bereft of the functioning political institutions required for reconstruction. Each in its own way, then, France and Germany were in their darkest hour in the mid-1940s.

By the 1960s, circumstances in the two countries had changed beyond recognition. France and Germany had constructed effective democracies and two of the world's most successful capitalist economies out of the devastation and poverty left in the war's wake.[2] In Germany, totalitarianism and militarism had yielded to a democracy that fulfilled the disappointed hopes of the Weimar Republic, turning the country from an international pariah into a model of political stability. The booming economy, supported by exports of high-quality consumer products, was creating enormous wealth, and an expanded welfare state helped sustain the social peace and political legitimacy. France, too, had become one of the world's most successful capitalist economies, leading observers to dub the period the *trente glorieuses,* or "thirty glorious years" of postwar growth. Politically, with the advent of the Fifth Republic in 1958, France left behind the parliamentary instability and ineffectiveness of the postwar Fourth Republic, which Charles de Gaulle had dismissed as a "regime of mediocrity and chloroform."[3] The new constitution provided a solution to the constant shifts between authoritarianism and democracy that had plagued the country during the nineteenth century. A new political elite, inculcated with a modernizing ethos, took the reins of the economy, engineering its complete transformation and providing the institutional "motor" whose absence Stanley Hoffmann has identified as the source of the economic stagnation of the Third Republic's "stalemate society."[4] Under the direction of Pierre Laroque, France also created the beginnings of a comprehensive welfare state,[5] which expanded gradually during the postwar period, compensating workers for the economic dislocation associated with rapid growth.

This chapter describes and explains this era of *welfare-capitalist expansion* in both countries. The welfare-capitalist models that developed during this period represented distinct national responses to the tasks of economic reconstruction and laid the groundwork for prosperity. Like many advanced industrial countries, France and Germany placed their faith in the capacity of public policy to promote growth and social stability.[6] Postwar policymakers worked to tame "the violence of the market" and create a mutually supportive relationship between collective and individual well-being.[7] This effort to transform economy and society reflected a repudiation of prewar classical economic orthodoxies, which held that the disruptive effects of economic cycles were unavoidable.

These responses to the challenges of postwar reconstruction and renewal were not entirely new, however, involving admixtures of tradition and innovation and turning many of the institutional arrangements of the past to new purposes. In the late 1940s, Jean Monnet, French commissioner of the Commissariat Général du Plan (CGP), created the first of a series of economic plans that returned the state to its historically dominant role in managing the economy. Since the time of Louis XIV's mercantilist Economics Minister Jean-Baptiste Colbert and until well into the nineteenth century, the French state had acted as a powerful motor of economic growth.[8] After World War II, the state once again became the primary locus of political-economic authority, as officials transformed the agrarian society of the nineteenth century into a vibrant, competitive, and prospering industrial economy. The Germans, similarly, returned to the bank-centered financial system that had helped drive industrialization in the mid- to late nineteenth century.[9] Following the political and economic chaos of the interwar period, after 1945 the banks once again became key motors of economic development, but in a context of a stable democracy and an export-driven economy supported by an extensive welfare state.

These transformations in the French and German models of welfare capitalism inaugurated a sixty-year period of continual institutional and policy adaptation. During the first three postwar decades, novel policies and institutions helped create a golden age of rapid economic growth. Then, as the French and German economies slowed in the 1970s, authorities devised a series of institutional and policy experiments in the hope of re-creating the earlier economic dynamism. In France after 1974, the center-right governments under Prime Minister Raymond Barre and President Valéry Giscard d'Estaing cut subsidies to large French multinationals and turned to promoting small and medium-sized enterprises (SMEs) as the way to return France to international competitiveness.[10] In the early 1980s, Socialist President François Mitterrand opted for an intensification of dirigisme, involving extensive nationalizations and expanded public spending. In Germany, policymakers in the 1970s responded to the darkening economic climate by promoting regional networks of internationally competitive firms and financial institutions. These efforts laid the groundwork for Germany's return to growth in the 1980s, when the country once again became an object of international admiration.

In the following sections, I describe the development of the transformed French and German postwar political economies and the emergence of novel institutional and policy arrangements during the postwar golden age and, later, in response to its decline. In both countries, authorities devised novel institutions and policy arrangements to support rapid economic growth while reconstructing and expanding their welfare states to preserve social and political stability and provide workers with stakes in the new economic order. The successes of the period were not attributable to economic policy alone, however. Rather, expanded social-policy arrangements provided essential support for the two countries' economic transformations.

New Variations on Old Themes: The Development of Postwar French Welfare Capitalism

Echoing elements of Colbert's seventeenth-century mercantilism, Revolutionary Jacobinism, and Vichy statist corporatism, postwar French dirigisme enshrined the state as the agent of social and economic change.[11] This institutional "restoration" reflected the venerable French view that "the state represent[s] an oasis of enlightenment and integrity amidst a desert of selfish, risk-averse societal actors" and that, by uniting "the multitude . . . in a single body," the state's pursuit of the "general will" on behalf of all citizens would, in Jean-Jacques Rousseau's famous formulation, "forc[e] them to be free."[12] In the postwar context, the notion of freedom would come to be inextricably bound up with that of economic prosperity as policymakers worked to transform the French stalemate society of the Third Republic, dominated by agriculture and small, risk-averse family firms, into a vibrant capitalist society.[13] Dirigisme thus represented a radical change from the prewar system, returning an activist state to what many saw as its rightful position as the engineer of the general welfare, from which all private weal was presumed to flow.

The postwar system was not merely a reinstatement of older statist models, however. Rather, it involved new mechanisms of intervention that were consistent with the demands of the postwar economic context. At first, policymakers emphasized the protection of domestic markets and the promotion of strategic economic sectors, such as coal, steel, and electricity, through the means of economic planning.[14] This strategy focused on developing segments of the economy "on which the increase in all other forms of industrial output was believed to depend."[15] This labor-exclusionary conspiracy in the public interest between the state and big business relied on a synthesis of Cartesian rationality and insularity to overcome the entrenched positions of Malthusian family firms and agriculture sheltered by the Third Republic. Protected from competition by high levels of tariffs and "by and large wish[ing] to be left alone,"[16] French companies before 1940 prioritized stability over growth and solvency over profitability. Lacking both the desire and the apparatus to change the French economy, the policymakers of the Third Republic focused their attention instead on subsidizing agriculture and particular, favored industries. This coddling posture was emblematic of the regime's general ethos of placating powerful economic interests for the sake of social and political stability, whose absence had produced more than a century of social unrest and political violence. With the exception of the short-lived leftist Popular Front in the 1930s, state economic policies during the entire period of the Third Republic aimed to preserve rather than transform the existing economic system, resulting, on the eve of World War II, in a stagnant and still-agrarian economy.

During postwar reconstruction, French planners, headed by Jean Monnet, endeavored to "increase production, expand trade, raise productivity to the level of the most advanced countries, assure full employment, and raise the standard of living."[17] The concentration of authority in the Planning Commission (CGP) was designed to rationalize the decision-making process, promote the efficient use of scarce resources, and obviate the pattern of dominance by particularistic ministries that had characterized the Third Republic. The First, or Monnet, Plan (1946–1953), as it came to be called, set detailed production targets and directed state resources to critical sectors, in particular steel, coal, transportation, agricultural machinery, and electricity.[18] The Second Plan (1954–1957) also prioritized heavy industry but enlarged its scope to include the entire manufacturing sector in the hope of removing "bottlenecks" to growth.[19] The Second Plan provided the general blueprint for subsequent versions, which were characterized by attention to the "*interrelationships* between different economic activities" and a growing emphasis on coherence in economic policy.[20] This new approach to economic policy met with an astounding degree of success, as growth targets were either met or surpassed, inaugurating an era of unprecedented economic dynamism.

Although the CGP represented the core of early incarnations of the postwar dirigiste model, over the ensuing decades this system underwent a constant process of innovation as responsibilities and mechanisms of intervention shifted in response to changing economic circumstances. As growth accelerated and the shortages of the immediate postwar period receded, France turned to a strategy of achieving growth through international competitiveness. The dominance of the CGP and technical ministries (e.g., labor, agriculture, and industry) declined in favor of the Ministry of Finance, which gradually extended its influence by funneling funds toward (or away from) particular firms and policy initiatives. By the mid-1950s, it had become a super-ministry, with extensive power over the entire economy.[21] This concentration of authority intensified with the advent of the Fifth Republic, whose strengthened executive provided authorities with increased leverage over a wide range of economic and industrial policies. It was also reinforced by the growing prominence of Keynesian economic ideas, as an embrace of deficit spending provided a rationale for the shift in the ministry's role from France's accountant to its primary paymaster. The inflation produced by high levels of public spending was combated on the domestic front through extensive price controls and, in the international arena, through periodic, aggressive devaluations designed to protect the price competitiveness of French exports.[22] Within the ministry itself, power was increasingly concentrated in the Treasury, or Trésor, which employed discretionary credit allocation and administered pricing to shape the character and direction of French economic development.[23] By the 1970s, the Trésor had become the "sanctuary inside the temple of the Ministry of Finance, the economic apex in a centralized state."[24] The result was an extremely insular policymaking process that excluded not only social groups, but also many government ministries, providing French economic-policy elites with an extremely coherent and powerful apparatus for intervening in the economy.

Just as the institutional resources available to governments evolved during the postwar period, so did the goals and modalities of economic policy. Although the overriding aim of rapid, industrially based growth remained a constant, changing economic circumstances and institutional contexts led French policymakers to alter the means by which they sought to achieve it. After the creation of the Fifth Republic in 1958, the Gaullist political establishment used France's strengthened political executive to accelerate the pace of economic modernization. The French economy having been opened to intra-European competition with the signing of the Treaty of Rome in 1957, economic imperatives were increasingly formulated in terms of promoting French competitiveness abroad. Accordingly, the sectoral plans designed to remedy industrial shortages and to facilitate postwar reconstruction gave way to a series of so-called *grands projets* in the public sector. These were combinations of "subsidies, captive markets, and the transfer of technologies developed in public research labs" designed to "catapul[t] French industry to positions of global leadership in such sectors as nuclear power, high-speed trains, and digital telephone switches,"[25] as well as aerospace and commercial aviation. During the late 1950s and early 1960s, the pressures associated with economic openness intensified amid growing concerns about the lack of competitiveness of small French firms and their residual Malthusian outlook. In an effort to overcome these two perceived obstacles to economic success, French authorities used forced mergers among firms in the private sector to create enormous "national champions." With the benefits of state largesse and supportive industrial policies, it was hoped, these massive conglomerates could compete with American multinationals and restore France to a position of international economic leadership.[26]

French policymaking after the war was not limited to promoting growth and the structural transformation of the economy, however. It also aimed to buffer French society from the economic dislocation resulting from rapid growth through the construction of an expanded postwar welfare state. Through the construction of a universal system of social protection, French policymakers aimed to rectify the inequalities of the system of mutual-aid societies, or "friendly societies," that had developed during the late nineteenth and early twentieth centuries. Organized and managed by workers, these organizations provided protection from potentially disastrous interruptions in their incomes due to work accidents, sickness, and old age. Although they represented progress, the societies failed to cover significant segments of the French working class, particularly the poorest workers.[27] Even for members, however, the level of protection varied widely and depended on the resources available in a particular industry and locality.[28] This fragmentary, residual system remained largely unchanged until 1940.[29] Just as policymakers during the Third Republic had failed to develop a coherent set of economic policies, they largely neglected social protection, which was seen as the burden of workers alone.[30] As a result, the development of France's welfare state lagged well behind that of other European countries, particularly Germany.

Entrusted to Pierre Laroque, who had been named director of social assistance in 1944, the construction of the postwar welfare state was initially inspired by the universalistic model that William Beveridge had seen through in Britain in 1942 and aimed to remedy the underdeveloped, fragmented character of French social protection. This project was not only consistent with the Keynesian economic ideas of the time; it also aimed to express wartime solidarity and give institutional expression and support to a new social order. In Laroque's words, "The plan for social security aims not merely at improving workers' material situation; it also, and especially, should involve the creation of a new social order in which workers can assume their full responsibilities."[31] This grand vision was echoed in the preamble to the 1946 Constitution, which asserted the right of all citizens to work and to obtain "the appropriate means of subsistence" from society in the event that they find themselves unable to do so.[32] The central tenets of Laroque's blueprint—unity (a single system financed by a single fund), universality (with respect to both the extent of coverage of the population and the risks against which workers were to be protected), and uniformity (the same benefits for all)—thus reflected a powerful social as well as economic logic.[33]

Laroque's invocation of workers as the welfare state's primary constituency reflected both the rapid expansion that the French industrial working class had undergone since the 1920s and the postwar vision of economic growth predicated on Fordist mass production. It also, however, provided intimations of a coming discrepancy between the universalistic vision that governed its creation and the institutional form that it assumed. Because the architects of the postwar French welfare state tended to equate citizens with workers, they assumed that a system aimed at protecting the latter would ipso facto benefit the former. Although it made sense in the postwar context of rapid growth and a growing working class, this conceptual primacy of workers as the welfare state's main constituency led to an institutional framework that fell well short of the solidaristic, universalistic goals envisioned by Laroque and his colleagues.[34] Both the structure of benefits and the institutions through which they were financed and managed perpetuated the uneven coverage that Laroque had hoped to rectify.

This "failure of the solidaristic welfare state" was also the result of a series of political battles between the architects of the new system and salaried employees (*cadres*) and affluent independents.[35] A 1930 social-security law had established a fixed income ceiling for obligatory participation in social-insurance schemes, and workers who earned more could opt out. French *cadres,* or white-collar management, and the self-employed had exploited this provision to negotiate a series of occupationally based benefits that were much more generous than those available to manual workers. As a result, these groups feared that the incorporation of their schemes into the nascent *régime général* after 1945 would both increase their financial burden and reduce the generosity of their benefits. Over the next three years, white-collar workers and the self-employed vigorously defended the independence of their funds. In 1948, Parliament responded with a law that preserved the independence of occupational pension schemes, dealing a serious blow to Laroque's vision of a universalistic welfare state. This development also validated the idea that social benefits should be financed through payroll taxes and that current benefits would be financed out of current contributions.

Although the postwar French welfare state thus failed to realize Laroque's universalistic aspirations, it clearly represented a major gain for many French workers relative to the prewar era. What is more, with the advent of the Fifth Republic in 1958, the French welfare state underwent a significant period of expansion, as coverage was extended to numerous additional segments of the population and a large number of additional benefits were created. For example, a unified unemployment-insurance fund (the Union Nationale pour l'Emploi dans l'Industrie et le Commerce [UNEDIC]), managed jointly by employers' and workers' representatives, was created in 1958. Complementary pensions, which only *cadres* had enjoyed since 1947, were extended to nearly all French workers in 1961. This pattern was duplicated for health care in 1966, with the creation of an independent, bipartite system of insurance for non-salaried, non-agricultural workers (the Caisse Nationale d'Assurance-Maladie des Travailleurs Salariés [CNAMTS]). By 1970, the vast majority of the French population was insured against the primary social risks, whether through the *régime général*, occupationally distinct social-insurance funds, or direct state benefits.

This combination of innovative social and economic policies and institutions in the years after World War II helped sustain the most remarkable period of economic growth in French history. Between 1950 and 1958, the aggregate rate of French economic growth was 41 percent, a figure that accelerated to an astonishing 123 percent between 1958 and 1973 under the Fifth Republic.[36] On an annual basis, growth averaged an impressive 4.9 percent between 1953 and 1961 and an even more striking 5.6 percent between 1961 and 1973. A major factor driving this growth was increased productivity rates, which rose by an annual average of 4.3 percent between 1953 and 1979, a figure that would be even higher if we exclude the years following the OPEC oil shock of 1973.[37] Real wages increased significantly until 1965,[38] notwithstanding the negative effects on purchasing power exerted by significant inflation and periodic currency devaluations. Despite these increases in real wages, moreover, unemployment remained negligible, averaging an annual 2 percent between 1952 and 1959 and only 1.8 percent between 1959 and 1969.[39] Moreover, the expanded social-protection system provided workers with additional economic support, thereby promoting social peace and the stability on which Fordist industrial growth relied. Not only was the French postwar economy producing unprecedented levels of wealth, but rising real wages and an expanded welfare state were providing large segments of the French population with an important stake in the system's economic success.

By the late 1960s, the millions of Frenchmen who had left the countryside for the rapidly expanding manufacturing sector in the late 1940s and 1950s thus enjoyed both rising incomes and greater protection from economic dislocation provided by an extensive pension system, health insurance, unemployment benefits, and the beginnings of a network of state-sponsored income-support policies. Economic growth boosted aggregate demand and payroll-tax receipts while facilitating continued capital accumulation by supporting social peace.[40] Plentiful employment moderated levels of income inequality in the 1960s, partially reversing earlier increases.[41] The revamped French welfare state and political economy thus provided the foundations of rapid growth while offering French citizens a greater share of the benefits of economic growth than they had ever before enjoyed.

From Devastation to Dynamism: The German Social Market Economy and the Economic Miracle

As in France, the construction of the postwar German political economy involved innovative variations on old institutional themes. The success of these new arrangements was even more remarkable in Germany, however, given the magnitude of the challenges facing postwar German authorities. Whereas most of France had been spared destruction by rapid surrender in 1940, German infrastructure lay in ruins, with at least 75 percent of most major cities either heavily damaged or completely destroyed. While casualties in France were relatively light, in Germany, the Holocaust, six years of combat on two fronts, and extensive Allied bombing had killed millions. While the French economy suffered from widespread shortages, the German economy barely existed, with what little exchange there was taking place on the barter system.

Rebuilding the German economy, society, and polity from the ground up was the unenviable task bequeathed to those who had remained relatively untainted by active participation with the Nazi regime. Konrad Adenauer, the first chancellor of the Federal Republic, was a typical member of the new elite. Mayor of Cologne during the 1920s, Adenauer was a Catholic whose spiritual homeland was the westward-looking, industrial Rhineland rather than militarist, agrarian Prussia, which he had always distrusted.[42] With the creation of the Federal Republic in 1949 and Germany's return to (relative) sovereignty, Adenauer's political experience, opposition to the Nazi regime, and relatively good relations with the Allied authorities made him an obvious candidate for the leadership of the newly created center-right party, the ecumenical Christian Democratic Union (Christlich Demokratische Union Deutschlands [CDU]). Adenauer's social Catholicism, which stressed social responsibility as an important component of faith, dovetailed nicely with the nascent Social Market Economy, which called for a synthesis of market capitalism with a generous welfare state and empowered non-state actors.

The concept of the Social Market Economy emerged from a synthesis of a number of earlier economic discourses. Among the most important was "Ordoliberalism," which developed during the interwar period and stressed the need for a "strong state committed to the restoration of a competitive economic order."[43] Like Keynesianism, Ordoliberalism developed as a response to the economic chaos of the interwar period, which its progenitors—notably, Alexander Rüstow and Walter Eucken—had interpreted through the lens of the failures of the Weimar Republic. Rüstow and Eucken blamed the collapse of the German economy in the 1920s on the capture of the state by parochial interest groups, which Rüstow demonized as "the wild beasts of pluralistic economic egoism."[44] As a result, they argued, economic policy under Weimar had favored the interests of powerful social groups, such as the Junker agrarian elite, over those of the economy as a whole, thereby undermining the legitimacy of Weimar democracy. They called for a strong state capable of creating a functioning market order but that, with this task completed, could allow market forces to govern.

One of Ordoliberalism's early adherents, Adenauer's Economics Minister Ludwig Erhard, was instrumental in developing many of the core concepts of the Social Market Economy. Trained as an economist, Erhard had become the economic director of the British–American Bizone in 1947 and was the architect of the creation of the deutsche Mark in 1948, which represented an important step toward economic stabilization. Originally opposed to redistributive social policies, the Ordoliberal doctrine advanced by Erhard and others was gradually reinterpreted through the lens of Adenauerian social Catholicism. This resulted in an acceptance of significant economic regulation and a developed welfare state, both of which were seen as essential for sustaining a market economy in the presence of the social strains of reconstruction.[45] In the hope of reconciling rapid economic growth with social peace, the architects of the Social Market Economy began to employ a relatively expansive notion of market-conforming policies, involving a managed economic order governed jointly by the state, large banks, firms (often organized into cartels), and quasi-monopolistic unions and employers' associations.[46] The result of this synthesis of Ordoliberalism and social Catholicism was an expression of "the balance between the liberal and the social democratic impulses in postwar Germany."[47] Somewhere between a command economy and a truly liberal order, the Social Market Economy embraced a number of illiberal arrangements in the interests of building capitalist prosperity.[48]

A similar mixture of liberalism and organized capitalism characterized the development of German neocorporatism, which, like French dirigisme, emerged in response to the postwar challenges of growth and reconstruction.[49] In contrast to the primacy of the French state, the German variant of corporatism was predicated on a set of "parapublic institutions."[50] In industrial relations, these institutions involved cooperative, mutually beneficial relationships among unions and employers. As Kathleen Thelen describes, in the immediate postwar period unions won seats on company supervisory boards, or works councils, which addressed questions relating to working conditions and the organization of production.[51] The government's extension of legal protection to these councils through the Works Constitution Act of 1952 was more an act of recognition than one of constitution, given that these institutions had already existed for years in a number of key sectors.[52]

The German network of firm-level works councils and the system of *Mitbestimmung*, or codetermination, that it underpinned was complemented by the emergence of cooperative, sectorally organized wage bargaining. Lacking coherence in the immediate postwar period, German collective-bargaining practices offered a strategic disadvantage to workers, whose isolation from their colleagues in other sectors weakened them in a number of important battles with employers. In response, IG Metall, the German metalworkers' union, spearheaded efforts to replace the haphazard pattern of wage negotiations with an organized structure and to develop a coherent union bargaining strategy. As a result, by 1956 IG Metall had become the de facto leader of all German wage bargaining.[53] By the 1960s, what Thelen calls the "dual system" of works councils and sectorally organized wage bargaining had been consolidated, providing important support for the cooperative ethos of negotiated adjustment that lay at the heart of the postwar German political economy.

The importance of such "parapublic institutions" in German industrial relations paralleled developments in other areas of the political economy. During the late 1940s and early 1950s, large German banks returned to their historical place at the center of the financial system. Under Otto von Bismarck, these banks, in cooperation with the German state, had provided significant financial support for investment in the rapidly growing industrial sector.[54] Broken up during the occupation by the Allies, who distrusted their economic influence and earlier support of the Nazi war campaign, the banks rapidly reconsolidated. Although this process was at first only tacitly permitted by Erhard's more general efforts to limit the federal government's power over the financial sector, the state later promoted bank reconsolidation through legislation, including a 1958 law that eliminated 1930s-era restrictions on the number of branches allowed to individual banks.[55] The result was a macro-corporatist financial system involving close collaboration among the recentralized business associations and the banks, which acted as "prefects" guiding the decisions of firms in whose performance significant cross-shareholding meant that they were heavily invested.[56] German banks thus not only emerged as the principal source of industrial finance, but they also became the primary stakeholders in, and important arbiters of, the trajectory of German economic development. The German banking system "ke[pt] a watchful eye on a new company, . . . restrain[ed] the speculative excesses of undisciplined investors, and . . . [had] the authority, ultimately, through their control of shareholders' proxy votes, to tell the managers of German industry where to get off."[57]

As with the financial and industrial-relations systems, the development of the postwar German welfare state was governed by a combination of historical legacies and innovation. Confronted with mass poverty and millions of refugees from formerly German territories to the east, the policymakers of the Federal Republic realized that an expanded network of social policies would be required to preserve the social peace on which economic growth depended. In many ways, the postwar German welfare state was modeled on the earlier, Bismarckian framework of social insurance, which provided workers with important administrative responsibilities. Nineteenth-century and early-twentieth-century social legislation, however, had "aimed predominantly to contain the worker movement, to reduce strife between workers and employers over industrial accidents, and to further national integration."[58] By contrast, postwar German social policy worked toward the *affirmative* goals of maintaining social peace and providing workers with a stake in German economic success.

Whereas the development of the postwar French welfare state involved the construction of novel institutions with little in the way of historical example, the welfare state's expansion in Germany was more a matter of extending existing arrangements and adapting them to altered circumstances. In the late nineteenth and early twentieth centuries, efforts by Bismarck and his successors to neutralize opposition to his policies of national unification and rapid industrialization had led to the creation of one of the most extensive European welfare states.[59] Bismarck's social policies were far from universalistic, however, with particular groups such as artisans and white-collar workers treated much more favorably than manual workers under a fragmented network of separate occupational schemes.[60] After the war, these historical discrepancies in welfare generosity led to demands, particularly from unions and the Social Democratic Party (Sozialdemokratische Partei Deutschlands [SPD]), for the creation of a universalistic welfare state along Beveridgean lines. As in France, however, resistance by white-collar workers and independents contributed to the defeat of solidaristic reform and the preservation of separate blue- and white-collar schemes.

Beginning in the mid-1950s, German policymakers undertook a series of initiatives designed to remedy this institutional fragmentation and distributional inequality. The first such initiative was Adenauer's 1957 pension reform, which was a response to discontent with the existing system's economic disparities, concerns about escalating state subsidies to the pension system, and the political pressures surrounding the federal election of the same year. Designed with the ambitious aim to share the wealth of an expanding economy with the retirees who had contributed to it during their working lives, Adenauer's measure replaced Bismarck's residual antipoverty benefits with pensions linked to rising aggregate wage levels. The new "pay-as-you-go" system was funded by contributions shared equally by employers and employees and financed current benefits (at a statistical norm of 70 percent of previous wages) out of current receipts. By indexing benefits to aggregate wage levels, which accounted for increasing rates of productivity, it also represented significant material gains for blue-collar workers.[61] The 1957 reform smoothed over social divisions by preserving the autonomy of the funds of artisans and other independents while placing them under the white- and blue-collar schemes.[62]

Sustained by the generalizing prosperity of the German of the *Wirtschafts wunder,* or "Economic Miracle," the pension system created in 1957 provided a touchstone for further extensions of German social policy.[63] For example, the Social Welfare Act of 1961 substantially expanded income support for the poor by increasing the generosity of means-tested benefits, which had previously covered only basic living expenses. This system of *Sozialhilfe,* or social assistance, was conceived as an effort to facilitate adjustment to economic dislocation by plugging gaps in coverage left by the occupationally based welfare system.[64] In 1972, a basic, state-managed pension benefit was established to provide income to those elderly poor who were not vested in an occupational program. Unemployment insurance, originally created in 1927, was significantly expanded by the *Arbeitsförderungsgesetz* (Employment Promotion Act) of 1969 and unified under the administrative auspices of the tripartite Bundesanstalt für Arbeit, or Federal Labor Office.[65]

In the 1950s and 1960s, the expanded German welfare state contributed to an impressive record of economic performance and social and political stability. Between 1950 and 1973, real annual economic growth averaged 5 percent, while unemployment rates averaged only 2.7 percent between 1952 and 1964 and a negligible .8 percent between 1965 and 1973. Productivity rates skyrocketed, and the average annual growth of 6 percent in real gross domestic product (GDP) per man hour between 1950 and 1973 was the highest of any major European country.[66] With its developing specialization in high-quality consumer and industrial goods, Germany became one of the world's largest exporters, with nearly a quarter of manufacturing goods sold abroad by 1959. Inflation, held in check by rapid productivity increases and the hawk-like stewardship of the Bundesbank, despite the bounding economic growth of the period, amounted to a mere 2.7 percent, the lowest rate in Europe.[67] Both the federal budget and the social-welfare funds enjoyed healthy surpluses, with the fiscal surplus averaging 2.2 percent of GDP between 1952 and 1972 and social-contribution rates remaining at a modest 26.5 percent of gross wages in 1970, despite two decades of social-policy expansion.[68] Social peace prevailed and strikes were rare, as unprecedented rights in collective bargaining and shop-floor management, combined with generous welfare benefits, induced workers to accept real wage increases that were below productivity gains.[69]

Paradise Lost: The Decline of the Golden Age and the Challenges of Economic Renewal

In the mid- to late 1960s, the felicitous political, economic, and social contexts that the postwar French and German models of welfare capitalism had enjoyed entered a period of crisis. The economic downturn mirrored developments across the advanced industrial world, where rates of productivity growth, business profitability, and output-to-capital ratios all began to slip in the late 1960s, resulting in a squeeze on profits and a decline in rates of investment.[70] Some have argued that this disheartening turn of events was due primarily to the saturation of increasingly internationalized markets for Fordist, mass-produced goods, which had been the mainstay of postwar growth in both Europe and the United States.[71] Others emphasize international factors, such as the collapse in 1969 of the Bretton Woods international monetary system, which had sustained balance-of-payment equilibria and helped control inflation.[72] Whatever the initial cause of the slowdown, however, nearly all observers agree on the determinative impact of the first oil shock in 1973, which led to a sharp spike in the price of primary industrial goods, a concomitant decline in business investment, increases in inflation, and a decline in rates of economic growth.

The effects of these shocks were sudden and dramatic. Annual growth rates, which had averaged 4.9 percent annually between 1950 and 1973 across the advanced industrial countries, dropped by nearly half, to 2.5 percent, between 1973 and 1979.[73] The average OECD unemployment rate rose from 2.9 percent in 1973 to 5.6 percent in 1979, spurred on by a secular decline in industrial employment.[74] Annual rates of inflation in Europe, which had averaged 3.4 percent between 1948 and 1969, jumped to 9.1 percent for the period between 1969 and 1979.[75] By the mid-1970s, policymakers had begun to search for effective policy responses to a sustained period of political-economic crisis that undermined the postwar arrangements that had previously proved so successful.

France and Germany were no exceptions to this pattern, as economic difficulties in each were punctuated by increasingly frequent social unrest. In France, the Gaullist strategy of economic modernization through labor exclusion and limits on wage growth had worked well in the felicitous economic context of the late 1950s and early 1960s. After 1965, however, increasing rates of inflation, declining real wage growth, and rising unemployment fueled workers' discontent, which eventually exploded into the near-revolution of May–June

1968.[76] In response, policymakers turned their attention from promoting rapid industrial growth to limiting its negative social and political side effects, as the "technocratic considerations of economic modernization increasingly took a backseat to the political imperatives of regime preservation."[77] In the 1970s, French authorities undertook a series of efforts to mute social unrest and preserve the Gaullist establishment's hold on power, which was also being challenged by an increasingly aggressive and coherent political left.[78] These political and economic pressures further undermined France's economic performance; unemployment and inflation rates continued to increase, and annual GDP growth rates declined to barely half their level during the heyday of postwar growth. In less than a decade, France had gone from an emblem of success and an object of admiration to an exemplar of inept economic management and social instability.

French authorities did not stand idly by as economic circumstances worsened, however. Rather, they embarked on a series of policy and institutional experiments designed to remedy some of the rigidities of the dirigiste system with a view to restoring the economic dynamism of the postwar period. Under President Valéry Giscard d'Estaing, elected in 1974, and Raymond Barre, who became prime minister in 1976, the government enacted a series of measures aimed at promoting the development of SMEs and encouraging economic competition to force French national champions to rationalize and modernize. For example, authorities made state aid to industry contingent on matching funds from private investors, strengthened antitrust regulations, and worked to foster the development of the market for private equity to wean French firms off of state aid. It was hoped that this turn to market mechanisms would, in Barre's words, produce "a profound transformation of structures and behavior across France."[79] The government created a new agency, the Comité Interministeriel pour l'Aménagement des Structures Industrielles (CIASI), to bail out firms in financial difficulty with a combination of private and public funds.[80] This experiment with structured liberalization, however, was undermined by the government's fears of rising unemployment, the electoral threat of a politically ascendant left, and the sheer weight of France's national champions. These conglomerates successfully pressured the state for aid, thereby effectively transforming CIASI's role from facilitating economic transformation to propping up uncompetitive lame ducks.[81]

With the election of Socialist President François Mitterrand in 1981 and a large Socialist Party majority in Parliament, France turned to a different kind of economic experimentation. If Giscard and Barre had tried to restore prosperity by attenuating the state's influence over the economy, Mitterrand sought to do so by extending it. The new administration employed a wide range of heavy-handed policies, including massive aid to industry and extensive nationalizations, and stepped up welfare spending, all aimed at restructuring and modernizing the French economy through a "rupture with capitalism."[82] While enabling the left to make good on its electoral promises to create jobs, boost workers' incomes, and promote consumption, this policy of "redistributive Keynesianism," it was hoped, would also help to reverse the post-1973 economic decline.

In Germany, too, the advent of hard times in the late 1960s led to a period of change, as authorities devised a series of novel institutions designed to foster economic renewal. In response to the recession of 1966–1967, for example, the newly elected "grand coalition" of the SPD and CDU/CSU (Christlich Soziale Union) established a framework of so-called *konzertierte Aktion,* or concerted action, which represented a partial departure from the precepts of the Social Market Economy and a qualified embrace of Keynesian demand management. As Peter Katzenstein describes, this arrangement involved a series of high-level meetings among the government, unions, employers, and the Bundesbank aimed at overcoming coordination problems, restarting growth, limiting real wage increases, controlling inflation, and spurring investment.[83] This attempt to fashion an overarching political-economic consensus, however, ultimately foundered in the aftermath of the first oil shock, when the Bundesbank undermined the government's expansionary fiscal policies by rapidly increasing interest rates, driving Germany into an even deeper recession in 1974–1975.[84] Although Germany continued to perform better than many of its European neighbors during the 1970s and early 1980s, these problems tarnished the Social Market Economy's record of adjustment and suggested the possibility that the postwar Economic Miracle might be coming to an end.

During the 1970s and 1980s, German authorities enacted a series of further institutional and policy changes designed to restore prosperity. Beginning in the mid-1970s, for example, they worked to reduce some of the rigidities of the bank-led system of industrial finance in an effort to boost export competitiveness. Officials in many German *Länder,* or federal states, promoted the development of SMEs by making more funds available for research and development, constructing new vocational-training centers, offering subsidized investment loans, and guaranteeing lending by small, regional banks. Such developments were most salient in Baden-Württemberg, where a historically high concentration of SMEs offered a superb laboratory for the development of public–private partnerships.[85] By the late 1980s, such efforts led to the emergence of a system of high wages and highly skilled, specialized workforces; a coherent strategy of producing high-quality goods for niche markets; and substantial information sharing among firms in particular sectors, which became a model in the eyes of many foreign observers.[86] Supported by a stable industrial-relations system and a celebrated vocational-training system, this production model helped preserve Germany's economic prominence and enabled the country to adjust better to economic austerity than many of its neighbors.[87]

France's and Germany's capacity for adjustment would be sorely tested in the 1980s and early 1990s, when both countries embarked on unprecedented projects of market making. For a combination of political and economic reasons, including a severe imbalance of payments,[88] upcoming elections, and a desire to maintain the country's leadership within the European Community, the French government made a dramatic "U-turn" in 1983, abandoning redistributive Keynesianism with the same alacrity with which it had embraced it in 1981. Over the next decade, French authorities would completely dismantle the edifice of dirigiste policymaking and embark on a period of radical liberalization and market creation. Similarly, following reunification in 1990, German authorities undertook the Herculean task of absorbing the formerly communist East and transforming it into a functioning market economy, working to rebuild a devastated economy and society from the ground up. In each case, market creation was supported by expansions of the welfare state designed to protect society from economic dislocation, thereby preserving social peace and making marketization politically feasible. While the outcomes of this period of "socialized marketization" would lead to new challenges, they were largely successful in achieving their principal aims of creating functioning market economies. I explore these transformations in greater detail in the next two chapters, beginning with a discussion of the French turn away from dirigisme.

3

Recasting France's Political-Economic Order

The Demise of Dirigisme and the Turn to the Market

On 10 May 1981, François Mitterrand became the first Socialist president to come to power in France since the advent of the Fifth Republic in 1958. This electoral revolution marked the end of the conservative Gaullist hegemony that had governed France during the previous two decades. It also embodied hopes for a new economic order in which the working class would be able to share more equitably in the fruits of economic growth. In the late 1970s, the industrial layoffs that had begun tentatively in the middle of that decade had accelerated dramatically, resulting in a jump in the unemployment rate from 2.8 percent in 1974 to 7.4 percent in 1981, a level unprecedented in the postwar era.[1] By 1981, it had become clear that the policies of constrained liberalization pursued by Giscard and Prime Minister Raymond Barre during the 1970s had failed to offer an effective response to France's employment crisis. Amid mounting public concern, the question of how to return France to prosperity was central to the campaign rhetoric and policy proposals of each of the presidential candidates. From Giscard on the right to Georges Marchais, leader of the French Communist Party (Parti Communiste Français [PCF]), on the left, each promised to find a durable solution to France's woes. Making political hay out of Giscard's failures, Mitterrand declared during the campaign: "Employment is the first of our obligations. I will devote my entire will to it."[2] With more than a million and a half unemployed, the French narrowly opted for the left's approach, giving Mitterrand a majority of 51.75 percent to Giscard's 48.25 percent in the run-off.[3]

The ensuing shift in the substance and orientation of French economic policy was no less dramatic than the change in personnel. From the earliest days of the campaign, Mitterrand had made clear how distinct his approach to restarting the French economy was from Giscard's. The core of the new administration's policy agenda dated back to the lead-up to the 1974 presidential election, which Mitterrand had narrowly lost to Giscard. In 1972, the Union of the Left, an electoral alliance of Socialists and Communists, had developed a "Common Program for Governing." In this platform, the left had pledged to undertake a fundamental break with capitalism through significant increases in public spending, massive nationalizations of the industrial and banking sectors, and an intensification of economic planning.[4] The narrowness of the right's victory in 1974—50.8 percent versus 49.2 percent—reflected the appeal of the Common Program to broad segments of the French electorate and the widespread conviction that France's problems required radical solutions.[5] In the 1981 campaign, the basic tenets of the Common Program were retained and incorporated into a "Socialist Project" penned by the Jacobin left of the Socialist Party (Parti Socialiste [PS]) under future Minister of Industry Jean-Pierre Chevènement. The document promised a rupture with "advanced liberal society" if the left were elected.[6]

When the left came to power in 1981, it moved quickly to implement this radically different approach to restarting the economy. Supported by a large Socialist majority in Parliament, Mitterrand and his government embarked on "the highest stage of dirigisme," using the powerful executive of the Fifth Republic to develop stepped-up industrial policies designed thoroughly to restructure the French economy while pursuing a "rupture with capitalism."[7] This policy of "redistributive Keynesianism" not only aimed to reverse the post-1973 economic decline by modernizing the French economy;[8] it also aimed to enact the left's electoral promises to create jobs, support consumption and incomes, and shelter workers from the increasingly widespread economic dislocation. The means by which this new agenda was to be implemented involved reorganizing the supply side of the economy, stimulating demand, "reconquering the domestic market," and relaunching research and development on a massive scale.[9] The government was thus attempting not merely to revitalize the economy, but to transform it.

Due to a combination of political and both domestic and international economic pressures, however, this brave new political-economic order collapsed nearly as quickly as it had begun. In 1982–1983, the government made an abrupt "U-turn," opting for policies of austerity in an effort to resolve a series of mounting economic problems that its policies had helped to create. This abrupt shift did not merely end the experiment with reflationary dirigisme, however. Rather, it initiated a period during which the entire postwar edifice of dirigiste policymaking would be dismantled. During the remainder of the 1980s, successive French governments embarked on an unprecedented project of market making, involving the abandonment of the system of preferential credit and industrial policies that had fueled the *trente glorieuses,* the replacement of bank lending with equity financing for French firms, and the introduction of a competitive financial-services sector.[10] This process of market-making accelerated under the center-right administration of Prime Minister Jacques Chirac, whose government entered into an uncomfortable "cohabitation" with President Mitterrand in 1986. Under Chirac, the French state lifted a series of controls over the labor market—notably, the 1974 "administrative authorization for layoffs"—privatized large numbers of nationalized firms, implemented major cuts in taxes and government spending, and undertook a wide-ranging deregulation of controls on capital and foreign exchange. In seven years, France had moved from the epitome of heavy-handed, *marxisant* statism to an acceptance of the market as the guiding principle for development.

Although clearly *liberal,* this move to the market was not *neoliberal* in inspiration, however, as the dismantling of dirigisme was accompanied by a significant expansion of the welfare state designed to preserve social peace and shelter workers from economic dislocation.[11] This period of socialized marketization, beginning in 1984, involved the creation of a wide range of income-support policies. In addition, successive governments rapidly expanded the early-retirement programs that had been introduced in the 1970s as means of reducing labor supply. They also instituted a number of "conversion poles," or locally based efforts to retrain laid-off workers, modernize infrastructure, and promote the creation of new firms in areas that had been most hurt by deindustrialization. This expansion of the welfare state not only supported the unprecedented project of market creation during this period; it was required to make marketization politically acceptable. Just as during the *trente glorieuses,* when the transformation of the country from a largely agrarian society into a vibrant industrial economy was facilitated by an expanded welfare state, in the less auspicious 1980s, the turn toward the market went hand in glove with the extension of the edifice of French social protection.

This chapter explores these seismic transformations of the French political economy during the 1980s. During this period, France undertook rapid economic liberalization supported by a major expansion and redeployment of the welfare state to preserve social peace and support the political legitimacy of the market-making process. I begin with the post-1981 embrace of "reflationary Keynesianism" and then explain why this "highest stage of dirigisme" was abandoned in 1982–1983. I then turn to an analysis of the twin processes of market creation and welfare-state expansion that followed the 1983 "U-turn." As opposed to most conventional accounts of the period, which focus on industrial and macroeconomic policies while largely neglecting developments in the welfare state, I argue that this redeployment of the French social-protection system was instrumental to the success of marketization. As during the period of postwar welfare-capitalist expansion, the dynamics of French political-economic change during this period cannot be explained without careful attention to developments in the welfare state and the broader political economy, as well as the mutually constitutive linkages between them.

The Swan Song of Dirigisme: Redistributive Keynesianism and the Marketization of the French Political Economy

In the heady days following its victory in 1981, the left moved quickly to transform the French economy and society. One of its first measures involved the reorganization of the supply side of the economy through a series of nationalizations of major industrial conglomerates and the bulk of the commercial and retail banking sector. This initiative, which represented the largest state seizure of firms since the immediate postwar years, involved both substantive and symbolic aspects. In substantive terms, the government sought to directly promote the growth of the segments of the economy on which economic growth and expanding employment were thought to depend most crucially. Symbolically, the government aimed to demonstrate its intention to follow through on its commitment to pursue a "rupture with capitalism." Fought tooth and nail by the right, these nationalizations were finally enacted in December 1981, after more than two months of acrimonious debate. When the nationalization program was completed in February 1982, the state controlled 24 percent of the employees and 60 percent of the annual investment in the industrial and energy sectors.[12] The extension of state control was even more dramatic in the banking sector, where the state controlled about 95 percent of the total turnover. In all, the share of the economy under state control had grown from 11 percent to 17 percent of GDP in the space of a few months.[13] In Mitterrand's words, this wave of nationalizations was designed to enable French firms to "play, as rapidly as possible, their rightful leading role in industrial policy." Nationalization was "a weapon for defending French economic production," through which to accomplish "what General de Gaulle did in the context of nuclear strategy: providing France with an economic striking capacity [*force de frappe*]."[14]

This grand vision of state-led transformation of the economy was equally characteristic of other aspects of the government's agenda. Under the leadership of Prime Minister Pierre Mauroy, the government adopted stepped-up industrial policies supported by massive increases in aid to industry. Together, these measures were designed to promote the recovery of troubled sectors and encourage the renewed expansion of industrial employment. Production targets were set for major sectors of the economy, with particular attention to those that had suffered most during the previous decade. In steel, for example, production was to increase from 18 million tons in 1981 to 26 million tons in 1986, and the target for coal output was set at 30 million tons in 1990, compared with 18 million in 1981.[15] Levels of aid to industry exploded as the government attempted to prime the pump of industrial production; for public-sector enterprises alone, subsidies amounted to 60 billion French francs (FFr) between 1982 and 1986, and total industrial subsidies rose from FFr 35 billion in 1981 to FFr 86 billion in 1985.[16] Not content with promoting employment in private industry and state-owned enterprises, the government directly created an additional two hundred thousand jobs in public administration between 1981 and 1983.[17] Together with the nationalization expenditures, these policies resulted in a massive increase in public spending, which rose by 27 percent in the government's first budget, prepared by Finance Minister Laurent Fabius.[18] Unsurprisingly, the sudden rise in spending resulted in an explosion of the budget deficit, which grew from 1.9 percent of GDP in 1981 to 3.2 percent of GDP in 1983.[19] In true Keynesian fashion, the government hoped that this massive injection of public resources into the economy would reap rewards in the medium term by increasing rates of economic growth, investment, and employment creation.

Not limited to the restructuring of industry, the government's agenda also focused on expanding social policies designed to shelter workers from economic precariousness and to support economic recovery by boosting aggregate demand. This "redistributive" facet of Mitterrand's program of "redistributive Keynesianism" entailed several distinct elements. The first set of initiatives involved significant increases in state benefits to poor or otherwise dependent citizens: Family allowances and housing benefits were raised,[20] the *minimum vieillesse,* or the basic pension benefit for the elderly poor, was increased by 62 percent between 1981 and 1983, and the minimum wage was increased by a full 10 percent.[21] Other, more symbolic measures were aimed at supplementing incomes by reducing unemployment. In 1982, as part of an effort to redistribute available work more broadly across the economy, the work week was reduced from forty to thirty-nine hours and a fifth week of legally required paid vacation was introduced.[22] In the same year, the age at which workers became eligible for full retirement benefits was reduced from sixty-five to sixty, and the number of participants in early-retirement schemes more than tripled between 1981 and 1983.[23] The fiscal drain caused by this ensemble of policies was partially paid for through highly progressive tax increases. In addition to implementing its campaign promise to introduce a "wealth tax" (the so-called *impôt sur la grande fortune* [IGF]), the government raised marginal tax rates for those in higher brackets and increased taxes on the profits of certain corporations.[24] These measures aimed to provide badly needed revenue while appealing to the government's leftist constituencies and satisfying the demands of the PCF, which saw the left's hold on power as a chance to shift revenue burdens from workers to capital. Whatever their palliative effects on the French budget, these tax increases were far from sufficient to restore it to balance.[25]

The degeneration of the French fiscal situation accompanied a mounting balance-of-payments crisis. Since the beginning of the Socialist-led administration, the attempt to restart economic and employment growth had been hampered by stubbornly high rates of inflation, the combined result of the aftermath of the 1979 oil crisis and the effects of stepped-up domestic spending.[26] Rising price levels in turn provided imports with a price advantage over domestically produced goods. The resulting "leakage" of domestic spending led to a surge in imports in 1982 and an explosion of the trade deficit, which rose from FFr 56 billion in 1981 to FFr 93 billion in 1982.[27] The trade deficit was worsened by the dire international economic environment. The government had assumed that the world would be restored to healthy rates of growth by 1983, which would have alleviated pressures on the French economy by boosting demand for exports.[28] These hopes were quickly disappointed when the advanced industrial countries were hit with their worst recession since World War II. To make matters worse, France's trading partners were raising interest rates to fight inflation,[29] accelerating the flight of French capital in search of higher returns.

The combined result of the mounting balance-of-payments crisis, capital flight, domestic inflation, and the exploding budget deficit was intense pressure on the French franc, which would eventually force the government to choose between pursuing its reflationary strategy and retaining its commitment to European institutions. As a member of the European Monetary System (EMS), the franc was allowed to fluctuate only within a certain band in terms of its value relative to other member currencies. The government had already devalued the currency in October 1981 to compensate for the inflationary pressures resulting from the sudden increase in public spending. As the value of the franc continued to fall in 1982,[30] and the government was faced with the prospect of a second devaluation, two schools of thought emerged among Mitterrand's advisers. The first, led by Chevènement and the PCF, called for a continuation of the government's spending policies coupled with a sharp devaluation of the franc, intensified exchange and trade controls, and withdrawal from the EMS, which would theoretically provide France with the autonomy in monetary policy required to continue its reflationary program. The second group, represented by Mauroy and Finance Minister Jacques Delors, favored a starkly different approach that involved retaining France's membership in the EMS and enacting a strict austerity policy to resolve the balance-of-payments crisis and end widespread capital flight.[31]

The second devaluation, undertaken in June 1982, was accompanied by the first steps to combat the overheating of the French economy and remedy the balance-of-payments crisis, measures that marked the beginnings of what would come to be known as the government's "U-turn" away from redistributive Keynesianism. The government introduced a four-month wage freeze (excepting the *salaire minimum interprofessionnel de croissance* [SMIC], or minimum wage) and a price freeze on almost all goods and services and promised to keep the budget deficit below 3 percent of GDP.[32] These "measures accompanying devaluation" also included a commitment to keep inflation below 10 percent in 1982 and below 8 percent in 1983.[33] In the short term, the reversal of policy orientation had the desired effects, as the rate of inflation of retail prices was reduced to 1.6 percent by October. Despite this initial success, however, these measures were insufficient, as pressures on the franc intensified and France's economic situation continued to worsen (economic growth in late 1982 declined to a mere .6 percent of GDP). Following a third devaluation (supported by a negotiated revaluation of the deutsche Mark), Mitterrand marked the victory of the Mauroy–Delors camp by opting for a program of "*rigueur*" involving an embrace of fiscal austerity and support for the franc. Public spending was reduced by FFr 24 billion; wage growth was capped at 8 percent (less than the prevailing rate of inflation); taxes were increased by FFr 40 billion (including increases in sales taxes, raised levies on the wealthiest taxpayers, and a "solidarity tax" of 1 percent designed to balance the social-security funds); and prices for public services were increased. By the end of 1983, France had completely abandoned "reflationary Keynesianism," opting instead for a strong franc, deflationary macroeconomic policies, and a balanced budget.

To be sure, economic considerations were central to the government's decision to undertake this precipitous U-turn. Although Mitterrand's long-standing political commitment to the European Community made him reluctant to pull France out of the EMS, even more important were the projected domestic economic consequences of such a decision, which would have resulted in an estimated 10–15 percent decline in the value of the franc and a trade deficit of more than FFr 2 billion per month.[34] Furthermore, Mitterrand and many of his advisers had become disillusioned about the economic potential of reflationary dirigisme, as a host of French firms, nationalized and private-sector alike, were failing to meet their production targets and suffering huge losses, which in turn impeded investment. As a result, state subsidies and industrial policies were increasingly devoted to the task of propping up uncompetitive lame ducks at the cost of diminished investment in sectors that stood a better chance of economic success.[35] Rather than creating jobs and increasing rates of economic growth, the government's policies had led to economic stagnation, major impediments to adjustment on the part of French business, and ballooning public and trade deficits.[36] They had also led to the overheating of the economy rather than restoring the country to prosperity. As Mitterrand would subsequently characterize the situation, "During this period we were like train conductors observing the rising engine temperature and wondering when we would have to ease up on the throttle."[37]

As Jonah Levy emphasizes, however, the decision to remain in the EMS and accept economic austerity was not dictated by economic factors alone. Rather, it reflected a number of political calculations and was ultimately a matter of choice rather than fate.[38] Public support for the government had been devastated by the economic crisis, and, with the legislative elections of 1986 looming, the left feared retribution at the polls.[39] The right was profiting politically from the dire state of the economy, which made its claims that the first government of the left in the history of the Fifth Republic was "unfit to govern" seem more and more credible. In this political context, the embrace of austerity was designed to demonstrate that the left could manage an advanced economy responsibly. Furthermore, the existence of a large Socialist Party majority in Parliament meant that the Socialists could afford to defy the PCF, whose votes had never been required for the government to legislate. Although Mitterrand and the supporters of the deflationary course realized that abandoning reflationary Keynesianism would be economically painful in the short term, they also felt that doing so would give France a chance of partial recovery by 1986 and, even more likely, by the next presidential election in 1988. Finally, the turn toward austerity and the market was not precluded by Mitterrand's personal convictions or any uncompromising ideological predispositions. Although partially informed by the left's euphoria at finally being in power, the government's embrace of reflation in 1981 had also reflected its desire to reward its political constituencies, as well as to steal political thunder (and legitimacy) from the PCF, which Mitterrand (along with many other members of the PS) loathed. Thus, to borrow Levy's formulation, if the "precipitants" of the U-turn derived from the international economy and the constraints of the EMS, the "drivers" of the shift in policy ultimately derived from domestic political concerns.[40]

Over the ensuing five years, the administration held firmly to its policies of austerity, marking the beginnings of a sea change in French politics. Between 1983 and 1986, the government not only completed its reversal of the reflationary policies of 1981 and early 1982; it also began to dismantle the entire edifice of dirigiste institutions and policymaking that had governed France for more than thirty years. This trend was accelerated by the left's unsurprising defeat in the 1986 parliamentary elections, which ushered in a neoliberal, center-right government under Prime Minister Jacques Chirac. The first Mitterrand government had attempted to restore prosperity through massive public spending, nationalizations, and stepped-up industrial policies; the Chirac administration worked to accomplish the same goal through tax reductions, spending cuts, extensive privatizations, and deregulation, all pursued with the aim of increasing economic flexibility and promoting investment. These initiatives significantly furthered the shift from the pursuit of a "rupture with capitalism" to, in the words of the Chirac administration, the quest for "a society of liberty and responsibility."[41]

The first set of initiatives involved a series of major tax cuts. The government reduced taxes on corporations by FFr 37 billion between 1986 and 1988, cut personal income taxes by FFr 31 billion, and, in a measure rich in symbolism, abolished the IGF, which since its inception had been denounced by both the right and employers as an ideologically motivated disincentive to investment.[42] In an effort to spur investment and promote the development of equities markets, the new administration introduced an amnesty for those who had moved their money abroad in response to the Socialists' tax increases. Aggregate personal and corporate income taxes declined from 8 percent of GDP in 1987 to 7.6 percent in 1988, and between 1986 and 1988 corporate tax ratios (or aggregate corporate taxes as a percentage of total corporate revenue) declined from 42.42 percent to 36.31 percent.[43] In addition to cutting a wide range of taxes, the government intensified the austerity policies begun under the Socialists. Government spending was slashed in a number of areas, from the civil service (a total of twenty thousand posts were cut during the government's two-year tenure) to the myriad agencies responsible for industrial policy and the budgets of government ministries.[44] Despite the government's tax cuts, these reductions in spending resulted in a full percentage-point decline in the budget deficit, from 2.7 percent of GDP in 1986 (down from a high of 3.2 percent in 1983) to 1.7 percent in 1988.[45]

The new embrace of fiscal discipline not only represented an effort to stabilize the French budget; it also reflected the government's desire to maintain the value of the franc. Despite a minor realignment of the franc–mark exchange rate in 1986, the franc remained significantly overvalued, placing competitive pressure on French exports. Rather than undertaking a second devaluation, however, in 1987 the government allowed the franc to fall through its floor in the EMS, leading the Bundesbank to intervene in the currency markets to prop up the franc and to revalue the mark.[46] The government's decision to refrain from a second devaluation marked an end to the postwar policy of "aggressive devaluations" and intimated the beginnings of the official strong-currency policy—the *franc fort*—that would become gospel under subsequent administrations.[47]

In keeping with its liberal agenda, Chirac's government also pursued a significant deregulation of the political economy. In the labor market, for example, it eliminated the "administrative authorization for layoffs," which since 1974 had required the approval of the labor inspectorate for a firm to reduce its workforce. The government also did away with all price controls; completed the Socialist Party's moves toward an end to credit rationing; and began to loosen foreign-exchange controls, which had been significantly strengthened in 1983 in response to the run on the franc. Finally, to promote the development of equities markets, the administration liberalized rules on the number of firms entitled to trade in stocks and bonds.[48]

Perhaps the most dramatic—and politically salient—of Chirac's initiatives, however, involved a large-scale program of privatization in the industrial and financial sectors. Between 1986 and 1988, the government sold off thirteen industrial and financial groups, six of which had been nationalized by the Socialists in 1982. Among the targets were household names such as TF1, one of France's major television stations; the investment banks Paribas and Suez; and Saint-Gobain, an important manufacturer of building materials.[49] Although the government had hoped to go even further with privatization, the scope (as well as the rapidity) of the sell-off was actually more extensive than Margaret Thatcher's privatizations in Britain, bringing FFr 70 billion into the state coffers, or FFr 20 billion more than the Socialists' 1982 nationalizations had cost.[50] Along with its policies of deregulation and its tax cuts, the government hoped that returning a substantial portion of the economy to private hands would stimulate innovation and investment and reduce unemployment, which in June 1986 amounted to 2.45 million workers, or about 10.5 percent of the workforce.[51] The results of the government's policies were somewhat disappointing: Job creation was sluggish at best; overall reductions in state spending were modest; and the trade deficit remained high.[52] Nevertheless, the amplitude of Chirac's policies of austerity, privatization, and deregulation represented a significant step toward the dismantling of the dirigiste edifice and a major acceleration of the turn to the market initiated under the Socialists.

At the same time, however, neither the advent of fiscal austerity and marketization under the Socialist Party nor their extension under Chirac's government or later administrations was ever truly neoliberal in inspiration[53]—at least, not in the sense that the term was commonly applied to Thatcher and Ronald Reagan. Even as successive French governments in the 1980s dismantled the institutions of dirigiste political-economic management, they undertook a substantial expansion of the French welfare state. As I show later, this extension of social protection entailed both a political and an economic logic. Politically, it reflected the desire to ensure social peace (the memory of May 1968 was still fresh) and to preserve political stability during difficult economic times. Economically, it facilitated industrial restructuring by absorbing surplus labor, thereby providing firms with increased flexibility as they adjusted. In short, the French abandonment of dirigiste industrial policy and the government's embrace of austerity required an expanded welfare state to provide the victims of economic dislocation with the means of subsistence that the labor market was increasingly incapable of furnishing.

From Dirigisme to the Socialized Market: The Expansion of French Social Policies in the 1980s

The expansion of the French welfare state during the 1980s represented the continuation and intensification of a policy trajectory that had begun during the previous decade. During the troubled 1970s, successive governments under Giscard sought ways to combat the inexorable rise in unemployment. As widespread layoffs suggested that mass unemployment was not merely a passing, conjunctural phenomenon, authorities feared a return of the kinds of unrest seen in May–June 1968 and turned to the welfare state as a means of preserving social and political stability. Between 1972 and 1980, for example, a series of early-retirement schemes was introduced, designed to "compensate for . . . premature poverty due to work situations or difficult economic circumstances" for older workers.[54] Aimed at those older than fifty-nine who were not yet eligible for standard pension benefits but were unable to find work, early-retirement schemes represented an attractive option. The programs proved enormously popular, and the number of early retirees increased from 59,000 in 1974 to 190,400 in 1980.[55] In 1980, the opportunities for early retirement were further developed through a measure that extended the right to benefits under the Fonds National d'Emploi (FNE) from workers in heavy industry to all workers laid off for economic reasons.

The extent of welfare-state expansion during this period was relatively modest, however, compared with that of the 1980s. After 1981, redistributive Keynesianism and then the abandonment of dirigisme led to a major extension of the French social-protection system. In 1982, the Socialist administration had accompanied the reduction of the standard retirement age from sixty-five to sixty with two measures that extended eligibility for early retirement to workers age fifty-five to fifty-nine—the so-called *contrats de solidarité-démission* and the *contrats de préretraites progressives*. These programs aimed to boost consumption and aggregate demand by providing firms with incentives to hire younger workers as replacements for early retirees.[56] In like fashion, in 1983 the government introduced "solidarity contracts," which provided early retirement for workers age fifty-five or older on the condition that firms replace recipients with younger workers.[57]

It was with the 1983 U-turn and the ensuing project of market creation, however, that the expansion of the French welfare state became a top policy priority. Following the abandonment of dirigisme in 1982-1983, unemployment skyrocketed, increasing from 7.4 percent in 1981 to a postwar high of 10.2 percent in 1985.[58] While the expansion of the welfare state during this period was conceived as a needed response to these severe economic dislocations, it also reflected an important political logic. Having gone back on its 1981 electoral promises to undertake a "break with capitalism," the left wished to avoid the perception that it had merely abandoned French workers to the vagaries of the market, *pace* Margaret Thatcher. Although Mitterrand had accepted the task of turning from state to market as the guiding principle of the political economy, he and his government under Laurent Fabius, who succeeded Mauroy as prime minister in 1984, were eager to be seen as protecting workers from market vicissitudes. Mitterrand expressed the left's wish to reconcile market forces and social justice in the following way: "The country will recognize, in the final analysis, that the left will bring not only more social equity, but also greater economic effectiveness than the right." Mitterrand's apparent eagerness to reconcile responsible economic stewardship with a concern for the human impact of the government's policies was echoed by Fabius, who claimed to represent "the modern left" wishing to "produce in order to redistribute."[59]

After 1983, as during the 1970s, early-retirement schemes became a favored tool for managing the labor market, but their overarching goal shifted from promoting consumption and net employment creation to removing workers from the labor market. In 1985, the national unemployment office, the Union Nationale pour l'Emploi dans l'Industrie et le Commerce (UNEDIC), introduced a measure that provided early-retirement benefits for workers age fifty-seven and a half or older who were receiving unemployment insurance, while abolishing the requirement that they engage in an active search for work. The same measure exempted all workers older than fifty-five and three months from restrictions on the size or duration of unemployment benefits.[60] This tacit acceptance of the limitations of the French labor market also informed a number of other state initiatives, including a transfer of funds from the FNE to the unemployment-insurance funds following the elimination of the administrative authorization for layoffs in 1986. In effect, both the government and the social partners responsible for managing early-retirement schemes had conspired in the conversion of these policies from temporary measures for assisting the unemployed into an entrenched network of benefits to compensate the growing number of older workers who stood little chance of landing a job.[61] Early-retirement programs were also quite popular with both the state and social partners: The state could use the schemes as a way to mute resistance to industrial restructuring while keeping down official unemployment statistics; employers were eager to shed workers at the expense of the welfare state; and workers were only too happy to retire early while receiving the bulk of their previous salary.

The attractiveness of this bargain for all parties obscured its essentially Faustian character, however. During the 1980s, the number of early retirees exploded, with the total number reaching seven hundred thousand in 1984 (compared with four hundred thousand in 1982) and then modestly declining to about six hundred thousand in 1989.[62] Even after the economic recovery of the late 1980s, the introduction of somewhat stricter eligibility criteria, and slight reductions in benefit levels, the number of participants remained about five hundred thousand in 1992, at an annual cost of about FFr 15 billion.[63] The effects on labor-market activity rates among older workers bear witness to the massive scope of French early-retirement programs during this period. At 53.6 percent in 1983 (following the reduction of the retirement age to sixty), the labor-force-participation rate of male workers age fifty-five to sixty-four slumped to 45.8 percent by 1990 and to 41.5 percent by 1995.[64] It was also far from clear that the programs would have any lasting impact on unemployment, since firms are reluctant to replace workers retired at the expense of the social-security system. In fact, in the long run such measures may actually increase unemployment, particularly in Bismarckian welfare states where they are largely funded through social contributions, which tend to impede job creation by raising non-wage labor costs.[65] Whether or not they are effective tools for combating joblessness, however, they clearly represent a politically attractive way for policymakers to reduce resistance to economic restructuring.

Although they were among the most important mechanisms for countering the economic effects of dirigisme's demise, early-retirement schemes were far from the only facet of French social protection to undergo expansion in the 1980s. After 1983, for example, the government designated fifteen "conversion poles," or local areas that had been particularly hard hit by industrial restructuring. In these localities, where heavy industries such as coal and steel had been the economic cornerstone during the postwar boom, the government offered "lubricant[s] to ease the transition from the voluntarist industrial policy of the early Socialist years to a more market-oriented strategy."[66] The first component of this strategy involved special provisions for early retirement, which was offered to workers as young as fifty in these areas. Moreover, two-year retraining periods, at full salary, were offered to those at risk of being laid off, thereby shifting the cost of supporting them from troubled firms to the state. Along with such efforts to ease the pain of workforce reductions, state authorities offered substantial subsidies to local authorities to modernize infrastructure, including roads and housing, and to promote the "conversion" of the local economy to high technology and other sectors with greater potential for growth. The government made the connection between the conversion poles and the abandonment of dirigisme more or less explicit, announcing their creation on the same day that it announced the planned "modernization" of the troubled coal, steel, and shipbuilding sectors. These programs involved massive financial outlays; in the former coal-mining town of Saint-Etienne alone, for example, a total of FFr 700 million was spent in only three years.[67] As part of the same effort to promote industrial restructuring, authorities partially reorganized France's vocational and technical training programs in the hopes of creating a pool of workers with skills that were in high demand.

The third major component of welfare-state expansion during the 1980s entailed the creation of antipoverty programs. When the dirigiste industrial policies that had been propping up many segments of French industry were removed, numerous firms were either allowed to fail or forced to rationalize to survive. As a result, hundreds of thousands of additional workers found themselves without jobs. In 1983, the number of unemployed surpassed 2 million (the level at which it had long been thought that France would become ungovernable), and the unemployment rate increased from 8 percent in 1982, to 8.3 percent in 1983, to 9.7 percent in 1984, to 10.2 percent in 1985.[68] Rising joblessness not only placed intense financial pressure on the payroll-tax-based French social-insurance system; it also represented a political problem for the government, as the emergence of a permanent economic underclass posed a major threat to social stability. The government's fears of social unrest and electoral disaster were both reflected in and intensified by the publication of a number of books on "social exclusion" and "the new poverty," which had become major public preoccupations.[69]

In response to these mounting concerns, authorities instituted a number of additional antipoverty benefits after 1983 designed to repair the widening tears in France's social and economic fabric. This policy trend began almost immediately after the 1983 U-turn, suggesting that, as with the creation of the conversion poles, the shift in policy orientation and efforts to compensate for its effects were closely linked. With the 1986 legislative elections fast approaching, the Socialists moved quickly to extend economic protection to thousands of laid-off workers—in the early 1980s, nearly one hundred thousand had lost their jobs in the steel, coal, automobile, and shipbuilding sectors alone—and, in the process, to construct some political cover for the government.[70] In 1984, for example, Fabius's government created the *allocation de solidarité spécifique* (ASS), a benefit for unemployed workers who had exhausted their eligibility for unemployment insurance. The creation of these kinds of means-tested benefits reflected a recognition that long-term unemployment was not only undermining the availability of income from work but was also eroding the rights of a growing number of workers to contributory, payroll-tax-based social insurance.

The expansion of income policies continued in 1988, when the government of Socialist Prime Minister Michel Rocard created the *revenu minimum d'insertion* (RMI).[71] The RMI, which established a right to a state-financed minimum income and offered job-placement services for recipients, constituted the first generalized antipoverty benefit in the history of the French welfare state.[72] This development represented a significant departure from the tenor of earlier antipoverty benefits, which had been focused on specific vulnerable populations such as the elderly poor, widows, and the long-term unemployed. By contrast, the RMI represented a guarantee of the basic means of subsistence for the entire population, irrespective of personal circumstances. The only restrictions on eligibility were that the recipient's income be below a set ceiling and that he or she be at least twenty-five years old. Reflecting the political consensus over the need for such a measure, the RMI passed through Parliament with unanimous support from both the left and the right. The rapid increase in the number of beneficiaries, which grew by an average of 15 percent per year between 1988 and 1995, bore out this perception. By the end of 2000, nearly 1.1 million French residents were receiving the RMI, with a total of 2.2 million people covered, either directly as recipients or indirectly as dependents.[73] As with the extension of early-retirement schemes and measures to facilitate industrial restructuring, the extension of income policies such as the RMI was not merely desirable in the aftermath of the dismantling of dirigisme, it was a social, political, and economic imperative.

Conclusion: The Social Predicates of French Marketization

In the 1980s, the Socialists' efforts to transform French society through state stewardship ended in unqualified defeat. Confronted with the monumental economic problems that their policies of autarkic Keynesian reflation had helped to produce, in 1983–1984 the Socialist administration abandoned its program of intensified dirigisme. Forced to choose between withdrawing from European monetary institutions and relinquishing his inflationary and redistributive policy agenda, Mitterrand opted for the latter alternative. The year 1983 not only marked the death of the Socialists' dreams of a state-directed "rupture with capitalism." Over the remainder of the 1980s and early 1990s, successive governments completely dismantled the entire dirigiste edifice of voluntarist industrial policies and discretionary credit allocation that had underpinned the country's astonishing economic successes during the *trente glorieuses*. The concomitant was an unprecedented project of market creation, whereby authorities exchanged technocratic dictates for market signals as the central principle of the French political economy.

While thus clearly *liberal*, this metamorphosis of the French economy and society was far from *neoliberal* in inspiration. Rather than merely abandoning workers to the market, authorities accompanied the shift toward the market with a major expansion of a wide range of social policies, in the process shifting responsibility for distributive economic tasks from defunct dirigiste industrial policies to an expanded welfare state. In the areas of early retirement, subsidies and other assistance for the economic transition of deindustrializing regions, and antipoverty programs, policymakers undertook major modifications to the welfare state to reconcile it with the new economic and political reality. One lesson of the French experience in the 1980s is that, *pace* Polanyi, a developed welfare state not only does not constitute evidence of failed adjustment, as neoliberals would suggest, but is also critically important for ensuring the social peace and political stability that liberalization and marketization demand.

The relevance of Polanyi's insight is not limited to the French case. Following reunification in 1990, German policymaking was characterized by an analogous pattern of market making accompanied by welfare-state expansion. In many ways, the German task of extending the purview of market forces was even more daunting. Whereas French authorities in the 1980s transformed a functioning, if troubled, capitalist system into a market economy, after 1990 German policymakers were left with an economic and social wasteland in the former East. If the French task had been one of changing the fundamental institutional and policy precepts of the economy, that German challenge was creating a capitalist economy and social order from the ground up. Over the ensuing decade, the German government would pour hundreds of billions of marks into the former East Germany to transform an area that had lost the majority of its jobs and industrial capacity more or less overnight. The state privatized huge segments of the Eastern economy, completely rebuilt the region's decrepit infrastructure, and dramatically expanded social and labor-market policies in the East in support of these seismic changes. These transformations and the policies that made them possible are the subject of the next chapter.

4

German Reunification and the Economic and Social Incorporation of Eastern Germany

He who wants a new world must first buy the old.

—DUTCH PROVERB

Less than a decade after the Socialist "U-turn" that marked the beginning of the end for French dirigisme, the reunification of the Federal Republic of Germany with the German Democratic Republic (GDR) utterly transformed the economic, social, and political life of the German people. The opening of the Berlin Wall on 9 November 1989 set off a year-long process of negotiations among East and West German elites and the four post–World War II occupying powers (France, Britain, the United States, and the Soviet Union), culminating in the formal reunification of the two countries on 3 October 1990.[1] On that November weekend, tens of thousands of East Germans poured into the streets of West Berlin to gaze upon the avatar of the prosperity of Western capitalism so long denied them and vilified by the Sozialistische Einheitspartei Deutschlands (SED), the ruling communist party of the GDR, as an outpost of Western imperialism and a vestige of Nazism. As East Berliners drove their dilapidated Trabants through the streets of West Berlin, thousands of people began to dismantle the Berlin Wall in celebration. Long-divided families were reunited, and Germans in the East and the West exulted at the prospect of finally beginning to leave behind the legacies of 1945. Though there were a few skeptics about the costs of the union, enthusiasm generally prevailed when reunification was accomplished in less than eleven months' time. Walter Momper, the mayor of West Berlin, aptly captured the spirit of the time: "At that moment I thought to myself how much suffering the Wall has caused, and that on this night the Germans were the happiest nation in the world."[2]

The motto among East Germans during this heady period—"*Keine Experimente* (No Experiments)!"—expressed their wish to acquire the full fruits of West German capitalism and democracy rather than "some third way between capitalism and Communism."[3] In fact, though, the transformation of East Germany into a market economy would entail an enormous experiment in nearly all areas of the political and economic life of the new *Länder*. In the years after 1990, German authorities worked to create a market economy in the former GDR, along with the supporting social and economic institutions that had allowed the postwar Federal Republic to prosper. Unlike the postwar experience in the West, however, where rebuilding had required decades of slow adaptation, German officials were attempting to accomplish this feat in the East within just a few years. In effect, this telescoped more than four decades of Western economic and social development into one, a project that would require extensive government intervention and financial support and would plant the seeds of growing state intervention later in the decade. In the words of Gerhard Ritter:

> One consequence of the massive state intervention in support of social and economic recovery was that the earlier tendency toward the shrinking of the state and the reinforcement of subsidiarity and economic actors' self-sufficiency [in West Germany] was turned on its head, and the state ultimately assumed responsibility for Easterners' subsistence.[4]

To a significant extent, the "conflictual corporatist" model that I describe had its genesis in those early post-reunification years.

The incorporation of East Germany entailed two major components, the first of which involved creating the predicates of the high-end West German Social Market Economy. In the five or so years following reunification, German authorities privatized those Eastern firms that were solvent enough to find buyers and oversaw the restructuring or bankruptcy proceedings of those that were not. Privatization took place quickly, with more than twenty thousand small firms and thirty-four hundred industrial concerns sold off by the end of 1991.[5] During the same period, Western institutions of social partnership, including collective-bargaining structures, works councils, and the system of vocational training, were likewise transferred to the East, a process fraught with conflict and subject to significant modifications with respect to the original Western blueprint.[6] Authorities also completely reconstructed the East's crumbling infrastructure—from electricity production and delivery equipment to the telecommunications network, the railway system, and the World War II–era system of roads and highways—a process supported through massive federal and regional outlays.[7]

This Herculean project relied on a major expansion of social protection in the East. Paralleling French developments in the 1980s, the absorption of the former GDR not only required the extension of the existing German welfare state to the new *Länder*; it also called for the creation of a number of new social and labor-market policies targeted specifically at eastern Germany. For example, in the early to mid-1990s, special early-retirement programs were introduced as a way to absorb the millions of workers whose jobs had suddenly disappeared.[8] In addition, a number of active labor-market programs were introduced, including direct job-creation programs and retraining schemes, most of which were extensively subsidized by the federal government. Similarly, immediately after reunification, a special provision for "short-time" work programs was introduced that preserved incomes for workers whose positions were all but fictional.[9] Both the federal government and the Federal Labor Office (Bundesanstalt für Arbeit [BA]) shared in the financing and administration of this expanded framework of social protection.[10] As in France during the 1980s, these expanded social policies not only facilitated the process of market creation; they were necessary for it to occur at all. Table 4.1 lists selected programs and their associated costs and scopes.

This chapter explores these linked processes of market creation and social-policy expansion in the decade following reunification. I begin by describing the processes and outcomes of the project of market creation in the East, including the privatization of the Eastern economy, the promotion of private investment, assistance for industrial restructuring, investment in infrastructure, and the transfer of the West German systems of social partnership and industrial relations. I then analyze the social- and labor-market policy instruments that facilitated this integrative process. Although the expanded social-policy arrangements that emerged from this period would create problems for later German governments, they were an essential component of the country's political-economic adjustment at the time. By supporting social peace and shoring up political support, the expansion of the German welfare state enabled Eastern Germany, albeit gradually and painfully, to adapt to the exigencies of modern capitalism.

Market Making from Scratch: The Integration of Eastern Germany into the Social Market Economy

One widely held interpretation of German reunification and its aftermath contends that the government merely abandoned the Eastern economy to the vagaries of the market, thereby permitting the destruction of the industrial base required for economic renewal and driving ill-adapted Eastern citizens into lives of poverty and desperation.[11] This account, however, fails to recognize the enormous resources and effort devoted by the German government to support-

TABLE 4.1 Programs for Economic Development and Social Welfare in Eastern Germany

Program/Policy	Description	Cost or Scope and Associated Dates
Fund for German Unity	Money to supplement Eastern social-security funds and finance infrastructure improvements	DM 115 billion (1990–1995)
Gemeinschaftswerk Aufschwung Ost	Regional assistance for industrial restructuring	DM 18.15 billion (1991–1996)
ETCs (employment and training companies)	Provision of short-term jobs and retraining programs to laid-off workers	40% of volume of all Eastern labor-market programs (1990–1993)
Kurzarbeitergeld	Subsidy for at-risk Eastern workers working reduced hours; provided 85%–90% of previous pay	Varied annually; peak of 2 million participants in 1991
BA job-creation schemes	Public employment projects in infrastructure improvement or public services	About 400,000 participants throughout the 1990s
Altersübergangsgeld	Special Eastern early-retirement scheme	More than 1 million participants (1990–1992); paid 65% of previous wages
Total West–East transfers		More than DM 1 trillion (1990–1998)
Annual West–East transfers		DM 139 billon–DM 189 billion (1991–1998)
Treuhand privatizations		DM 230 billion (1990–1994)
Reconstruction of Eastern postal and telecommunications systems		DM 200 billion (1991–2000)

ing the transition of East German society. With the collapse of the GDR, the Eastern economy was completely devastated, and hopelessly uncompetitive firms, which had long been shored up by the East German state, stood no chance of survival in an advanced capitalist economy open to intense competition from Europe and the rest of the world. To make matters worse, the collapse of the Soviet bloc had obliterated the bulk of East Germany's traditional export markets.[12] In response, the German government moved aggressively to privatize thousands of Eastern firms, foster the development of a self-sustaining means of industrial finance, and rebuild the crumbling Eastern infrastructure to provide the new *Länder* with the same supportive arrangements that had contributed to West Germany's postwar boom.

As early as 1992, it was clear that the transition of the East to a functioning market economy would require a long period of Western tutelage and the immediate transfer of resources that far exceeded earlier optimistic estimates.[13] Industrial production in the East declined by 40 percent between 1990 and 1992; real rates of unemployment soared to about 37 percent (including both the registered unemployed and those participating in job-creation and retraining schemes); the active labor force declined from 10 million in 1989 to 4.4 million in early 1993; and 3,500 firms had been bankrupted by the end of 1994.[14] This rapid collapse left widespread bitterness and pessimism in the East and resentment in the West caused by the perception that Western Germans were being forced to foot the bill. This situation put substantial political pressure on Chancellor Helmut Kohl, who in the run-up to the 1990 national elections had promised a "flowering landscape" in the East within two years with no tax increases.[15] By 1993, it was evident that both of these commitments had been wildly unrealistic and that Germany had only just begun a slow, painful, and expensive process of creating a functioning market economy.[16] Kohl's promise both reflected and reinforced the political imperatives of rapid reunification, though available resources were far from adequate to fulfill these expectations. Ultimately, although Easterners got their wish for the wholesale transfer of West German policies and institutions to the East, the cost would have to be borne in equal measure by German taxpayers and the German welfare state over a period of two decades. Though rapid reunification made political sense, its social and economic effects reflected Oscar Wilde's observation that "when the gods wish to punish us they answer our prayers."

The resources that were actually required, and that the politics of rising expectations demanded, were further increased by the terms of the 1990 Treaty for German Economic, Monetary, and Social Union. The centerpiece of this treaty was the currency union, which exchanged the Ostmark for the deutsche Mark (DM) at a one-to-one rate on amounts up to DM 4,000 and at a two-to-one rate for higher balances. While it appeared to be the only politically viable option at the time, and although some form of currency union was an essential component of the long-term economic integration of Eastern Germany, the decision to establish effective parity between the two currencies would have serious repercussions. It immediately made East German firms uncompetitive by forcing them to pay workers and suppliers at a grossly inflated real rate, resulting in the disappearance of most of the markets for their goods and massive layoffs.[17] The result was a huge budgetary shortfall, since the 1990 Unification Treaty had provided only DM 35 billion for the task.[18]

Earlier optimism gave way to the sober realizations that Kohl's "flowering landscape" would be slow to bloom and that his promise not to raise taxes would be untenable. Beginning in 1990, the German government began to marshal the resources that the Eastern social and economic transition would require. In May 1990, it created the Fund for German Unity with assets of DM 115 billion to supplement Eastern social-security funds and infrastructure investment and then instituted a Solidarity Tax of 7.5 percent on all income-tax payers while raising the value-added tax (VAT) and excise taxes on gasoline and tobacco.[19] Despite this additional revenue, the federal budget deficit spiked to 3.2 percent of GDP in 1993.[20] Between 1991 and 1998, annual transfers to the East increased from DM 139 billion to DM 189 billion.[21] Between 1990 and the end of 1996, transfers from West to East totaled more than DM 1 trillion, with federal transfers running an annual 4.5 percent of German GDP.[22]

Among the most important components of the government's response was a wide-ranging effort to privatize the thousands of firms previously owned by the East German state.[23] In March 1990, the government created the Treuhandanstalt, a public trust responsible for the management and sale of GDR state assets. The Treuhand assumed control of 45,000 Eastern industrial establishments, which were held by 8,000 separate enterprises and had employed about 4 million workers.[24] In 1990, the estimated value of Treuhand holdings was DM 1 trillion, a figure that was revised downward at the end of 1991 to DM 600 billion.[25] These holdings included not only Eastern industrial enterprises and factories, but also 60 percent of the forests in the territory of the former GDR, hundreds of buildings that had been owned by the East German secret police, or the Stasi, and about 800 properties owned by the Partei des Demokratischen Sozialismus (PDS), the successor party to the SED.[26] The Treuhand was assigned the unenviable task of selling these assets, though many of them, including thousands of antiquated factories, had no real value.[27]

The privatization program, which policymakers initially had hoped would provide much needed cash for reconstruction, quickly turned into a significant liability, forcing the German government to subsidize the Treuhand. By the end of 1994, the enormous financial needs of those firms undergoing restructuring had resulted in a net *loss* of DM 230 billion.[28] While the bulk of the subsidies came from the federal government, authorities secured some assistance from large German banks, which issued loans to troubled Eastern firms in exchange for a guaranteed interest margin and the Treuhand's assumption of all default risks. Many non-German banks also made significant loans to firms undergoing privatization.[29] Although this assistance was insufficient to cover the losses incurred by privatization, it reflected the urgency of the task and the low market value of the assets in question rather than incompetence or corruption, as some have suggested. In any event, given the costs of supporting firms waiting for buyers, a slower process would have been even more expensive.

Widespread criticism of its balance sheet and of privatization's negative effects on employment notwithstanding, the Treuhand deserved substantial credit for successfully completing a monumental task in less than five years' time while endeavoring to minimize the resulting pain. By late 1994, when the agency was dissolved, it had fully or partially privatized 8,389 enterprises and had slated another 3,713 for liquidation. From this latter group, however, about 6,000 relatively productive units were to be sold, preserving 30 percent of the jobs in these firms. In addition, many privatization contracts contained clauses that guaranteed nearly 1.5 million jobs and established DM 207 billion in private investment commitments.[30] In an effort to develop a productive base of SMEs in the East, moreover, about one-fifth of all privatizations were conducted as management buy-ins or buy-outs, giving a nascent regional small-business elite a vested interest in returning these firms to productivity.[31]

In spite of the Treuhand's best efforts to pursue a program of privatization with a human face, however, it was powerless to prevent the bulk of post-1990 layoffs. By 1994, when the Treuhand completed its mission and closed its doors, nearly 3 million Eastern workers, or 72 percent of the pre-unification workforce, had lost their jobs. In the first quarter of 1991 alone, 360,000 Eastern workers were laid off, followed by an additional 440,000 in the second quarter. In June of that year, 842,300 people were unemployed in the former GDR, with another 2 million working in part-time positions. After 1990, industrial output collapsed to about 60 percent of its pre-reunification level and had recovered to only 68 percent by July 1993. By 1994, the nominal unemployment rate (not counting participants in various government job schemes) had risen to 15.2 percent in the new *Länder,* with the total number of registered unemployed reaching more than 1.1 million.[32] In some particularly troubled areas, *registered* unemployment rates reached 25 percent.[33] In fewer than five years, East Germany had gone from the showcase of the Eastern bloc to the basket case of the advanced industrialized world.

Faced with this dismal economic situation, the government moved quickly after 1990 to complement the program of privatization with a number of measures designed to allow East German firms to begin to adjust to market forces. The first component of these efforts involved the dedication of extensive funds to Eastern industrial restructuring and the promotion of private investment, including money to assist firms with the modernization of production techniques, investment subsidies, and various tax breaks for East German enterprises. Such programs were begun under the auspices of the Treuhand, immediately following (and even prior to) formal reunification. Following the Treuhand's dissolution in 1994, the German federal and *Länder* governments took the reins of these programs, many of which were administered by the Gemeinschaftswerk Aufschwung Ost (Joint Task Force for Recovery in the East), a regional assistance program created in March 1991.[34] Between 1991 and 1996, DM 18.15 billion was furnished to Eastern industry through this program.[35] Taken together, these initiatives amounted to a large-scale industrial policy for the East, a kind of policy orientation not seen in Germany since the immediate aftermath of World War II.[36]

The government's investment in economic restructuring initially concentrated on the Eastern manufacturing sector,[37] which had been hardest hit and was most exposed to international competition. At nearly 30 percent of Eastern GDP in 1990, manufacturing output had plummeted to less than 15 percent by 1993, making only a slight recovery thereafter.[38] In the machine-tool industry, which had been a critical component of the GDR's economy, Germany's share of world production increased from 18.9 percent in 1990 to 25 percent in 1991 (representing the addition of a large number of East German firms) but then, despite an upturn in overall East German manufacturing, rapidly declined to 18.2 percent by 1993, as many of these firms collapsed or were liquidated.[39] The effects on the East German steel industry were also particularly brutal, with production declining by 73 percent in the first year after reunification.[40] In response, the government undertook a series of subsidization programs designed to allow the core of Eastern industry (or what was left of it) to survive while firms restructured. The largest share of subsidies to Eastern industry, disproportionately aimed at export-oriented firms, came in the form of preferential credits and investment grants designed to promote fixed-capital formation, with the rest composed of tax bonuses for equipment investment, special depreciation allowances on capital formation, and support for research and development.[41]

These efforts to promote industrial restructuring were accompanied by large investments in Eastern infrastructure, which was crucial to firms' production and distribution capacities. In 1990, every aspect of the physical and technological infrastructure of the former GDR, from telecommunications to roads and the postal and rail networks, lay devastated by years of neglect. It was nearly impossible to make a direct telephone call to the West from many parts of East Germany; water and electricity shortages were widespread; numerous buildings still bore the scars of World War II–era damage, and the road system was dilapidated and, in many places, non-existent. Over the ensuing decade, the German government worked to repair what could be fixed, reconstruct what could not, and build from scratch the major infrastructural components that did not yet exist. For example, the Federal Railways (Bundesbahn) and the national postal system each devoted DM 100 billion during the 1990s to repairing, upgrading, and extending their networks in the East.[42] The telephone system was completely modernized, and digital and high-speed cables were installed. By 2000, the network in many Eastern areas was more technologically advanced than that in the West. The modernization of the electricity network, involving both the extension of power lines and the conversion of East Germany's inefficient brown-coal fields, benefited from a nationwide modernization program spurred by the liberalization and privatization of the national electricity market.[43] The highway system was completely modernized, benefiting tourists, residents, and commercial distributors alike.

The final component of recent government efforts to create an Eastern Germany in the image of the West German Social Market Economy has involved the transfer of Western institutions of social partnership,[44] including both the systems of collective bargaining and firm-level works councils. Initially, many feared that liberalization and privatization, coupled with soaring unemployment, would provide employers with a major strategic advantage, resulting in an imbalance in the collective-bargaining system, frequent industrial conflict, and a "race to the bottom" and hollowing out of collective-bargaining institutions nationally.[45] As Lowell Turner describes, however, the collective labor institutions of the Social Market Economy successfully took root in the East. This implantation of Western industrial-relations institutions began in 1990 and 1991, when major German unions and employers' associations, particularly those in the critical metalworking industries (IG Metall and Gesamtmetall, respectively), succeeded in building collective-bargaining frameworks and firm-level works councils in a number of important industries, including machine tools and automobiles.

That said, the establishment of social partnership in Eastern Germany has been far from a seamless or instantaneous process, marked instead by significant conflict and a cumulative process of experimentation and adaptation. In 1993, Eastern employers' efforts to renegotiate the wage provisions of an existing contract sparked a major strike by IG Metall, which demanded an accelerated adoption of East–West wage parity. The strike was settled relatively quickly with an agreement that gave workers a much higher pay increase than employers had demanded, as well as an agreement to phase in wage parity. The union's success enshrined its status as an effective bargaining agent in the East, validating the model of social partnership and collective bargaining in Eastern Germany. In Turner's words, "For Germany as a whole . . . the strike settlement of 1993 appeared to have pushed forward the long-term development of a country truly unified, not just territorially, but economically, socially, and politically as well."[46]

Although Turner's optimistic account was perhaps warranted by early successes in creating industrial-relations institutions, recent developments have given some cause for concern about the depth of these institutions' implantation. For example, many Eastern wage agreements contain *Öffnungsklauseln,* or "opening clauses," which allow employers to petition for exemptions from certain provisions of existing contracts, including deferrals of wage increases and temporary reductions in pay rates when warranted by local conditions or a particular firm's circumstances. Other alterations include firm-specific renegotiations of work time, such as a deal between IG Metall and Volkswagen in

1993 that reduced the work week to four days to allow the struggling company to reorganize.[47] Such controlled flexibility has also characterized more recent Eastern wage agreements, particularly in the chemical and automobile industries.[48] Although one could argue that these modifications of German industrial-relations practices were necessary, some observers have interpreted them as evidence of the slow erosion of the collective-bargaining system in the East. Such concern has been reinforced by recent declines in the membership rolls of employers' associations and unions, particularly but not exclusively in the new *Länder*, as well as the increasing frequency of violations of collective-bargaining guidelines.[49] That said, it is important to emphasize that a system of social partnership, which is critical to the functioning of the high-end German economy, has been successfully introduced in the East, in a political-economic context that was far from propitious.

Each of these post-1990 developments—the adoption of Western institutions of social partnership, state aid for industrial restructuring and infrastructure improvements, support for private investment, and the privatization of the Eastern economy—reflects the importance of government activism in integrating the new *Länder* into the Social Market Economy. This monumental task arguably represents the most rapid and extensive project of market creation in the history of postwar Europe and was unlikely to succeed in the absence of significant public support. Just as the German government has played a critical role in facilitating industrial restructuring, moreover, it actively worked to help Eastern workers adjust. Over the first post-reunification decade, authorities substantially expanded social policies designed to ensure social peace and stability as the East slowly adapted to the exigencies of capitalism. As I describe in the next section, this adaptive process of welfare-state expansion has involved two major components. First, it has entailed the integration of East Germans into the pre-existing West German welfare state. Second, it has involved the creation of new programs targeted specifically at Eastern workers. This extension of social protection was not merely a token of Westerners' largesse toward their poor Eastern cousins. Rather, it was a necessary counterpart to the creation of a viable market order in the former GDR and to the survival of the Social Market Economy in any recognizable form.

The Social Aspects of Market Creation: Economic Adjustment and Welfare-State Expansion in Post-reunification Germany

Following reunification, East Germans were not merely left without a functioning economy; they were also deprived of the cradle-to-grave welfare system that had been one of the GDR's most vaunted features. Once the euphoria of 1989 had given way to the sober reality of 1991, it quickly became clear that a successful transition to a market economy would require the rapid extension of the German social-protection system. At stake were both the social peace required for successful marketization and the legitimacy of the Social Market Economy. Understandably problematic for any country in the throes of such a profound transformation, the situation was particularly worrisome in Germany, where fears of a resurgence of neo-Nazism fueled by poverty and unemployment found confirmation in a series of acts of violence against foreigners in 1991. The words of the SPD's general-secretary in the early 1990s succinctly captured elites' preoccupations at the time: "It is very difficult to know what to say to the East Germans I meet who keep telling me that all politicians are useless and that they are to blame for everything. I must say I am very concerned. Disappointment, anger and bitterness run deep."[50]

The extension of social protection to Eastern Germany formally began with the signing of the Unification Treaty, which provided for the transfer of all German social, political, and economic institutions, including those of the German welfare state, to the new *Länder*. Translating this commitment into practice, however, would prove far more complicated. When the erstwhile GDR became part of the Federal Republic, the country's population jumped from 65 million to 81 million, representing a nearly 25 percent increase. In addition to dramatically increasing welfare expenditures, this sudden rise in the number of beneficiaries required a major upgrade in the East's social infrastructure, including the construction of new administrative offices for the BA and other social agencies. Existing welfare institutions were ill-equipped to handle these needs, and pre-reunification legislation, such as the 1989 pension reform, had not accounted for reunification's effects. The government's first attempt to deal with these new pressures involved an injection of funds into the Eastern social-security budget in 1991 equal to about one-third of all West–East transfers.[51] This measure was far from adequate, however, and total public social expenditures ballooned from 23.2 percent of GDP in 1990 to 27.6 percent in 1993, while the federal budget deficit grew from .1 percent of GDP in 1989 to 3.5 percent in 1993.[52] These alarming numbers reflected in equal measure the extent of the need for social protection in the wake of reunification and existing institutions' inability to address it.

In response, German authorities complemented the extension of the existing welfare state to the East with the creation of new, Eastern-specific social programs for the millions of workers who nearly overnight had found themselves without sources of income. Expanded early-retirement schemes were one important component of this strategy. In 1990, the last government of the GDR had introduced an early-retirement program from which about 400,000 workers had benefited. The Unification Treaty replaced this scheme with a "transition allowance" (*Altersübergangsgeld*), financed through social contributions and administered by the BA, which provided benefits equal to 65 percent of previous wages to about 600,000 Eastern workers age fifty-five and older, and the total number of participants climbed to more than a million by 1992.[53] In addition, as citizens of a united Germany, Eastern workers had recourse to pre-existing Western early-retirement benefits, including those provided by the 1989 pension reform, which became effective in 1992. In 1996, early-retirement provisions were extended still further through a law allowing workers age fifty-five or older to work part time while receiving standard pension benefits.[54] After a sharp increase in the first years after 1990, the number of early-retirement recipients gradually declined as Eastern workers who had benefited from the short-term provisions of the Unification Treaty were absorbed into the standard pension system.[55]

With the waning of Eastern early-retirement programs as a means of labor-supply reduction, authorities created a number of new policy instruments designed to absorb displaced Eastern workers. Chief among these arrangements was a series of active labor-market policies, including a broad array of job-training and employment-creation schemes. For example, during the post-1990 period, the government, unions, and employer associations agreed to the creation of a series of employment and training companies (ETCs) throughout Eastern Germany. These new agencies, which provided short-term jobs and retraining programs for laid-off workers, were administered and largely financed by the BA. Originally, Treuhand companies themselves were intended to subsidize dismissed workers by employing them in efforts to refurbish deindustrialized areas. As pressures intensified for firms to restructure, however, companies were eager to sever ties with former workers to clean up their books and make themselves more attractive to prospective buyers. The solution was the ETCs, which were made responsible for acting as temporary employers to help workers find jobs,[56] whether in the private sector or in one of the BA's numerous job programs. They thus acted as a buffer between the GDR's defunct command economy and the inhospitable world of capitalism.

In first half of the 1990s, ETCs became the favored instrument for facilitating workers' adjustment. At the end of 1993, about four hundred were operating in the new *Länder,* employing about ninety thousand people, a figure that represented roughly 40 percent of the volume of state-sponsored jobs in the East. Although about half of these companies were still formally connected to Treuhand companies in 1993, ETCs increasingly assumed an independent existence as firms were privatized. These agencies were formally entities of private law, though their stakeholders included a large number of local authorities, private firms, and trade-union officers, all of whom had a clear stake in their success.[57] Because workers in ETCs were still officially employed, trade unions could preserve membership while demonstrating their commitment to their rank and file, and struggling Eastern firms could lay off workers at the expense of the state. In this way, ETCs provided a means of ensuring social peace while achieving the politically desirable goal of reducing the number of registered unemployed.[58] This convergence of interests resulted in the rapid expansion of ETCs after 1993, despite the pressures that such payroll-tax-financed programs placed on the economy's capacity for job creation.[59]

ETCs were far from the sole instrument for absorbing dislocated Eastern workers. Another component involved the post-reunification creation of a "short-time work benefit" (*Kurzarbeitergeld*), which allowed workers at risk of being laid off to work fewer (sometimes close to zero) hours while receiving 85–90 percent of their previous pay. The benefit was funded by the federal government and the BA (which together covered wages up to 68 percent of the previous salary) and supplemented by firms (which paid the remaining 17–22 percent). As early as 1991, an estimated 18.5 percent of employed Eastern workers were receiving it.[60] This program was intended to subsidize the economically displaced until they were eligible for retirement, could be placed in an ETC, or, ideally, found a new job in the private sector. Many did, and this program saw its number of beneficiaries decline from a peak of nearly 2 million in 1991 to about 38,000 in 1996.[61] Other, similar policies were also introduced, including numerous schemes that placed people in social-service or infrastructure projects. At the end of 1992, nearly 400,000 Easterners were employed in these programs, a level that remained constant through the 1990s.[62]

This ensemble of early-retirement programs, active labor-market policies, and direct subsidies such as the *Kurzarbeitergeld* sheltered a substantial number of Eastern citizens from truly dire economic straits. In 1992, when participation in early-retirement schemes was at its height and the bulk of job-creation and retraining schemes had gone on line, more than 2 million Eastern workers were covered by related programs, with another 1.2 million people receiving standard unemployment benefits.[63] In 1991 alone, nearly 400,000 jobs were created through ETCs and other employment-creation programs. By the end of 1995, nearly *half* of the East German working-age population had participated in some sort of active labor-market policy or the *Kurzarbeitergeld* program,[64] and active labor-market policies were absorbing about 40 percent of the total Eastern outflow from the unemployment rolls.[65]

As one might expect, these programs were quite expensive and represented an enormous fiscal commitment. In 1991, 23 percent of Eastern GDP was spent on job creation and retraining schemes.[66] Between 1991 and 1994, social expenditures by local authorities in the new *Länder* increased by a factor of four, reaching 70 percent of the level of such expenditures in the West, compared with 22 percent in 1991, despite the East's much smaller population.[67] The share of the German GDP spent on labor-market programs grew from 2.26 percent in 1989 to 4.1 percent in 1993, with the proportion devoted to active labor-market policies increasing by more than half, from 1.03 percent to

1.58 percent of GDP.[68] Between 1990 and 1995, total German social expenditures grew from 24.8 percent to 29.6 percent of GDP, reflecting both the shocks of reunification and deteriorating labor-market conditions in the early to mid-1990s.[69]

Despite their enormous cost, however, there can be little doubt that these policies were essential to the economic adjustment of the former GDR. The economic dislocation that resulted from the transfer of the West German legal system and economic institutions to the East created an immediate and pressing need for social protection that the pre-existing German welfare state never could have provided adequately. High rates of unemployment in the East bore witness to the indispensability of this expansion of the German welfare state. In the mid-1990s, the sum of registered unemployment and rates of participation in job-creation and retraining schemes in Eastern Germany was still more than 40 percent. In the absence of policies capable of absorbing displaced Eastern workers, unemployment rates thus would have far exceeded that of the United States at the height of the Great Depression, creating unmanageable social and political pressures. Although the post-1990 expansion of the welfare state did not solve East Germany's economic woes, and though it significantly increased strains on the German economy, it remained, in the words of one union official, "the best of all possible bad solutions."[70]

Conclusion: Prospects for Eastern Germany in the Era of Managed Austerity

To be sure, the ordeal of economic and social adjustment in the former GDR is far from complete, and the economic results of the initiatives described in this chapter have been mixed. The recovery of the Eastern manufacturing sector accelerated in the early to mid-1990s, with total output increasing by 15 percent in 1993 and by another 28.5 percent between 1995 and 1998.[71] Between 1992 and 1994, the Eastern economy grew by more than 8 percent, although Eastern growth rates had declined to West German levels by 1997.[72] Per capita output also recovered, increasing from 30 percent to 56 percent of West German levels by 1996, although East–West economic convergence along this indicator slowed after 1997. Real wages, productivity rates, and incomes also continued to rise, with average household incomes reaching 75–80 percent of Western levels by 1998.[73] Although such positive trends resulted in part from continued transfers from the West,[74] they were also the products of the development of Eastern SMEs and improvements in East German capital stock and infrastructure.

Such positive indicators suggest that the new *Länder* are continuing to develop the institutions required to make development self-sustaining, though continuing economic difficulties in the region warrant a cautious assessment of its future prospects. Unemployment continues to be significantly higher, with a jobless rate of 14.7 percent in the East in July 2008 compared with 7.3 percent in Western German *Länder*.[75] Poverty and economic precariousness remain major problems,[76] and many Eastern firms continue to experience competitive difficulties. In 2000, real per capita GDP in the East was only 60.5 percent of that in Western Germany, or 27 percent below the European Union average, and in 2003, Eastern productivity rates had recovered to only 72 percent of Western levels.[77] Some observers have blamed this disappointing performance on the market distortions created by the government's prioritization of large-scale industry, including significant industrial overcapacity, increases in relative prices for non-tradable goods, and a neglect of the development of SMEs and the service sector.[78]

This mixed outlook for Eastern Germany, however, should not detract from the extent and scope of the region's economic and social transformation. The fact that economic adjustment in the East remains a work in progress is a testament to the monumental nature of the task rather than evidence of a lack of focused attention. Forty years of dictatorship and central planning had left a devastated economic and social landscape, crumbling infrastructure, and a population with no experience with the norms of a capitalist economy or with democratic political processes. During the past two decades, German authorities have privatized an Eastern economy whose assets few wanted to buy, promoted industrial restructuring on a massive scale, supported the erection of a functioning system of social partnership and collective bargaining, and completely rebuilt the Eastern infrastructure, which now rivals or, in some cases, exceeds the quality of its Western counterpart. This process of market creation has been supported by a major expansion of social- and labor-market policy instruments in the new *Länder*. As in France during the 1980s, German market making in the 1990s went hand in glove with welfare expansion, and a robust welfare state remains essential to the East's ongoing economic adjustment.

More recently, policymakers in both countries have turned to reforming and rationalizing the policies and institutions that enabled the two countries to accomplish their market-making projects. Beginning in the early 1990s, existing welfare policies came under increasing pressure from aging demographic profiles, sluggish economic growth, and high rates of unemployment, all in the face of constraints imposed on government expenditures by European Economic and Monetary Union (EMU). In response, French and German authorities have adopted a strategy of *buttressed liberalization,* involving significant reforms in labor-market policies and social-insurance policies such as pensions and health care. Liberalization and rationalization in these areas have been supported by the creation of a variety of new policy instruments and the devotion of significant resources to reducing unemployment and alleviating poverty through means-tested income support.

In the next three chapters, I explore recent reforms in each of these policy areas in turn, beginning with developments in labor-market policies. In this area, officials in both France and Germany have undertaken significant modifications of existing arrangements with a view to resolving the two countries' common dilemma of "welfare without work." These reforms have involved efforts to reduce non-wage labor costs and subsidize job creation, introducing job-search requirements for unemployment-insurance recipients, promoting part-time employment, and limiting dysfunctional early-retirement programs. Although policy outcomes and reform dynamics have varied, in both countries adjustment has involved mutually supportive changes in the welfare state and the broader political economy while intensifying the process of political change that has driven the reform process.

5

Modernizing the French and German Labor Markets in an Age of Austerity

The night cometh when no man can work.
—New Testament, John 9:4

In the three decades following World War II, vibrant economic growth and expanding employment throughout Western Europe were sustained by an enhanced role for public policy. The shared European hope was to guide and regulate the power of capitalist accumulation to rebuild the continent's devastated economies and conquer mass unemployment, fear of which had been branded into the collective consciousness by the Great Depression. Like many of their neighbors, France and Germany devised novel institutional arrangements involving "a variety of independent forces combin[ing] to increase the available powers of control over the economic system and at the same time to keep the volume of demand constantly at a very high level."[1] Particularly in France, these emerging paradigms were characterized by Keynesian countercyclical demand management through deficit spending and the "automatic stabilizers" of progressive income taxes and expanded welfare states.[2] The French

Portions of this chapter include revised versions of material presented in "From 'Welfare without Work' to 'Buttressed Liberalization': The Shifting Dynamics of Labor-Market Adjustment in France and Germany," *European Journal of Political Research* 47, no. 3 (May 2008): 334–358, by Blackwell Publishing; "Rethinking Corporatism and Consensus: The Dilemmas of German Social-Protection Reform," *West European Politics* 26, no. 3 (January 2003): 41–66, by Taylor and Francis (copyright © 2003 Routledge); "The Myth of the Frozen Welfare State and the Dynamics of Contemporary French and German Social-Protection Reform," *French Politics* 2, no. 2 (August 2004): 151–183, by Palgrave-Macmillan Journals (available online at http://www.palgrave-journals.com/fp/journal/v2/n2/pdf/8200055a.pdf); "The Better Part of Valour: The Politics of French Welfare Reform," *Journal of European Social Policy* 9, no. 4 (Winter 1999): 311–330, by Sage Publications Ltd. (all rights reserved, copyright © 1999, available online at http://online.sagepub.com). Used by permission.

variant of Keynesianism worked to stimulate economic growth through technocratic planning, industrial policy, and deficit spending while maintaining export competitiveness through periodic currency devaluations.[3] The Keynesian revolution came later and was more qualified in Germany, where growth and full employment were sustained through neocorporatist institutions that underpinned the "virtuous circle of high profit, high investment-led growth cycles" of the postwar Economic Miracle.[4] Despite differences in the timing and extent of Keynesianism, both countries were thus heavily influenced by Keynes's legacy of promoting growth and full employment through active government.

Following the oil shocks of the 1970s and the failure of French "redistributive Keynesianism" in the early 1980s, however, Keynesian policies fell out of favor in France and Germany as policymakers turned to market making as the means by which to address unemployment. Far from remedying the problem, however, these market-making projects actually exacerbated unemployment, which reached unprecedented levels in the early 1990s. The return of the specter of mass joblessness led in turn to new approaches to labor-market policy. In contradistinction to the macro-level strategies of the earlier period, these new policy orientations have focused on micro-level labor-market activation designed to promote job creation, such as subsidies and tax breaks for employers and boosting incentives for the unemployed to find work.

Since the early 1990s, French and German authorities have focused their attention on combating the problem of "welfare without work," itself the partial legacy of the social-policy expansions of the 1980s and early 1990s. Although they ensured social peace and limited economic dislocation in the wake of marketization, these expanded arrangements yielded a new set of problems, such as high non-wage labor costs that impede job creation. These policy dysfunctions have helped to produce high rates of unemployment, which in turn have led to enormous costs for the welfare state and significant drains on the economy's productive capacity. To make matters worse, aging demographic structures have placed considerable pressures on state budgets, even as the advent of the fiscal-policy restrictions associated with European Economic and Monetary Union (EMU) have constrained social spending.[5]

Over the past twenty years, increasing political pressures to address these trends have led French and German authorities to undertake a series of ambitious reforms involving efforts to preserve the core of their welfare states while reconciling them with the imperatives of growth, job creation, and fiscal responsibility. In contrast to the 1980s and early 1990s, when passive policies such as unemployment insurance and early retirement predominated, since the early to mid-1990s authorities have prioritized active policies designed to promote workers' reintegration into the labor market. This approach has entailed reducing non-wage labor costs by subsidizing employers' share of social contributions, increasing pressure on the unemployed to accept work by tightening restrictions on unemployment benefits, encouraging part-time and temporary employment, and cutting early-retirement programs.

These reforms have not represented a simple abandonment of workers to the vagaries of the market, however. In contrast to prevailing conceptions of the labor market as "commodifying," policymakers have pursued a strategy of what I call "buttressed liberalization" of social protection, in which the labor market itself constitutes a focus of economic distribution, as authorities work to reconcile expanding employment with preserving a meaningful social-protection system.[6] In so doing, French and German governments have looked to job creation as a means by which to address the needs of a population for whom austerity has meant limited employment opportunities, as well as to defuse the political pressures arising from economic precariousness. Whereas earlier approaches embodied the notion of social protection *against* the labor market, in other words, recent reforms have exhibited a paradigmatic shift toward protection *through* it, involving the promotion of employment rather than dependence on the state.

Work as Welfare: The Dual Imperatives of Labor-Market Reform and Social Protection

The centrality of the labor market in contemporary French and German reform finds its origins in the emergence of high levels of unemployment in the late 1980s across advanced industrial democracies.[7] As elsewhere, jobless rates in France and Germany began to rise in the mid-1980s, fueled by the deep recession of the period and accelerated in France by the abandonment of dirigisme. There, joblessness climbed steadily after 1973, passing the barrier of 2 million unemployed in 1982, beyond which the country had been thought to be ungovernable, with the rate of unemployment reaching an alarming 10.2 percent by 1985.[8] Although the German model proved more effective at preserving jobs, by the mid-1980s the scourge of mass unemployment had crossed the Rhine, with jobless rates reaching 8 percent in 1985, the highest level since the immediate postwar period. As described in Chapter 4, however, it was reunification that drove Germany into a full-blown labor-market crisis, with unemployment reaching a postwar record of 11.7 percent in 1997.[9]

The difficulties posed by rising unemployment were not limited to the labor market; they also entailed a distinct set of challenges for the French and German welfare states. Because these systems finance the bulk of welfare benefits through payroll taxes, rising unemployment results in reduced revenue for social protection. A decline in payroll-tax receipts in turn creates pressures for increased contribution rates to balance the books, leading to higher non-wage labor costs that in turn place additional pressures on the labor market. This vicious circle between welfare financing and employment means that unemployment not only represents a direct threat to workers' incomes; it also undermines the social benefits, in particular the unemployment insurance, on which they increasingly have been forced to rely. The social partners who administer social-security funds have traditionally found it easiest to rely on increases in payroll-tax rates, rather than cutting benefits, to remedy the imbalance between revenues and expenditures. In so doing, they are able to appear as responsible stewards of welfare funds while using them to finance the costs of economic adjustment and protect the high wages, profits, and generous benefits available to their "insider" constituencies. Though politically expedient, this approach raises non-wage labor costs, thereby dampening the economy's capacity to create new (often low-wage and/or unskilled) jobs for "outsiders" searching for work.[10]

The problems plaguing the French and German labor markets in the 1990s extended beyond the level of unemployment to its composition. Beginning in the 1970s, the edifice of industrial employment created by the postwar boom began to erode in both countries. Between 1973 and 1990, industrial jobs declined from 32 percent to 25.3 percent of the workforce in Germany and from 25.4 percent to 17.5 percent in France.[11] These industrial jobs, which had long represented stable and well-paid employment for the working class, were increasingly replaced by service-sector jobs for which wages and job security tended to be significantly lower. As the two economies gradually deindustrialized, their incidence of fixed-time and part-time employment rose dramatically, resulting in generalizing economic insecurity.[12]

Furthermore, unemployment and precarious, poorly paid jobs tend to be concentrated among particular groups, such as women and younger and older workers. Colored by the legacies of male "breadwinner" models that went hand in glove with the prevalence of male-dominated industrial employment, the growth of early-retirement schemes in the 1980s, and outdated vocational training systems, France and Germany had some of the lowest labor-market-participation rates in the OECD for women of all ages and for workers of both sexes in the 15–24 and 55–64 age brackets.[13] The result was increasingly precarious terms of employment, and growing numbers of citizens were excluded altogether from the labor market. Authorities have worked to respond to this trend of generalizing economic precariousness as they have struggled to promote the labor market's capacity to adjust to economic austerity.[14]

In the wake of the marketization of the French and German political economies in the 1980s and 1990s, the linked dilemmas of unemployment and economic exclusion became even more critical. These problems have resulted in intense political pressure on policymakers, as high rates of unemployment increasingly have been interpreted as evidence of governmental failure. With the completion of earlier market-making reforms, authorities thus had both the economic opportunity and the political motive to tackle the dilemma of welfare without work. Finding an effective way to do so, however, was problematic.

Even as unemployment continued to rise, EMU deprived officials of traditional tools of macroeconomic management, such as devaluation and expansive public spending. French and German authorities were thus caught in the unenviable position of confronting rising unemployment even as their capacity to address it diminished. Nonetheless, governments in both countries felt that their political credibility crucially depended, in the words of one French party leader, on "not being resigned in the face of unemployment" and that the very "political identity" of the political establishment was at stake.[15] Representing a reverse analogue to Paul Pierson's observation that undertaking welfare retrenchment entails significant political liabilities, in this case policymakers increasingly saw too *little* activism as the politically most dangerous option.

Since the early 1990s, unemployment has moved to the forefront of French and German political debates. Since the mid-1990s—notably, in the French presidential elections in 1995 and 2007 and in the general elections in 1998, 2002, and 2005 in Germany—elites have repeatedly promised to reduce unemployment.[16] Though unfulfilled for much of the 1990s, such promises increasingly reflected a shift in the content of policy reforms late in the decade and, by the mid-2000s, increasing success at revitalizing the labor market. This shift to a strategy of buttressed liberalization has involved a combination of liberal initiatives, such as stricter conditions for receipt of unemployment benefits, and illiberal ones, including stepped-up active labor-market policies, the use of public resources to restructure training and job-placement services, and the subsidization of private-sector job creation. As unemployment has exposed the incapacity of inherited models to facilitate adjustment to economic austerity, authorities have developed innovative labor-market policies that reflect a strategic shift toward pursuing economic equity through rather than against the labor market.[17]

This new approach to labor-market policy has been colored by nationally specific institutional frameworks and political and economic discourses. For example, with the coming to power of Lionel Jospin's Socialist-led government in 1997, reductions in weekly work time became central to French policy debates, while in Germany this debate has been largely limited to the metalworking sector. Similarly , the French state's autonomy has enabled authorities there to intervene more directly to encourage employers to create additional jobs and to increase workers' access to employment. By contrast, the anti-interventionist biases of the German Social Market Economy and the reservation of wage-bargaining authority to the social partners (*Tarifautonomie,* or wage independence) has led authorities to adopt different means of intervention.[18] German governments first tried to encourage the social partners to undertake needed reforms, but the failure of this strategy increasingly led to direct intervention and confrontation with unions and employers. Though French and German responses to unemployment have been colored by institutional legacies, pressures for reform have created space for shifts in relationships among the state, employers, and unions as they compete for influence and legitimacy.

During the past decade, the transition from a "subsidization society" to an "employment society" at the center of the buttressed liberalization strategy has required a fundamental rethinking of the labor market and its linkages to the welfare state. Just as the solidification of the postwar boom and the process of market creation in the 1980s and early 1990s involved momentous changes in the French and German labor markets, so, too, have more recent reforms. The evolution of French and German labor-market policy during the past decade has entailed shifts in both the goals and the substance of policy as authorities have worked to reconcile responsible economic stewardship with just (and politically viable) distributive outcomes. In the process, employment has joined income derived from the welfare state as another primary "good" to be distributed and redistributed, with the availability of jobs becoming a central component of governments' visions of reform.

Below, I undertake a detailed discussion of recent French and German labor-market reforms and authorities' strategies for combating the dilemma of welfare without work. I begin with France, where the past decade and a half has witnessed the emergence of a novel micro-level strategy for labor-market revitalization. The implementation of this vision, however, has been far from seamless, repeatedly coming up against resistance on the part of unions and employers' associations, each of which has objected sharply to a number of government initiatives and fought to preserve and to extend their influence in the policymaking process. In Germany, the state has adopted an increasingly aggressive stance, working to compensate for the failures of tripartite labor-market institutions—for example, introducing a number of state-managed job-creation and training schemes. This strategy has called into question some of the foundations of German neocorporatism, in which the circumscribed power of the state has traditionally relegated it to a role of "first among equals." As the policies of the French and German labor markets have shifted, then, so, too, have the political relationships through which these outcomes are mediated.

New Strategies for Revitalizing the French Labor Market

In the early 1990s, French policymakers confronted an economic environment of slowed growth and rising rates of unemployment, which had both structural and conjunctural components. As we have seen, French unemployment began to rise in the 1970s as firms began to lay off workers in large numbers.[19] After 1983, these layoffs accelerated as French firms reduced their workforces in the wake of the abandonment of dirigisme. As a result, unemployment, which had been a mere 2.7 percent in 1973, rose to 6.3 percent in 1980, then to an unprecedented 10.5 percent in 1987 and to an even more alarming 12.3 percent by 1994.[20] In the 1970s, the prevalent conception of unemployment had seen the problem as a "temporary disturbance" resulting from macro-policy mistakes and the OPEC oil shocks.[21] As time went on, however, rising joblessness eroded faith in the inherited model of planning and industrial policies that had underpinned the *trente glorieuses* and had treated full employment as a natural by-product of responsible and enlightened economic stewardship.

The emergence of mass unemployment in the 1980s created pressures for alternative policy approaches, and authorities began to cast about for a solution to what was quickly coming to be viewed as a major social and political crisis. The first component of this response involved the "administrative authorization" for layoffs, introduced in 1975, which required approval by the Labor Inspectorate to ensure that workforce reductions were undertaken for justifiable economic reasons.[22] The lifting of this restriction by Prime Minister Jacques Chirac's neoliberal administration in 1986 yielded an additional surge in job cuts by companies under increasing competitive pressure and an explosion of cases in labor courts between aggrieved workers and firms, who now had merely to "consult" works councils before reducing their workforces.[23] This withdrawal of the state from the labor market was qualified in 1989, when the Socialist government of Michel Rocard passed the *loi Soisson*. This measure codified the requirements and procedures for so-called *plans sociaux* for firms laying off more than ten workers, requiring efforts on the part of firms to avoid layoffs and compensation for workers who did lose their jobs.[24]

The most substantive component of the state's efforts to socialize the effects of workforce reductions during the 1980s was the expansion of early-retirement schemes. These programs aimed to reduce unemployment (and preserve social peace) by subsidizing the early exit of older workers from the labor market in the hope that this would create openings for the young and the long-term unemployed. These programs exploded after 1981 with the advent of Mitterrand's Socialist administration and the expansion of the national employment fund, the Fonds National d'Emploi (FNE),[25] and particularly following the post-1983 dismantling of dirigisme. By the end of the 1980s, they were removing more than 200,000 workers annually from the labor market, with the total number of participants numbering more than 700,000.[26] In the mid-1980s, the costs of these programs became unsustainable for the national unemployment-insurance office, the Union Nationale pour l'Emploi dans l'Industrie et le Commerce (UNEDIC), forcing the state to assume a greater degree of financial responsibility.[27] Despite the costs, however, early-retirement programs offered clear benefits for policymakers, employers, and workers: Workers were able to retire early with a minimal loss in income; firms were able to externalize the costs of their restructuring onto the state; and governments could limit the social unrest attendant to economic dislocation. The result was a cozy, if tacit, consensus that subsequent policymakers would have difficulty breaking.[28]

Even as French authorities turned their attention from expanding social policies in support of liberalization to reforming these arrangements in the mid-1990s, and as demands for the state to "do something" about unemployment were increasing,[29] they had at their disposal fewer tools with which to address joblessness. No longer able to dictate labor-market outcomes or to limit firms' recourse to layoffs by administrative fiat, policymakers were obliged to seek new ways to promote job creation in the face of growing demands on the state, greater firm autonomy over questions of labor allocation, and a fragmented union movement unable coherently to represent workers' economic interests.[30]

In 1993, conservative Prime Minister Edouard Balladur adopted a strategy that combined selective, targeted labor-market liberalization with state subsidization of employers' social-security contributions in an effort to promote job creation by removing disincentives to hiring. The 1993 Five-Year Law on Employment (*la loi quinquennale sur l'emploi*) permitted firms to negotiate work-time adjustments with workers on an annual rather than weekly basis and offered partial contribution exemptions to employers who reduced annual work time by 15 percent combined with a proportional creation of jobs. This law effectively gave employers greater authority over the allocation of manpower within the firm and reinforced the pre-existing trend of negotiating part-time work on the level of individual contracts rather than through sectoral or national collective bargaining.[31] The hope was that providing firms with flexibility along with attractive social-contribution exemptions would encourage them to create jobs even as they modified their workforces in response to fluctuations in demand.[32] Representing a further break from heavy-handed labor-market regulation, this measure constituted a model for reforms under later governments.[33]

In 1996, Prime Minister Alain Juppé's administration passed the *loi Robien*, which reinforced the dual approach of subsidization and liberalization that had characterized the Five-Year Law. The new law further liberalized the wage-bargaining process, permitting firm- and branch-level negotiations and reducing the mandated work-time reduction from 15 percent to 10 percent for a given accord. It also provided more generous financial incentives to employers, offering a 50 percent reduction in social-security contributions the first year after an accord and 40 percent each year thereafter in exchange for a 10–15 percent reduction in the number of hours worked annually and a proportional creation of new positions.[34] This law comprised two major "wings," each of which was designed to address a particular aspect of long-term unemployment. The first, or "offensive," wing was aimed at firms that *created* jobs by reducing work time. The second, or "defensive," wing applied to firms that avoided layoffs, thereby preserving existing positions.[35]

Although, like its predecessor, the *loi Robien* continued to confront the difficulty of ensuring that firms would create jobs, its more aggressive (and more generous) approach had a significant impact on the French labor market. With 160 accords signed in its first six months, the measure encouraged the acceleration of firms' ongoing expansion of part-time and fixed-time work.[36] Although more than half of the deals fell under the law's defensive wing,[37] by May 1997 the measure had resulted in 1,100 conventions concerning 120,000 jobs. Unions greeted the measure with misgivings, fearing that it would merely encourage firms to "annualize" work time rather than create new employment or protect their members from layoffs. However, faced with the choice of signing on to greater flexibility or having similar conditions imposed without negotiation (through the proliferation of part-time and fixed-time contracts, for example), union representatives usually chose to accede.

The government of the left elected in 1997 adopted a somewhat different approach, which nonetheless represented significant continuity with respect to the mechanisms employed by earlier administrations. Under Socialist Prime Minister Lionel Jospin and Labor Minister Martine Aubry, the government enacted a series of measures that aimed to facilitate social dialogue over labor-market reform, reduce levels of unemployment, and increase opportunities for workers. The first major component of the government's labor-market agenda, the *programme emploi-jeunes* (Program for Youth Employment) offered generous subsidies to public-sector firms or agencies to hire workers between age sixteen and twenty-five, paying 80 percent of the minimum wage, or *salaire minimum interprofessionnel de croissance* (SMIC).[38] This measure was enacted in the hopes of reducing joblessness among young workers and better preparing those leaving school, in order to help heal a generational component of France's "social fracture."

The second facet of the government's labor-market program, and the one that would become its touchstone, involved two measures that extended financial incentives to employers while mandating a reduction of the work week to thirty-five hours. The first Aubry Law, passed in 1998, increased social-contribution exemptions to employers but made them contingent on a firm's or sector's negotiation of a thirty-five-hour weekly work-time limit, accompanied by proportional job creation.[39] The second law, passed in 2000, introduced an exemption on social-security contributions that rose with salaries up to 1.8 times the minimum wage (fixed above that level) and established annual limits on work time and overtime for firms or sectors that negotiated new contracts.[40] The laws thus aimed to create jobs through a combination of coercion and incentives, as opposed to the right's reliance on incentives alone. At the same time, the measures were part of the government's efforts to appeal to its constituencies on the left and embodied its self-image as "the counter-current of ultra-liberalism."[41]

Such rhetoric reflected the laws' partially political inspiration, an attempt by the new government to shore up support among its leftist constituencies and to ensure the loyalty of the new "plural left" government (composed of Socialists, Communists, and Greens) in Parliament. Having made the thirty-five-hour week one of its central campaign promises, the government settled on the reforms as the core of its economic-policy agenda.[42] Authorities realized, however, that the law would have to limit costs to employers if the measure were to lead to any significant job creation. The administration's "bait-and-switch" strategy permitted it to keep its electoral promises while painting itself as fighting the narrow self-interest of "ultra-liberal" employers,[43] even as it crafted the laws to encourage employers to create jobs.

Though a political boon in many ways, the measures also had significant negative political effects for the government, souring business–government relations for the next five years. The government unveiled the first law, without any prior consultation with the social partners, at a national conference in 1997 that had been called ostensibly to demonstrate the government's commitment to social dialogue. In response, Jean Gandois, president of the main employers' association, the Confédération Nationale du Patronat Français (CNPF), resigned in protest. Gandois refused to be a party to what employers considered to be a law that was authoritarian, expensive, and ineffective.[44] Employers then embarked on a high-profile campaign against both the laws and the government's overall policy agenda, a confrontational posture reflected in its changing its name from the CNPF to MEDEF, for Mouvement des Entreprises de France.

This aggressive public strategy harked back to campaigns that employers had begun to undertake during the previous decade. During the postwar boom, the CNPF, which was dominated by large firms, had pursued its legislative agenda through back-room lobbying with key actors in the government. This strategy had been part and parcel of a cozy relationship with the Gaullist establishment. Beginning in the 1980s, however, with the arrival of Yvon Gattaz as its president and the election of an administration of the left, the CNPF broadened its target constituency to include SMEs and adopted a combative stance vis-à-vis the government. In like fashion, MEDEF after 1997 began to act as a sort of undeclared ultra-liberal political party, publicly working to influence both elections and government policy.[45]

Despite their open hostility to the Aubry Laws, employers actually benefited considerably from the measures, which took a page from the strategy of labor-market subsidization and flexibilization begun under the right. According to one Labor Ministry official familiar with behind-the-scenes negotiations between employers and the government, the discrepancy between MEDEF's public reaction to the law and its private support for its provisions reflected "a lot of bad faith."[46] In apparent confirmation of this assessment, employers privately admitted that they objected primarily to the fact that the state had encroached on what they (as well as many unions) felt should be the social partners' right to negotiate wages and work time, rather than the actual substance of the measures.[47] Not only did the laws increase employers' social-contribution exemptions and offer them greater discretion over the allocation of labor; they also accelerated the shift from national to sectoral and firm-level collective bargaining, a development that employers have long favored. It was precisely these provisions that enabled the law to create jobs, for, as demonstrated by the experience of the Five-Year Law, no reform can create significant employment without active cooperation from business.[48] By the end of 2002, the laws had resulted in the creation or preservation of an estimated 350,000 jobs.[49] Even as the left enacted measures that benefited employers, it gained support from broad segments of the public by expanding workers' vacation time and encouraging social dialogue.

Recent administrations have undertaken a partial reversal of the Aubry Laws. In 2002, the conservative government of Jean-Pierre Raffarin introduced the *loi Fillon,* which permitted employers to negotiate a return to a thirty-nine-hour work week, raised annual limits on overtime, and blocked the application of the thirty-five-hour week to SMEs that had not already negotiated an accord. The center-right administration of President Nicolas Sarkozy and Prime Minister François Fillon, elected in May–June 2007 on promises to "break with the ideas, the habits and the behavior of the past,"[50] has stepped up efforts to liberalize France's labor market, beginning with a series of reforms of the Aubry Laws. Nearly immediately after the election of Sarkozy to the presidency in May and a comfortable parliamentary majority for the center-right in the Assemblée Nationale in June, the government adopted the Law Promoting Work, Employment, and Purchasing Power. This package of reforms aimed to provide renewed impetus behind labor-market reform, centering on a liberalization of the rules governing overtime and supplemental work time. Henceforth, in firms or sectors with governing bargains under the thirty-five-hour laws, all hours worked beyond thirty-five per week are to be exempt from social-security contributions, the *contribution sociale généralisée* (CSG), and income tax.[51]

In July 2008, the government went even further, adopting an extensive reform of the Aubry Laws that significantly dilutes them through provisions that are broadly consistent with the dual strategy of labor-market liberalization and subsidization. The Renewal of Social Democracy and Reform of Work Time increased the annual number of allowable working days from 218 to 245, effectively abolishing many of the extra days off (so-called *Jours RTT*). Additional days worked beyond 218 will be compensated at an additional 10 percent of the applicable wage, and companies are to be allowed to negotiate work time directly with workers' representatives. Following the law's adoption, Labor Minister Xavier Bertrand proclaimed that the government was "responding to ideology through pragmatism," implicitly indicting the left's approach to labor-market reform as overly voluntarist and sclerotic.[52] Such rhetoric notwithstanding, the government's approach to labor-market revitalization follows substantively in the tradition of the previous Socialist administration, even if it has been marked by sharply different ideological packaging and a different conception of the importance of restrictions on work time. The Confédération Française Démocratique du Travail (CFDT) and Confédération Générale du Travail (CGT) were predictably upset at the reform and led the campaign throughout the spring to prevent the government from implementing it. But Sarkozy's comfortable majority in Parliament, divisions between the CGT and the CFDT, the continuing disarray of the Socialist Party in the aftermath of its defeat in 2007, and Sarkozy's careful cultivation of union and employer support allowed the government to overcome opposition.[53]

As discussed later, the government was also assisted politically by the fact that the CFDT, the CGT, MEDEF, and the Confédération Générale des Petites et Moyennes Entreprises (CGPME), representing small and medium-size enterprises, had signed a "common position" on the half of the reform relating to "social democracy," calling for a reform of the rules by which unions were to be considered "representative" of workers.[54] Though all of the unions objected to the section of the law relating to work time, the government's clever packaging of the two measures into a single reform, and the linkages between the two sets of issues implied by this synthesis, weakened the unions' ability to fight it effectively. Though the work-time provision contravened the unions' desire to preserve the Aubry Laws, they found themselves in the politically untenable position of cooperating with a reformist government in some contexts and proclaiming themselves the defenders of the working class in others. Having agreed to negotiate with the government on an accord on greater labor-market flexibility and having signed the "common position" on union representation, reform-oriented unions like the CFDT could do little to block the reform, particularly given their longstanding public commitment to social dialogue.[55]

Measures relating to work time and non-wage labor costs have dovetailed with a number of recent attempts to reshape the demand side of the labor market, particularly with respect to unemployment insurance. These reforms have involved a combination of pressure on the unemployed to find and accept available jobs and the expansion of less generous, means-tested benefits for those without unemployment insurance. This trend began with the 1992 *allocation unique dégressive* (AUD), which made unemployment benefits decline as income rose, in the hope of increasing incentives for the unemployed to find work.[56] Those whose right to benefits has expired or who have inadequate contribution histories have access to the *allocation de solidarité spécifique* (ASS), a means-tested, flat-rate benefit for the unemployed. While its meagerness (up to 980 Euros [€] per month for a single person in 2008, minus other income) limits the attractiveness of long-term unemployment, the program has filled an important gap in a Bismarckian system of unemployment insurance based on contribution histories.[57] The AUD and the ASS also reflected a move away from an insurance principle to means-tested benefits in the hopes of preserving a safety net (most clearly embodied in the *revenu minimum d'insertion* [RMI], as discussed in Chapter 7), while facilitating workers' return to employment.

Recent battles over unemployment insurance have been driven by a changing set of relationships between the state and interest groups, a shift in which MEDEF's Refondation Sociale (Social Refoundation) campaign in the late 1990s was a critical turning point. This agenda reflected employers' growing assertion of influence over the policymaking process and their attempt to convey an image of (liberal) social-mindedness rather than parochialism. In December 2000, MEDEF announced that the Refondation Sociale would center on the critical areas of unemployment insurance, vocational training, health insurance, and pensions. In addition to influencing public debates, the campaign also reflected MEDEF's attempt to reclaim the initiative in the face of what both employers and unions viewed as the government's growing intrusion into the purview of the social partners. In the words of Ernest-Antoine Seillière, MEDEF's president at the time, "Of course, the State has social responsibilities, but that does not mean that it should carry them out in an authoritarian way, with sole regard to its own initiative."[58] For Denis Kessler, the intellectual father of the Refondation Sociale and MEDEF's erstwhile *éminence grise,* the campaign was not only about countermanding the government's ostensibly illiberal impulses. More fundamentally, it was about a "quest for rules" governing social dialogue and a clarification of the respective responsibilities of the state and social partners.[59] The Refondation Sociale represented employers' effort to assert their influence and a reaction to dysfunctions in France's system of social partnership, which had long been characterized by state dominance, ideological and politically marginalized trade unions, and relatively passive employers' associations.

The continuing battle over labor-market reform inaugurated by the Refondation Sociale is not merely a fight over policy content. It is also a conflict over the legitimacy of the government and the social partners. The 2000 debate over unemployment insurance took place against the background of acrimonious conflict between MEDEF and the government. Even as employers complained about the government's "Jacobinism" and "authoritarianism," Prime Minister Jospin begged the public not to "expect everything from the state."[60] This plea reflected the government's view that the dysfunctions of French social partnership were forcing it, as the sole institution with broad legitimacy, to step in to fill the vacuum of authority and address France's labor-market crisis.

The Refondation Sociale's dominance of public debate over social-protection reform paralleled the significance of the unemployment-insurance reform to which it led.[61] In June 2000, MEDEF and the CFDT struck a bargain that limited access to benefits and imposed significant new obligations on job seekers. The resulting *plan d'aide et de retour à l'emploi* (PARE) ended benefit degressivity but made receipt of benefits contingent on a signed contract between job seekers and the Agence Nationale pour l'Emploi (ANPE) or the national employment office, the *projet d'action personnalisé* (PAP), making benefits contingent on a personalized job-search program.

Following the conclusion of union–employer negotiations, however, the government refused to ratify the agreement, arguing that the measure insufficiently extended coverage and that defining rights to benefits should remain the state's prerogative. Labor Minister Martine Aubry's objections, however, were more jurisdictional than substantive, since she and her closest advisers privately supported the basic policy direction represented by the deal. After several iterations of the reform, the conflict between MEDEF and the government was finally resolved by a phone call from Jospin to Seillière at midnight on a Sunday to defuse it. Jospin felt compelled to intervene to secure a reform that all sides (with the predictable exceptions of Force Ouvrière [FO] and the CGT) supported and to prevent MEDEF's withdrawal from the administration of France's social-security funds, which the association had threatened if legislation did not hew closely to its demands.[62]

The fight for legitimacy and political influence between the government and MEDEF, however, did not end with the PARE. Partially in response to perceptions of its impotence in the face of increasing layoffs and partially to reclaim political initiative from MEDEF, in late 2001 the government adopted the *loi sur la modernisation sociale* (Law on Social Modernization), whose title was a not-so-subtle reference to MEDEF's Refondation Sociale. The legislation was politically inspired, a response to both the approach of the 2002 presidential elections and layoffs at high-profile companies such as Michelin, Danone, Marks and Spencer France, and Moulinex. The politically charged atmosphere surrounding these layoffs resulted from the fact that many companies were laying off workers while making healthy profits and the widespread sense that they were reducing their workforces in response to the short-term concerns of shareholders. The redundancies were also often undertaken with great brutality, with thousands laid off with little warning.[63]

Although this largely symbolic law pleased constituencies on the left, it also came at a significant political cost. In addition to MEDEF's predictable outcry, the government confronted broader resistance among France's corporations, with fifty-six chief executives publishing a manifesto in *Les Echos* decrying the law as "a trap for workers."[64] Employers objected to the law's restriction of the definition of "economically motivated layoffs" and its extension of the period during which firms wishing to dismiss workers were obliged to consult with workers' representatives. In reality, however, these measures created few new substantive obstacles to workforce reductions. Under increasing pressure to respond to unemployment, the government was effectively shoring up its political credibility through symbolic politics while alienating the firms whose cooperation was needed to reduce unemployment. Motivated by opposition to such measures, the center-right administration of Jean-Pierre Raffarin focused on modifying what it saw as the excessively regulatory impulse of its leftist predecessor. Following its election in 2002, the government acted almost immediately to rescind portions of the contested *loi sur la modernisation sociale,* suspending the extension of the period during which firms must consult with works councils but preserving the provision that strengthened firms' obligation to compensate or retrain laid-off workers.[65]

In 2005, the center-right administration of Prime Minister Dominique de Villepin battled unions and employers over control of the agenda for reforming the labor market. The government's most controversial measure was the so-called *contrat première embauche* (CPE), or Contract for First Hires, which loosened restrictions for small and medium-sized enterprises on firing workers younger than twenty-six in the hope of spurring job creation. Though employers tepidly supported the measure, all major unions and many student groups vigorously opposed what they saw as a way to increase the precariousness of employment. Demonstrations in spring 2006 brought more than a million people out into the streets. Many protests turned violent and resulted in dozens of arrests and significant property damage in Paris and other major cities. The scale of the protest and pressure from President Jacques Chirac forced the prime minister to withdraw the measure.

In late 2007, the Sarkozy administration began a public debate on the need for further tightening of restrictions on unemployment insurance and requirements that recipients actively search for work. In April 2008, at the behest of the government, which threatened to impose reforms through legislation if the social partners did not agree to reforms themselves, unions and employers began negotiating a new convention on unemployment insurance to replace the one set to expire at the end of the year. Both the government and MEDEF wished to tighten the rules governing benefits, particularly with respect to the definition of a "reasonable job offer," which the unemployed person would be obliged to accept. Though the PARE had imposed new job-search requirements and restrictions on benefits, the government felt that such restrictions were not sharp enough to stimulate labor demand significantly, especially given that only fifteen hundred workers were sanctioned every month out of a total of 1.9 million unemployed. In the words of Economics Minster Christine Lagarde, redolent of language used by Gerhard Schröder, "The unemployed have rights, to be sure, but they also have obligations."[66]

Frustrated with the social partners' lack of agreement, the government decided to impose reforms consistent with the demands of MEDEF and, to a lesser extent, the CFDT.[67] Hoping to reduce unemployment to 5 percent by

2012, the government's proposal required a benefit recipient to accept a job offered by the ANPE if it required up to a two-hour round-trip commute and corresponded to the person's qualifications. After a three-month period, the person would be obliged to accept a reduction in salary of 5 percent through the sixth month and 20 percent between the sixth and twelfth month of unemployment. Thereafter, all jobs were to be considered "reasonable" with respect to compensation that paid at least the level of unemployment benefits defined at a level of 57 percent of the most recent wage. The final *loi sur les droits et les devoirs des demandeurs d'emploi,* which was adopted by Parliament in an overnight session on 17–18 July and took effect on 1 October 2008, defined a "reasonable job offer (*offre raisonnable d'emploi*)" as one that offered 95 percent of a worker's most recent salary after three months of unemployment benefits, 85 percent after six months, and the level of unemployment insurance after a year. The job had to involve skills consistent with the job seeker's qualifications, and the job seeker had to be willing to commute at least two hours, round-trip. If the person rejected two such "reasonable offers," benefits were to be suspended, initially for a period of two months and then indefinitely.[68] This increased pressure on the unemployed would be accompanied by an "intensified, individualized" job-counseling program offered to each worker (the *projet personnalisé d'accès à l'emploi* [PPAE]) following the merger of UNEDIC and the ANPE in 2009.[69]

The tightening of restrictions on unemployment insurance and the political dynamics of the debate surrounding the initiative reflect significant continuity relative to the 1990s while also indicating some important differences between Sarkozy's approach and that of earlier governments. The unions railed against the measure and the government's lack of consultation, with the CFDT criticizing it as "unjust because it focuses on punishing the most vulnerable among the jobless, those who have been looking for work the longest," and the FO blasting it as another step in the "logic of liberalism, aiming to stigmatize, always and constantly, the unemployed person as the primary author of his regrettable situation."[70] The government's decision to impose reform through legislation shows that the state has been able to reclaim some of the initiative in the reform process that it had ceded to the social partners during the Jospin, Raffarin, and de Villepin administrations, because of divisions on the left, public opinion that has become more accommodating of reform,[71] and a government whose preferences are consistent with employers'. That said, the government's constant threats to legislate in the absence of a deal among the social partners reflects unions' and employers' now established place at the bargaining table, as well as a discourse that increasingly sees unilateral state imposition as illegitimate.

Recent French labor-market reform has thus involved gradual liberalization punctuated by episodes of partial re-regulation; expanded incentives for employers to create jobs; greater pressure on the unemployed to accept available work;

and the expansion of some forms of financial support for the jobless.[72] The positive effects of a decade of reform have been considerable for both France's workers and the labor market more broadly. Even as growth during the early 2000s slowed significantly relative to the late 1980s, the number of jobs created per point of GDP growth increased dramatically, from about 183,000 in the late 1980s to 268,000 in the late 1990s. What is more, a large number of total jobs created (832,000 between 1997 and 1999 alone) have been the direct products of labor-market reforms.[73] Part-time jobs as a share of total employment increased from 12.2 percent in 1989 to 14.7 percent in 1999 and to 17.2 percent in 2006, as did the share of temporary jobs, from about 8 percent of employment in 1989 to more than 10 percent in 1999 and to 13.5 percent in 2006.[74] Both of these trends represent increased labor-market flexibility and a prioritization of access to remunerative income. The rate of decline of activity rates among workers age fifty-five to sixty-four has slowed,[75] and rates of participation in early-retirement programs have been significantly curtailed.[76] Furthermore, rates of increase in workers' hourly productivity grew from an annual average of 1.2 percent between 1991 and 1996 to 1.5 percent between 1997 and 2001.[77] In October 2005, due in part to the effects of active labor-market policies, French unemployment dipped below 10 percent.[78] By the fourth quarter of 2007, it had declined to 7.5 percent, the lowest since 1983.[79]

While labor-market reform during the past decade has thus had a number of important economic effects, it has also been driven by significant changes in French political dynamics. Recent outcomes (see Table 5.1) have been defined by a battle between the state and social partners for influence and legitimacy in the policymaking process, a pattern that I call "competitive interventionism." This new pattern marks a major departure from the traditional dynamics of French statist labor-market governance. Rather than merely responding to government proposals—with either support or hostility—as in the past, French unions and employers are also taking the initiative in a wide range of policy areas, working both to shape the content of policy outcomes and to influence the reform agenda and the character of political debate. As the economic context has shifted during the past two decades, an emerging coalition among moderate unions and employers has been unwilling to leave the business of policymaking to the state. At the same time, other, "negative" coalitions have arisen to block measures that the French electorate sees as illegitimate.

Since the election of French President Nicolas Sarkozy in 2007, the prevailing relationships between the state and social partners have continued to evolve in ways that have reinforced this competitive interventionist dynamic. Just as the Refondation Sociale began a period of ascendance by the social partners as important players in the reform process, the activism of the Sarkozy "hyper-presidential" administration has led to a series of bargains among the social partners that aim to defend and consolidate that influence. From the earliest

TABLE 5.1 Major French Labor-Market Reforms, 1993–Present

Program/Law	Year	Provisions
Five-Year Law on Employment	1993	Subsidized employers who reduced work time by 15%; facilitated annualized working hours; prioritized firm-level bargaining
Loi Robien	1996	Permitted firm- and branch-level wage bargaining; subsidized social contributions for firms who reduced hours and created jobs
Programme emploi-jeunes	1997	Offered subsidies for firms hiring workers age sixteen to twenty-five; paid 80% of the SMIC
First Aubry Law	1998	Mandated thirty-five-hour work week, negotiated on firm and sectoral levels; offered subsidy to employers who reduced total working hours
Second Aubry Law	2000	Introduced additional social-contribution exemptions; increased annual work-time and overtime limits
Plan d'aide et de retour à l'emploi (PARE)	2000	Made receipt of unemployment insurance contingent on job search and placement contract; ended degressivity of unemployment benefits
Loi sur la modernisation sociale (partially suspended in 2002)	2001	Tightened restrictions on "economically motivated" layoffs; mandated negotiations on thirty-five-hour week before *plan social*
Loi Fillon	2002	Permitted negotiated return to thirty-nine-hour work week; quashed further application of Aubry Laws to SMEs
Loi sur la rénovation de la démocratie sociale et réforme du temps de travail	2008	Increased number of allowable workdays and redefined rights of union representation
Loi sur les droits et les devoirs des demandeurs d'emploi	2008	Tightened rules for receipt of unemployment insurance; defined and made obligatory acceptance of "reasonable job offers"

days of his administration, Sarkozy's strategy has involved demanding that the social partners negotiate reforms and threatening to impose legislation if they fail to do so. As we have seen, the government adopted this approach with the reform of the Aubry Laws and the recent reform of the rules governing unemployment benefits.

In contrast to these two instances, however, in the case of reforms that have redefined the rules according to which much social dialogue takes place, the government largely implemented the preferences of employers and key unions. In late 2007, the government called on the social partners to clarify and systematize bargaining over wages and social-protection reforms by revamping the rules determining which unions are considered legitimate representatives of workers' interests. Since the immediate postwar period, French collective bargaining has been based on rules that grant the right of worker representation to five key unions—the CGT, the CFDT, the FO, the Confédération Française des Travailleurs Chrétiens (CFTC), and the Confédération Générale des Cadres (CGC)—irrespective of actual membership in a particular sector or firm. This fact has led to the perverse effect that unions can negotiate wage bargains that apply to firms or sectors in which they have few, if any, members. The "quest for rules" invoked by Denis Kessler in 2002 has continued, and both the social partners and governments have sought ways to bolster unions' bargaining position and to provide order within a chaotic and disorganized system of social partnership. Doing so would both consolidate employers' and (some) unions' place at the policymaking table and enable governments to confer legitimacy on a reform process in which workers and firms alike can be said to have had a real voice. From the government's perspective, the goal was to "make the social partners responsible" and to create "long-term investments" in a constructive system of social dialogue.[80]

The reform of "union representativeness"—the second half of the Law on the Renewal of Social Democracy and Reform of Work Time—went a long way toward providing this kind of order. It represented what one adviser to the prime minister called "a real revolution" that "completely transforms" the French system of social partnership.[81] The measure implemented the "common position" signed by MEDEF, the CGPME, the CFDT, and the CGT in April 2008. This position was the product of more than two months of tense negotiation between unions and employers, with the government repeatedly threatening to use the "sword of Damocles" by imposing reform in the absence of an accord.[82] At first, a deal seemed unlikely, given the distance between the positions of the CFDT, which had long favored such a reform; the CGT, which was much more skeptical; and MEDEF, which seemed opposed to any reform that did not reduce all bargaining to the firm level. To everyone's surprise, negotiations in March resulted in a narrowing of differences between MEDEF, which became more open to some recognition of the importance of sectoral-level negotiations (which tend to favor the unions), and the CGT, which for the first time seemed open to signing an accord that shifted the locus of much bargaining to the firm. One reason for the shift involved the resolution of an internal conflict in MEDEF, which pitted the organization's president, Laurence Parisot, against the Union des Industries et Métiers de la Métallurgie (UIMM), which organizes employers in the metalworking sectors and has long been MEDEF's hard-line neoliberal power broker. Following a financing scandal in which the UIMM was found to have misdirected organizational funds, Parisot successfully consolidated her authority by issuing a declaration of new ethics rules for MEDEF and marginalizing UIMM representatives in the organization's executive council.[83]

This internal coup allowed Parisot to limit the influence of liberals within MEDEF and to seek a compromise on an accord with the CFDT and, surprisingly, the CGT. Though normally opposed to any dilution of sectoral in favor of firm-level bargaining, the CGT took a page from the CFDT's playbook by acting more like a constructive partner in the reform process than an obstructionist protest organization aiming to resist the predations of capitalism. By signing an accord that compromised some of its traditional orthodoxies, the CGT aimed to reinforce the organization's position in the French system of social partnership, even at the cost of validating some aspects of employers' preference for firm-level bargaining.[84] The "common position," signed in April 2008 by MEDEF, the CGPME, the CFDT, and the CGT, and then adopted substantively unchanged by the government, was celebrated by Sarkozy as an example of "social dialogue [that] has never been as intense or as constructive as it has been during the last several months."[85] The reform is widely seen as a "true revolution" in the system of social partnership and continues the redefinition of roles of the government and social partners that began in earnest with the Refondation Sociale.[86] The law abolishes the privileged position of the five main unions and replaces it with rules that establish unions' right to represent workers through firm- or sectoral-level professional elections. To do so, a union must win 10 percent of the votes in a firm or 8 percent in a particular sector. For an accord to be valid, it must gain the signature of at least one union representing at least 30 percent of the workers in a firm or sector, and unions with at least 50 percent of the votes must accept the deal.[87] This reform effectively replaces the old system of collective representation, which enabled any of the "big five" unions to sign an accord in any sector, with a more majoritarian system in which unions' right of representation is a function of their ability to garner support among workers.

The CFDT's and CGT's signing of the accord reflects their support of a deal that validates the leadership of large unions and marginalizes smaller ones, such as the CFTC and unions beyond the "big five," which will almost certainly be unable to obtain the necessary votes. But some observers see the accord as a Faustian bargain that consolidates the power of the CFDT and the CGT even as it officially recognizes the primacy of firm-level bargaining, which tends to fragment worker representation.[88] Though the long-term effects remain unclear (it will not become effective on the national level for five years), it clearly reflects a continuation of two important components of the "competitive interventionist" dynamic. First, it consolidates large unions' place at the bargaining table and strengthens their role as officially sanctioned negotiators in the policymaking process. Second, by clarifying the role of unions and employers in collective bargaining on the national level, it provides a partial answer to the longstanding "quest for rules" in this area, thereby furnishing a context that is likely to encourage good-faith negotiation among the government and social partners.

If the law on union representativeness has not turned France into a neocorporatist country, it nonetheless represents a further step away from the traditional system of statist labor-market regulation. Gone are the days when the French state functioned as the sole impetus for labor-market reform, and the CFDT, the CGT, and MEDEF in particular are likely to continue to exert a powerful influence over the character of debates and the substance of reforms. Changes in both recent labor-market policies and the political bargains underpinning them are the cumulative products of a long period of gradual, incremental readjustment of a policymaking model to a new set of political and economic circumstances. Though France has not fully liberalized its labor market, it has undergone a paradigmatic shift in terms of both the degree of public acceptance of liberalization and prevailing understandings of the state's and social partners' respective roles in the process.

State Activism in a Corporatist Setting: Reforming the German Labor Market

In Germany, authorities' strategy for reviving the labor market has been colored by a different constitutional distribution of authority and distinctive labor-market institutions. The constitutionally enshrined principle of *Tarifautonomie,* or wage independence, reserves to employers and unions the authority to bargain collectively over work time and wages. Powerful firm-level works councils composed of employers' and workers' representatives control shop-floor decisions over the organization of production. Tripartite labor-market institutions—in particular, the Bundesagentur für Arbeit (BA; previously the Bundesanstalt für Arbeit), or Federal Labor Office, have long dominated labor-market policymaking, and the social partners' responsibilities for managing the country's social-security funds have limited the state's ability to restructure labor-market policies such as unemployment insurance.[89] Since the early 1990s, these limitations on state authority have forced successive governments to confront both firms' de facto control over employment decisions and the social partners' substantial de jure control over significant aspects of the policymaking process. As a result, in working to reduce unemployment, the state has tried to wrest authority from neocorporatist labor-market institutions, which have failed to devise effective responses. While French labor-market reform has been characterized by the social partners' increasing contestation of state dominance, in Germany battles over reform have involved the emergence of a logic of "conflictual corporatism," with increasingly aggressive attempts by governments to reshape a policy domain over many aspects of which they do not enjoy direct control.

The outcome of this new state assertiveness has been a significant alteration in the way the German labor market is governed, as well as important changes in the plight of the unemployed. To be sure, the neocorporatist labor-market institutions—above all, the BA—continue to govern a good deal of labor-market policy, from vocational training to unemployment insurance and to job-creation schemes. At the same time, German governments have worked to promote active labor-market policies, which have traditionally remained underdeveloped, while exploiting windows of political opportunity created by tripartite labor-market institutions' failure to reduce unemployment. During the past decade, German labor-market policy has become bicephalous, with expanded state-administered and state-funded policies working alongside established neocorporatist organs. With regard to the unemployed, governments have preserved the core of social insurance while imposing stricter requirements and broadening incentives for them to find jobs. Officials have worked to reshape the supply and demand sides of the employment nexus with a view to pursuing redistributive goals through rather than against the labor market.[90] They have done so despite mounting opposition from unions and the new Linke, or Left Party, and realizing that many reforms would take time to be effective. As one highly placed labor-market-policy official put it, "One cannot wash one's hands without getting wet."[91]

As described in Chapter 2, Germany's neocorporatist labor-market institutions worked quite well during the era of full employment that accompanied the postwar *Wirtschaftswunder,* requiring only minor adjustments to the industrial economy and the welfare state. As explained in Chapter 4, however, German reunification, on the heels of a slowdown in economic growth and rising unemployment in the late 1980s, exposed major structural weaknesses in German labor-market institutions. As unemployment continued to rise in the mid-1990s, it became increasingly clear that Germany's labor-market arrangements were poorly equipped to manage adjustment to an economic climate of slowed growth, the continued burdens of restructuring the Eastern economy, and a secular shift away from the industrial-production model that had served the country so well in the decades after the war. Furthermore, the adaptive welfare-state expansion that had supported Eastern Germany's transition to a market economy had led to an explosion of social expenditures, even as unemployment continued to erode social contributions. By 1996, GDP growth had slowed to .8 percent, and unemployment, which averaged 8.7 percent after reunification in 1990, reached 10.3 percent in 1996 and an unprecedented 11.4 percent in 1997.[92] The virtuous circle between the labor market and social policy had turned vicious, as rising joblessness led to increasing social-security deficits and slowed growth undermined the positive relationship between wages and profits. In short, it had become abundantly clear that the economy was suffering from deep-seated problems of which structural unemployment was both an exacerbating factor and a politically sensitive symptom.

These alarming economic trends, coupled with languid responses by neocorporatist labor-market institutions, created the impetus for vigorous state efforts to reform the German labor market. Rather than addressing high non-wage labor costs and a vocational-training system that had not adjusted to an increasingly service-dominated economy, the social partners contented themselves with balancing the books by increasing social-contribution rates, which rose from 37.3 percent of gross wages in 1990 to 41.7 percent by 1999.[93] Even more alarmingly, a full 32.8 percent of jobless workers between 1995 and 1999 had been on the rolls for more than a year, reflecting the ineffectiveness of the BA's job-placement services.[94] The BA's labor-market policies had long served largely "to maintain people inactive outside the labor market" rather than reinsert them into it, relying on extensive make-work schemes and early-retirement programs to limit the labor supply.[95] In 1998, in addition to more than 3.4 million unemployed (according to restrictive definitions), nearly 1.7 million were involved in BA make-work schemes (430 million), training courses (402 million), or early-retirement programs (809 million).[96] Germany suffered from ineffective labor-market policies perpetuated by social partners more concerned with their own institutional prerogatives than with promoting reform.

In the mid-1990s, Germany's lackluster employment performance and the continuing strains of reunification created an impetus for a greater degree of policy activism on the part of the center-right government of Chancellor Helmut Kohl. As was discussed in Chapter 4, the government had already enacted the beginnings of an activist labor-market policy by creating myriad job-creation schemes in the East, including a 1993 modification of the *Arbeitsförderungsgesetz* (Employment Promotion Act). This amendment aimed to create a secondary labor market by introducing certain exceptions to existing sectoral wage bargains to permit lower wages in the hope of creating jobs. It operated through federal subsidies to cover wages for new hires above the level of unemployment insurance, up to a ceiling of DM 15,120 (€7,731) per year, as long as the worker was paid no more than 90 percent of the weekly minimum wage set out in a governing wage agreement. By 1996, the law had created 60,000 jobs in the struggling Eastern economy. Although the government hoped to extend the measure to Western Germany, employers and unions refused, with IG Metall filing a lawsuit claiming that the provision was a violation of *Tarifautonomie*. In the end, the government acquiesced, accepting that the law would lapse by the original deadline of 1997.[97] At the same time, the law inaugurated a more activist government approach to labor-market policy, a strategy that would continue to develop under the center-left government of Chancellor Gerhard Schröder. That said, the social partners' resistance to the measure reflected the difficulties faced by German governments wishing to shape the labor market through state policy and showed that any administration wishing to do so would have to contend with the entrenched prerogatives of unions and employers.

The "Red–Green" coalition of Social Democrats and Greens that governed from 1998 to 2005 went well beyond its center-right predecessor's responses to Germany's employment crisis. By 1998, unemployment had become the central economic question on the national political agenda, and public demands to address it had become increasingly vocal. Schröder pledged, if elected, to reduce German unemployment from nearly 4 million to fewer than 3.5 million by the end of the government's first term in office. With the unemployment rate at a postwar record of 11.4 percent, the government had its work cut out for it. Its first major initiative involved an effort to resuscitate the Bündnis für Arbeit (Alliance for Jobs), harking back to earlier, neocorporatist patterns of labor-market policymaking. The Bündnis had been designed as a standing forum for the government and social partners jointly to develop effective labor-market reforms. Initiated by Kohl in 1995 in response to demands from IG Metall, the arrangement soon fell apart due to employers' insistence on more extensive measures than those envisioned by the forum's first major proposal, which involved an agreement by unions to accept flat wage rates in exchange for the creation of 300,000 jobs and a 5 percent increase in the number of apprenticeship slots.[98]

When Schröder revived the Bündnis in 1998, it seemed at first to augur a period of renewed consensual labor-market policymaking, particularly given the historical alliance between the SPD and the trade unions, which had initiated the idea. These hopes would remain unfulfilled, however, as Bündnis meetings tended to degenerate into disagreements over the respective prerogatives of the state and social partners. Initially, the government embraced the Bündnis as a way to avoid responsibility for unemployment, and employers hoped to use it to secure wage restraint, but neither unions nor employers were prepared to make major concessions.[99] As a result, the government realized that any significant reform would have to take place outside traditional neocorporatist channels, and the failure of the Bündnis represented the beginning of the end for this historical model of labor-market governance.[100] Some observers suggest that the Bündnis für Arbeit had really been a red herring—a high-profile, token gesture toward consensual politics rather than a substantive policy initiative. Neither employers (who wished above all to increase labor flexibility and limit their tax burdens) nor unions (who were most concerned with protecting the wages of their older industrial membership) had much interest in making sacrifices to reduce unemployment. In early 2003, the government finally allowed the Bündnis to dissolve, publicly recognizing a failure that had been clear for some time.[101]

The collapse of the Bündnis both reflected and accelerated the government's turn to a labor-market strategy that centered more on state intervention than negotiation. This new forcefulness was nicely formulated in the words on a plaque on the desk of one government labor-market expert, citing the German author Christa Wolf's dictum that "nothing makes us more tired than the deeds that remain undone."[102] Having made reducing unemployment one of his central campaign promises, Schröder, along with Labor Minister Walter Riester, formerly (and ironically, given his subsequent disregard for unions' concerns) head of IG Metall, launched a series of important policy initiatives. Soon after the election, Schröder gave rhetorical form to his government's new approach, combining an emphasis on the "rights and obligations" of the unemployed with a strategy of "*Fordern und Fördern* (demanding and supporting)" their reactivation in the labor market. This formulation hinted at the government's strategy of assuming substantial authority from the BA, as well as its agenda of applying pressure to the jobless to accept available employment. Schröder famously declared, "Whoever is able to work but refuses an appropriate job should have his support cut. There is no right to laziness in our society!"[103] For decades, unemployment insurance and job-placement services, for which employees furnish 50 percent of the financing, had been considered benefits previously paid for and therefore owed to workers as a matter of right. By contrast, both the rhetoric and the policies of the Schröder government suggested a growing emphasis on state initiatives and making "rights" previously taken for granted contingent on workers' acceptance of obligations.

One of the government's keystone policy initiatives was the JOB-AQTIV Gesetz, or the Law for Job-Activation, Qualification, Training, Investment, and Placement (*Vermitteln* in German), which entailed elements of coercion as well as an effort to expand employment opportunities. It mandated the restructuring of the BA's job-placement services and adopted an aggressive, contractual stance toward the unemployed. Regional and local branches of the BA were obligated to create a personalized profile for each job seeker, offering appropriate job openings and providing tailored advice and counseling services. In return, the unemployed person was obligated to accept "reasonable" job offers and to make a concerted effort to find work. The law also introduced new vocational-training programs for workers and new entrants to the job market, expanded subsidies to employers to encourage hiring by reducing non-wage labor costs, and instituted job-creation schemes aimed at improving public infrastructure.[104] Resisted by trade unions, the law also showed Schröder's willingness to contravene the preferences of his traditional political allies. As the government worked to create a *Leistungsgesellschaft,* or "performance society," it reinterpreted the concept of the *soziale Marktwirtschaft,* working to develop the "market" without abandoning the "social."[105]

The government's labor-market strategy also entailed a dramatic extension of active labor-market policies, an area traditionally neglected by Bismarckian welfare states such as Germany's. A central target of such policies was the stubborn problem of youth unemployment, which reflects a long-run imbalance of labor supply and demand. Joblessness among workers younger than twenty-five rose significantly in the 1990s, reaching a level of 10.4 percent in 1998, 476,000 youth being without either jobs or apprenticeship places. Between

1991 and 1998, the number of applicants registered with the BA for apprenticeship slots grew from 541,790 to 796,400, while the number of available positions decreased from 830,940 to 603,900.[106] Between 2002 and 2005, the number of available apprenticeship places continued to decline, and the number of unemployed workers younger than twenty-five continued to increase, from 512,864 in 2002 to 621,829 in 2005.[107]

The ongoing campaign against youth unemployment is emblematic of the federal government's efforts to move into the political space created by the failure and immobility of neocorporatist labor-market institutions. In 1998, the government passed the *Sofortprogramm zum Abbau der Jugendarbeitslosigkeit* (Immediate Program for the Reduction of Youth Unemployment), known as JUMP. This law created new training and apprenticeship programs, introduced wage subsidies for firms that hire young unemployed workers, and instituted additional job-counseling services. It devoted DM 2 billion (€1.02 billion) annually to the goal of creating 100,000 new jobs for workers younger than twenty-five.[108] Of the total DM 2 billion allocated in 2001, moreover, a full DM 1.2 billion (nearly 90 percent of the German government's share) came from federal tax revenues. Furthermore, whereas the BA has traditionally administered such programs with almost total autonomy, JUMP was managed jointly by BA and the Labor Ministry.[109] In this way, both the content and the funding of the initiative flowed from the federal government and the Labor Ministry rather than from the BA and social partners.[110]

The interventionist character of the JOB-AQTIV Gesetz and the law on youth unemployment paralleled shifting patterns of labor-market-policy financing. In fiscal year 1999, the federal government (not counting contributions from the *Länder* and municipalities) financed more than 37 percent of the BA's budget (most of the rest came from employers' and employees' contributions).[111] In the same year, the government financed a full 29 percent (DM 43.6 billion, or €22.3 billion) of the total cost of DM 150.3 billion (€76 billion) for *all* labor-market polices, compared with €16.2 billion in 1995.[112] Then, in 2001, the government increased its share by providing the BA with an additional DM 1.2 billion (€614 million) to offset the costs of its JUMP reform. During the same period, the BA's outlays for *active* labor-market policies rose substantially, with a record DM 44.1 billion (€22.5 billion) budgeted for 2001, despite a reduction in the total number of unemployed during the same year.[113] In 2002, the federal government supplied 29 percent of the BA's annual funding, more than a third of which was paid as a lump sum to cover the agency's deficit.[114] From 1998 to 2002, then, the federal government raised its already high level of *overall* funding for the BA's labor-market policies while the total share of funds devoted to *active* labor-market policies increased significantly relative to expenditures at the end of the Kohl administration in 1998 (from 34.6 percent to 43.6 percent).[115] Between 2003 and 2006, the federal government's expenditures on labor-market policies more than doubled, reaching a high of €38.7 billion before declining slightly, to €33.4 billion, in 2007 due to renewed economic growth and a decline in unemployment.[116]

The Schröder administration also prioritized the subsidization of low-wage jobs by reimbursing social contributions and granting income-tax exemptions for low-wage workers. In 1999, the government introduced a measure that extended the obligation to pay social-security contributions to "casual" workers (employees, disproportionately women, working fewer than fifteen hours per week, who were previously exempt) while shifting public revenues to the social-security system by reimbursing the taxes and contributions of workers who earn slightly more than DM 630 (about €320) per month.[117] The hope was to collect social-security contributions from (and therefore to extend social protection to) lower-wage workers; to improve the collection of contributions from the so-called *Scheinselbständige,* or "supposedly self-employed" (those who claim the status of self-employment as a shelter from taxes and social contributions); and to continue to encourage the creation of low-wage jobs. During 2000 and 2001, the debate over low-wage subsidies was renewed, with many claiming that the threshold was still too low to have much effect on unemployment. Despite rising budget deficits, the government debated raising this threshold once again, at an estimated additional annual cost of DM 2.8 billion (€1.43 billion). The Greens had pushed for a ceiling of DM 1,740 (€890), more than double the then-current threshold. Although the SPD rejected this level as too costly, both parties agreed that the level should be increased as unemployment passed the psychologically significant mark of 4 million in January 2002.

Government intervention was not limited to assuming a greater financing burden and introducing new policy instruments, as the Schröder administration modified a range of labor-market regulations, including one concerning employees' right to part-time work. As of January 2001, employees could, without their employers' approval, convert their full-time jobs into part-time jobs.[118] While unions were pleased with the law's protection of social-security coverage of part-time workers, employers were outraged and campaigned aggressively against the reform. Companies from small firms to major industrial concerns objected not so much to the promotion of part-time employment (the use of which has long been on the rise in Germany),[119] but, rather, to the creation of a legal *right* to it and the intrusion by the state into the domain of wage contracts, a move that they perceived as a threat to *Tarifautonomie.* A leading figure in the German employers' confederation complained that the government's intrusion was typical of its "top-down" approach and represented a danger to historical models of social partnership.[120]

The government also embarked on a series of experimental policies designed to facilitate job creation. Inspired by the experience of the social-liberal government in Denmark, in August 2001 Schröder introduced a "job-rotation" measure, which involved the temporary replacement by the unemployed of existing workers, who were to use the time off to upgrade their skills through job-training or other continuing-education programs.[121] The "vacationing" workers would receive normal unemployment benefits during their training period. In return for their participation, employers received state subsidies of between 50 percent and 100 percent of the total wage costs for each participating worker.

Some of the most dramatic changes in German labor-market governance, and further development of the "conflictual corporatist" model, followed in the wake of a series of scandals at the BA, involving the discovery that the office had grossly inflated its job-placement statistics.[122] In 2002, the highest German administrative regulatory agency found that the BA had falsified as many as 70 percent of cases, placing the ineffectiveness of neocorporatist labor-market regulation in stark relief. In the agency's words, it was doubtful whether the statistics issued by the BA could "be used as the basis for the law-making and budgetary decisions of the Bundestag and the government." Riester euphemistically admitted that "it cannot be ruled out that workers in the labor office had an interest in falsely reporting statistics on successful job placement." The scandal led to the resignation of BA President Bernhard Jagoda and major reforms of the BA's administrative structure. In March 2002, the government created a three-person executive board appointed directly by the federal government to govern the BA. In the summer, the government established the Hartz Commission to make further recommendations on labor-market reforms, partly taking responsibility for labor-market policy out of the hands of the BA and giving it to a select group of experts from government ministries, employers' associations, and unions. Although nominally tripartite, the commission's recommendations were statist in inspiration, calling for the reinforcement of state control of labor-market policy, greater state funding for active labor-market policies; the development of state-run, temporary job agencies to promote more flexible employment; and extensive reforms of the BA's placement and training services.[123]

Between 2002 and 2005, Schröder's government stepped up efforts to revitalize the labor market even further. Under the banner "Agenda 2010," the administration introduced a series of ambitious reforms that aimed to promote job creation, reduced non-wage labor costs, and liberalized regulations on shop hours and economically motivated layoffs. Announcing the measures in March 2003, Schröder proclaimed, "There are sometimes measures that must be pushed through, which arouse little enthusiasm, for me or for others. They must nonetheless be undertaken."[124] The reforms reduced the length of eligibility for primary unemployment insurance (*Arbeitslosengeld*) to twelve months for all workers, with the exception of those older than fifty-five, who enjoyed eighteen months of eligibility. The controversial Hartz IV reform (so called because it was the fourth area of reform initially proposed by the Hartz

Commission) reduced unemployment-assistance benefits (*Arbeitslosenhilfe*), paid to workers whose eligibility for the more generous unemployment insurance has expired, to the level of *Sozialhilfe,* the basic antipoverty program. This reduced monthly benefits from 75 percent of previous wages to a few hundred Euros per month. Nor was their import lost on the German electorate, sparking massive protests during 2004, with tens of thousands of Germans marching for weeks through the streets of several major cities. The reforms' unpopularity contributed to the defeat of the SPD in the 2005 elections, which forced the party to cede the chancellery to Angela Merkel, leader of the CDU, and to share power in a "grand coalition."[125] Clearly, Agenda 2010 showed the government's willingness to run significant risks to avoid the greater political costs of ignoring Germany's labor-market problems, as well as its readiness to impose reform on a skeptical public and recalcitrant social partners.

The proposals elicited sharp criticism from the left wing of the SPD, who promised to fight "meter by meter" to secure modifications of the reforms' major provisions.[126] Opponents offered an alternative set of proposals, including a wealth tax to finance a new €100 million fund to assist the long-term unemployed. So strident were the conflicts within the SPD that the party called an exceptional conference for June, a few weeks after Schröder had threatened to resign if the measures were not approved. Although the left succeeded in having its proposals placed on the agenda for the annual SPD conference in November, the government's measures were approved after weeks of negotiations between the government and opposition.[127] Despite this short-term victory, the Agenda 2010 reforms created greater problems for Schröder and the SPD. In the 2005 elections, a new far-left party, the Linkspartei, was founded by left-wing Social Democrats disillusioned with the reforms' liberal character. Not only did the Linkspartei contribute to the SPD's defeat in the 2005 election; its successor party, Die Linke, has increased pressure on the SPD, publicly attacking it as a traitor to social justice and helping to drive its poll numbers down to levels not seen in decades.[128] Just as with his earlier labor-market measures, Schröder's approach with Agenda 2010 was one of imposition rather than consensus, involving a willingness to incur significant political risks to push through reforms.

The CDU–SPD grand coalition led by Chancellor Angela Merkel has struggled to maintain the momentum in labor-market reform generated by the Red–Green coalition. Though their political credibility depends in large part on their handling of the unemployment issue, the CDU and the SPD have different conceptions of reform, and any adopted measures represent the narrow middle ground between their respective priorities. The administration's record to date has been mixed, with ambitious reform proposals resulting in relatively modest reform outcomes. For example, a widely touted health reform was diluted in response to opposition from doctors and the SPD, and tax reforms have been tepid, at best, with the best-known measure increasing the rate of VAT as a way to reduce pressures on payroll taxes rather than rationalizing the system as a whole.

The paucity of ambitious reforms by the current administration, however, represents an anomaly in the recent pattern of growing state intervention that has resulted from the inclusion of both major parties in the government rather than a qualitative change in the pattern itself. If elections in 2009 place one of the two major parties clearly in charge, the same economic pressures and political incentives that gave rise to the shift in policymaking dynamics under Kohl and Schröder should lead to a more impositional posture by the state and renewed political conflict between the government and producer groups. Indeed, as I discuss in Chapter 7, battles within the coalition over the introduction of a minimum wage and an expansion of the long-term-care benefits point in this direction, with the SPD hoping to use the CDU's ostensible intransigence as a campaign issue.[129] Not only have reforms of the BA significantly eroded the social partners' authority over labor-market policy; public demands that the government reduce unemployment and the discrediting of the tripartite system of labor-market governance will provide few incentives for policymakers to revert to the older incrementalist pattern. As in France, the climate of economic austerity has shifted the incentives facing German governments and other key political actors, as well as their understanding of their own interests. These shifts have led to a qualitative change in the dynamics of prevailing political relationships and a shift in the effective distribution of political authority, replacing the older model of consensual gradualism with a new pattern of conflictual corporatism in which the state is punching its weight and the social partners have lost influence.[130]

Despite the slowing of the pace of reform under the grand coalition, recent policy initiatives, particularly the prioritization of active labor-market policy, have begun to remedy some of the German labor market's most trenchant problems. Long-term unemployment began to decrease in 1998,[131] as did the rate of unemployment among older workers. While these measures have not fully remedied Germany's unemployment problem, they have clearly begun to have the desired effect, despite the strictures of EMU. Between March and October 2005, for example, the number of unemployed fell by more than 200,000, and the decline of 94,000 in October alone was the greatest in that month since reunification in 1990.[132] Such encouraging trends have continued, with a net decline of 383,000 in the number of registered unemployed between June 2005 and June 2006.[133] In 2006, both the number of unemployed and the unemployment rate continued to fall, and in September 2007, unemployment declined to its lowest level in twelve years, with 3.54 million workers, or 8.4 percent of the active labor force, without a job, representing a decline of 700,000 unemployed in a year.[134] By November 2008, despite the deterioration

TABLE 5.2 Major German Labor-Market Reforms, 1993–Present

Program/Law	Year	Provisions
Modification of *Arbeitsförderungsgesetz* (Employment Promotion Act)	1993	Introduced federal subsidies for wages above level of unemployment insurance; permitted wages lower than levels set in sectoral contracts
Sofortprogramm zum Abbau der Jugendarbeitlosigkeit (JUMP)	1998	Expanded training programs and counseling services for young workers; introduced federal wage subsidies for hiring unemployed youth
"Job-rotation" program	2001	Permitted temporary replacement of workers by the unemployed, who receive jobless benefits and enroll in training schemes
JOB-AQTIV Gesetz	2002	Made unemployment benefits contingent on job-search contract between workers and BA; created new retraining and job-creation programs; expanded employer subsidies
Hartz Commission reforms	2002–2003	Created temporary employment agencies; new funding for activation programs; reformed BA; promoted self-employment
Agenda 2010 reforms (some initially proposed by the Hartz Commission)	2003–2005	Limited eligibility for unemployment insurance and health-contribution rates; equalized unemployment assistance with basic income support; loosened restrictions on shop hours and protections against layoffs in SMEs

of the international economy, the German jobless rate had declined to 7.1 percent, representing just under 3 million registered unemployed, the lowest level since 1992.[135]

Despite these positive recent developments, however, jobless rates remain relatively high by historical standards, and the issue of unemployment has lost none of its political salience, which will only increase in 2009 as the effects of the worldwide recession filter through the German labor market. That said, continuing high rates of unemployment have led recent German governments to undertake increasingly coherent and comprehensive efforts to promote labor-market adjustment (see Table 5.2). Faced with an ineffective system of tripartite labor-market governance, state officials have gradually assumed a variety of responsibilities that formerly lay within the domain of the social partners,[136] devoted greater public resources to the labor market, and developed a range of novel and aggressive policies to battle unemployment. Rising joblessness highlighted the system's incapacity for self-regulation, creating a vacuum of influence and credibility that the state has begun to fill.

The past decade and a half has witnessed the emergence of a public vision of social and economic justice that links the goals of providing workers with access to stable, remunerative employment and correcting the perverse labor-market effects of Bismarckian social policies. As authorities have worked to address these problems, moreover, the institutional fabrics of the German political economy and system of social partnership have adjusted, reflecting the fluidity and negotiability of inherited political institutions and distributions of authority. Changes in German labor-market policy represent an important component of ongoing processes of change in the political economy as a whole and the continuation of postwar patterns of adjustment in the German model of welfare capitalism. If employers' perennial call for a "Renewal of the Social Market Economy" unquestionably reflects their interests, it also shows that German welfare capitalism and the political relationships that underpin it have continued to change.

Conclusion: Labor-Market Reform and the Politics of "Managed Austerity"

Since the mid-1990s, policymakers in France and Germany have responded aggressively to the labor-market dysfunctions that represent the Achilles' heel of their Bismarckian systems of social protection. As levels of unemployment remained stubbornly high, placing acute pressures on the payroll-tax funding of social policy and on overall economic performance, modernizing the French and German labor markets moved to the center of both countries' political agenda. The primacy of labor-market policy has been reinforced by mounting political pressure to address unemployment, which is seen as evidence of governmental failure and represents a profound social fracture between the employed and those left behind by economic modernization. As the postwar model of lifetime employment has given way to a more complex and multifaceted world of work, policymakers have developed novel approaches to promoting labor-based income. From promoting part-time work to relieving pressures on non-wage labor costs, encouraging the acquisition of new job skills, and adjusting the rules of unemployment insurance, French and German authorities have adopted a similar posture of reform. As the labor market has assumed a central place in governments' political-economic agendas, earlier conceptions of a welfare state protecting workers against the market have given way to efforts to promote their access to income within it.

That said, the broadly similar policy trends in France and Germany have been the products of distinct and evolving political dynamics. Confronting divergent institutional legacies and systems of social partnership, authorities in each country have faced unique challenges in their efforts to adjust their labor markets. In France, where the state traditionally has played the central role, authorities have been forced to yield authority to an aggressive neoliberal employers' association and reformist unions. In Germany, by contrast, the state has become increasingly assertive, despite a political framework in which its authority is constrained and in which the social partners have entrenched institutional authority over many aspects of labor-market policy. As growing economic pressures have yielded a climate of recrimination and political conflict, elites in both countries have been forced to fight a two-front war, simultaneously struggling to promote labor-market adjustment and battling for legitimacy with employers and unions over both whose vision of labor-market reform should prevail and which actors should enjoy the authority to enact it. In a pattern seen in other areas of social-protection reform, the political space created by economic pressures for labor-market reform has yielded a parallel process of renegotiation of the French and German systems of social partnership and relationships between the state and social actors.

These experiences return us to our broader theoretical argument that the development of national models of welfare capitalism must be studied through attention to the linkages among a wide range of political and economic institutions and areas of policy. Not only have recent labor-market reforms shaped and been shaped by developments in the French and German welfare states; they have also been driven by changes in the two countries' broader political economies and systems of social partnership. As during the 1980s and early 1990s, when the French and German systems of social protection were expanded in response to the economic demands of market making, more recently, austerity has driven reforms that redefine the relationship between the welfare state and the labor market.

While these new pressures have led to important adjustments in the French and German labor markets, they have also yielded a series of reforms of traditional social insurance. Pensions and health care, the heart and most expensive components of the French and German Bismarckian welfare states, have undergone major reforms, as policymakers have worked to respond to the slowed growth and rising unemployment that have challenged traditional arrangements. Such fears have been heightened by the deepening international recession and economic crisis, which have intensified pressures for the expansion of support for the unemployed and economically vulnerable as governments debate the necessary scale and scope of neo-Keynesian stimulus packages and regulatory changes designed to avert another Great Depression. Here, too, the solutions of the past have become the problems of the present, leading to major pressures for reforms in these arrangements and shifts in the bargains that underpin them.

6

The Shifting Politics of French and German Social-Insurance Reform

The French and German social-insurance systems were essential components of the two countries' postwar settlements. Revamped after World War II, pensions and health care were expanded over the following three decades and provided essential support for rapid economic growth by facilitating workers' adjustment to new economic circumstances and providing them with a politically salient stake in economic performance. The restructured systems were designed to plug gaps in income streams for workers, who generally enjoyed job stability and rising wages. By compensating workers for medical costs and ensuring income for the aged, these two keystones of the postwar French and German welfare states supported social peace and political stability while abundant receipts from social contributions ensured plentiful resources to fund them.[1]

In the early 1980s, however, these arrangements came under increasing pressure from shifting demographic profiles and the erosion of the climate of

Portions of this chapter include revised versions of material presented in "Rethinking Corporatism and Consensus: The Dilemmas of German Social-Protection Reform," *West European Politics* 26, no. 3 (January 2003): 41–66, by Taylor and Francis (copyright © 2003 Routledge); "The Myth of the Frozen Welfare State and the Dynamics of Contemporary French and German Social-Protection Reform," *French Politics* 2, no. 2 (August 2004): 151–183, by Palgrave-Macmillan Journals (available online at http://www.palgrave-journals.com/fp/journal/v2/n2/pdf/8200055a.pdf); "The Better Part of Valour: The Politics of French Welfare Reform," *Journal of European Social Policy* 9, no. 4 (Winter 1999): 311–330, by Sage Publications Ltd. (all rights reserved, copyright © 1999, available online at http://online.sagepub.com). Used by permission.

full employment. The economic crisis of the 1970s and the mass unemployment that developed in its wake eroded the social contributions on which the French and German pension and health systems relied. Following the French abandonment of dirigisme in the early 1980s and German reunification in 1990, these pressures intensified, as mass layoffs and slow growth began to represent serious threats to the two systems. Strains were exacerbated by the fact that governments had expanded social protection in support of market making, providing needed lubrication for economic liberalization.[2] Early-retirement programs were broadened to absorb surplus workers; new active labor-market policies were created; French income-support programs were expanded; and the German health and pension systems were extended lock, stock, and barrel to millions of impoverished Eastern workers.

By the early 1990s, it had become clear that these extended arrangements were no longer sustainable. In both countries, slow or even stagnant growth, bounding social expenditures, and ominous demographic trends led policymakers and observers alike to worry about the future solvency of the welfare state. By 1993, social expenditures had reached a record 29.7 percent of GDP in France and 27.6 percent in Germany.[3] By 1995, the proportion of the population age sixty-five or older had increased to 15 percent and 15.8 percent in France and Germany, respectively, up from 12.8 percent and 13.3 percent in 1970.[4] Future prospects were even bleaker. The demographic dependency ratio, which compares the number of retirees with the working-age population, had increased to .37 in Germany by 1996, with the contributions of 1.6 workers available to support each pensioner, and was estimated to rise to about .7 by the year 2030, with just over one worker per retiree.[5] In 2000, about 16 percent of the population in both countries was sixty-five or older, a figure projected to rise to 29.2 percent by 2050 in France and to about 30 percent in Germany by 2040.[6] In Germany, the number of people older than sixty-five was projected to increase from 25 percent of the working-age population in 1999 to about 55 percent by 2050.[7] Even in the 1990s, however, these developments were contributing to rapidly rising expenditures for pensions and health care. In 1995, health-care costs reached all-time highs of 9.6 percent and 9.5 percent of GDP in Germany and France, respectively. The numbers for pensions were even more alarming, at 11.1 percent of GDP in Germany, projected to rise to 18.4 percent by 2040, and 10.6 percent in France, predicted to rise to 14.3 percent.[8] Not only were spending levels in the 1990s indicative of an urgent need for reform, therefore, but projections suggested that the very survival of the two countries' social-insurance systems might be at risk.

French and German authorities faced the challenge of bringing social spending under control,[9] as well as the more fundamental task of adjusting their welfare states to an enduring climate marked by economic austerity and aging populations. During the postwar boom, pensions and health care became the centerpieces of the French and German social contracts, institutionalized promises by the state to care for society's most vulnerable members. As welfare states were expanded, authorities could demonstrate their commitment to share the benefits of economic growth equitably. As a result, workers had come to see Bismarckian social-insurance policies as entitlements, paid for in advance through their payroll taxes.[10] For all of these reasons, meaningful pension and health reform involved significant political risks to governments and to the system's legitimacy.[11]

At the same time, French and German policymakers felt increasing pressure to respond to mounting public insecurity about the future solvency of pensions and health care. Beginning around 1990, these issues assumed a central place in public debates, and a series of studies assessed the two countries' social-insurance systems,[12] painting dire pictures of the imbalance between expenditures and revenues. Authorities faced the challenge of recalibrating their pension and health systems without provoking massive political unrest. As we shall see, their doing so has depended in part on successfully projecting an image of being at once economically responsible and socially minded while convincing voters of the urgency of an issue that, to many of them, seems remote.

Successful reform strategies have been defined in part by the institutional incentives and constraints presented by the character of political institutions and historical relationships between the state and social groups in each country. In Germany, political concertation between left and right is often encouraged by often-fragile parliamentary majorities and the threat of a veto in the upper house of Parliament, the Bundesrat, in which the German *Länder* are represented and which is frequently controlled by parties outside the governing coalition. As a result, when concertation does take place in social insurance, it tends to occur between the government and parts of the opposition but against the social partners. In France, by contrast, an ideologically divided, bipolar party system; a dual executive that gives a separately elected president the power to dissolve Parliament and call new elections; and the concentration of power in the lower house of Parliament and in the political executive tend to preclude such interparty alliances, forcing governments to negotiate with the social partners. Accordingly, as we shall see, impositional reform strategies, particularly those that are coupled with an open refusal to negotiate and a paternalistic idiom of political arrogance, tend to fail. As in the case of labor-market reform, in both countries competition over social-insurance reform and the broad policy agenda has driven important changes in political relationships and policymaking dynamics. In France, traditional statist policymaking has been replaced by a "competitive-interventionist" logic of conflict between the state and social partners, both of which are vying for influence. In Germany, the traditional neocorporatist model has given way to a model of "conflictual corporatism," with growing state assertiveness and declining influence on the part of the social partners and the political opposition.

The importance of such institutional considerations can be seen in recent efforts by French and German governments to reform their pension and health-care systems. Significant reform came earlier in France than in Germany, beginning with conservative Prime Minister Edouard Balladur's modifications of the French health and private-sector pension systems in 1993, accomplished through a willingness to negotiate with the social partners. While divisions among doctors enabled his successor, Alain Juppé, to reform health care in 1995, Juppé was forced to retract proposed changes to the politically volatile *régimes spéciaux* in the wake of massive union protests. By contrast, Prime Minister Jean-Pierre Raffarin enacted significant reforms in public-sector pensions in 2003 by adopting a modified version of Balladur's concertational strategy, and François Fillon's post-2007 government under President Nicolas Sarkozy succeeded in reforming the *régimes spéciaux* by consulting with trade unions and compromising on details while exploiting divisions among unions and favorable shifts in public opinion. In each case, the success or failure of reform depended on the government's ability to foster an atmosphere of cooperation and exploit divisions among opponents, rather than simply trying to impose reform.

In Germany, by contrast, recent developments have reflected a concentration of authority in the central state that parallels recent patterns in labor-market reform. In 1992, the government of Chancellor Helmut Kohl successfully enacted a major health reform by enlisting the support of the opposition SPD against the resistance of the German medical profession. In the case of pensions, the SPD's resistance resulted in a period of policy stagnation until 1997, with the exception of a very modest reform in 1989. This stagnant pattern changed dramatically in 2000, when SPD Chancellor Gerhard Schröder, over the objections of unions, the CDU, and the left of his own party, enacted the first comprehensive reform of the German pension system since 1957. In this case, Schröder exploited divisions in Parliament and ensured the support of two CDU-led *Länder* in the Bundesrat by making a series of concessions that would benefit them rather than those demanded by the CDU leadership. In both France and Germany, effective reform strategies thus have been defined by each country's political-institutional landscape and by evolving relationships between major political parties and between the state and social partners.

Statist Legacies and Political Competition in French Pension and Health Reform

Since the early 1990s, governments have undertaken a series of efforts to rebalance revenues and expenditures and ensure the viability of the French social-insurance system. Authorities have limited replacement rates, introduced incentives to deferred retirement, and increased contribution periods in the pension system, while in health care they have increased patients' co-payments, imposed parliamentary caps on expenditures, and reduced reimbursement rates. While the state remains a key player in the reform process, policy outcomes have been increasingly colored by shifting relationships among the state, unions, and employers, themselves the legacies of decades of state dominance and economic crisis. Authorities have had to contend with the social partners' authority over the management of social-insurance funds, as well as their capacity to channel public opinion in opposition to proposed reforms.[13] The political and legal influence of unions and employers has not completely blocked reform, however. Instead, it has forced policymakers to choose carefully among available political strategies and to negotiate (or appear to negotiate) reforms with organized interest groups rather than merely imposing them from above. Table 6.1 presents major French health and pension outcomes.

Learning to Dance: Edouard Balladur and the Success of Negotiated Welfare Reform

French health and pension reform gained significant momentum under the post-1993 government of conservative Prime Minister Edouard Balladur, which made welfare reform a central plank of its agenda. In health care, Balladur confronted rapidly rising costs and unemployment-related declines in social contributions, as well as the newly adopted Maastricht restrictions on public expenditures. He and Health Minister Simone Veil crafted a series of proposals designed to balance expenditures and contributions and pursued reforms under the mantle of societal consensus and negotiated adjustment. Balladur recognized the importance of soliciting input from unions, doctors, and the public at large, while arguing that "all parties involved know that things cannot continue as they are. . . . I hope that our nation will find itself in a better position in two years than it does today; it is this that will legitimate our plan and our place of power."[14] This emphasis on responsibility and accountability resonated with the French public, 51 percent of whom felt that the government's welfare-reform package was "going in the right direction."[15]

In his way stood the French medical profession, jealous guardian of its liberal tradition. Laid out in the 1927 *charte médicale,* the profession's governing philosophy was based on patients' choice of physician, freedom of prescription and treatment by doctors, and payment by patients directly to doctors for services rendered. The terms of reimbursing patients and compensating doctors since 1936 had been defined in conventions signed by doctors and social-insurance funds.[16] The spectrum of French doctors' unions facing Balladur had developed over several decades around varying conceptions of *la médicine libérale* and was marked by important divisions between specialists and

TABLE 6.1 French Health and Pension Reforms, 1993–Present

Year	Policy Area	Proposed Reforms	Outcomes
1993	Pensions	Reformed private-sector basic and supplementary pensions; increased calculation period from ten to twenty-five years and contribution period from thirty-seven and a half to forty years; increased *contribution sociale généralisée* (CSG) to fund pensions for the unemployed and the poor; changed benefit indexing from wages to prices	All reforms implemented
1993	Health	Imposed binding spending constraints on doctors; trimmed hospital expenditures; introduced additional reimbursement controls; increased patient charges; cut some hospital beds; reformed hospital administration	All reforms implemented
1995	Pensions	Applied 1993 reforms to public-sector pensions; created *remboursement de la dette sociale* (RDS)	All pension reforms withdrawn; RDS implemented
1995	Health	Constrained negotiations between doctors and sickness funds through parliamentary spending limits; created collective penalties for doctors who violate caps; increased patient contributions and reduced reimbursement rates; reduced hospital budgets' annual increase; created new insurance charges; registered new specialists	Most reforms implemented; collective penalties, insurance-form charges, and registration of additional specialists withdrawn
2003	Pensions	Aligned rules for most public-sector pensions with those for private sector; gradually increased required contribution period to forty-one years; increased contribution rates; indexed benefits to prices; liberalized regulations on part-time work for pensioners; reduced incentives for early retirement	All reforms implemented; minor concession to unions allowing workers beginning their career at sixteen to retire after forty years of contributions; *régimes spéciaux* for rail and electrical workers excepted
2004	Health	Shifted some health financing to the CSG; instituted a mandatory €1 patient charge for office visits; required a visit to a "*médecin traitant*" before fully reimbursable visits to specialists; reorganized CNAMTS	All reforms implemented
2008	Pensions	Aligned *régimes spéciaux* with 2003 rules for other public-sector pensions; increased required contribution period to forty-one years; created a penalty, to increase to 5% by 2020, for each year of missing contributions; indexed benefits to prices and calculated based on last six months of salary	All major provisions implemented; minor concessions included delaying implementation and up to two-and-a-half year penalty for early retirement with forty years of contributions

generalists. The most prominent doctors' union, the Confédération des Syndicats Médicaux Français (CSMF), was organized in 1928 around the defense of the liberal principles laid out in the 1927 *charte*. Controlled by specialists, the CSMF consistently resisted the erosion of doctors' prerogatives by the state. The even more liberal Fédération des Médecins de France (FMF), which was organized in 1925 and in 1928 joined the CSMF, rejected even the relatively informal convention-based expenditure regulations accepted by the CSMF and broke off in 1961. When the FMF signed the national convention in 1982, the Syndicat de la Médicine Libérale (SML) emerged to uphold the liberal principles that it saw both the CSMF and FMF as having betrayed. Finally, the Fédération Française des Médecins Généralistes (MG France), the generalists' union recognized only in 1989, supports giving generalists control over access to specialists.

The French health system revolves around the Caisse Nationale d'Assurance-Maladie des Travailleurs Salariés (CNAMTS), which administers 16 regional and 128 local funds,[17] is co-governed by union and employers' representatives, and traditionally negotiates annual conventions with the specialist-controlled CSMF and FMF. Covering the vast majority of the French population, it wields enormous influence in shaping health policy.[18] In contrast to the ambulatory sector, the hospital system is dominated by public institutions directly managed and funded by the Ministry of Health. In 1983, the introduction of *budgets globaux,* or annual spending caps, increased the state's influence over the sector, but this control was limited to some extent by the rising number of private-sector hospitals, most of which are not subject to the *budgets.*[19] This complex public–private mix renders the French health system both expensive and difficult to reform.[20] Due to the fee-for-service system in the ambulatory sector and the state's responsibility for its deficits, doctors traditionally have had little incentive to control costs. Spiraling ambulatory costs have been the single most important component of rising health expenditures in France, which has the highest levels and rates of growth in Europe. In 1960, France spent 4.2 percent of GDP on health care (as opposed to 3.9 percent in Britain and 4.7 percent in Germany). By 1993, this figure had more than doubled to 9.8 percent of GDP (in contrast to 8.6 percent in Germany and 7.1 percent in Britain).[21]

Balladur focused his 1993 health reforms on the ambulatory sector. His nuanced strategy was designed to achieve the politically difficult task of limiting physicians' autonomy. First, he pitted specialists' interests against those of generalists, maintaining the independence of the convention system while refusing to implement generalists' demand for control over patients' access to specialists. Second, he implemented reforms individually, thereby avoiding the appearance of an assault on the profession as a whole. Finally, his consensual rhetoric, which emphasized the importance of good-faith negotiations, defused much of the tension surrounding his reform initiatives. This approach permitted the government to dilute resistance among doctors while creating coalitions of support behind individual reforms, which, taken together, constituted a reform of a scope not seen since the immediate postwar period.

In June 1993, Simone Veil, recognized as a shaper of consensus, presented the government's plan to Parliament. The package aimed to cut health expenditures by FFr 30 billion (€4.57 billion) by reducing the level of patient reimbursement from 75 percent to 70 percent, increasing patients' daily hospital charge by FFr 5, and removing 60,000 hospital beds. It also called for the negotiation of a new convention that would set binding ceilings for global health expenditures, backed up by Veil's threat to impose a solution in the absence of an agreement between doctors and the CNAMTS. Veil's preservation of the autonomy of negotiations between physicians and the CNAMTS aimed to minimize resistance, which was already constrained by divisions within the medical sector.[22]

Although the emphasis on consensus was a hallmark of the government's strategy, Balladur and Veil also made a series of hard-nosed political calculations. By refusing to implement the contracts long demanded by the still weak MG France and retaining the specialist-dominated framework of negotiation, Veil successfully exploited cleavages among doctors to validate the supremacy of the CSMF and the FMF.[23] Her consultative approach, moreover, played nicely with the specialists' liberal ethos, and their support obviated the need to garner the consent of generalists.

Veil employed a divide-and-conquer strategy in her campaign to reform the public hospital system, isolating hospital from ambulatory physicians in an effort to minimize resistance to a reform that was likely to focus recrimination squarely on the government. While Veil's exploitation of cleavages under the mantle of consensus allowed her to deflect blame for the government's ambulatory reforms, her isolation of hospital physicians obviated the need for such a strategy in her efforts to cut hospital expenditures. Though hospital physicians vocally objected to the measures, her pursuit of hospital reforms *after* the ambulatory convention had been signed deprived them of potential allies. As a result, hospital physicians' cries of injustice fell mostly on deaf ears, permitting passage of the initiatives into law with minimal modifications.

The reform was matched by success on the even riskier terrain of pensions, long considered sacrosanct by both unions and much of the French public. Given an average annual increase in expenditures of 2.2 percent during the 1980s and alarming demographic projections, the system was clearly in urgent need of reform in the early 1990s.[24] The centerpiece of the pay-as-you-go, earnings-based pension system is the Caisse Nationale d'Assurance-Vieillesse des Travailleurs Salariés (CNAVTS) of the *régime général,* which provides a basic benefit for most private-sector employees, workers in state-owned enterprises, social-security employees, and salaried agricultural workers. The system of mandatory, complementary pensions (the *régimes complémentaires*) is divided between the Association Générale des Institutions de Retraite des Cadres (AGIRC), covering executives and managers, and the Association des Régimes de Retraites Complémentaires (ARRCO), providing benefits to non-managerial workers in the private sector. These complementary pensions are governed by collectively negotiated conventions and managed, in the case of the AGIRC, by employers and independent administrators, and in the case of the ARRCO, by employers' and workers' representatives.[25] In addition, a variety of separate *régimes spéciaux* cover particular groups of functionaries, such as workers in the national railway system (Société Nationale des Chemins de Fer Français [SNCF]), the Parisian metropolitan public-transport system (Régie Autonome des Transports Parisiens [RATP]), the merchant marine, and the Bank of France. In the early 1990s, the *régimes spéciaux* accounted for 30 percent of French pension expenditures, while the *régimes complémentaires* represented about 24 percent.[26] The remainder of the system consists of autonomous funds for a variety of agricultural workers and the self-employed.[27] In addition, the Fonds National de Solidarité (FNS), created in 1956, funds minimum old-age pensions (*le minimum vieillesse*) and was used to finance Mitterrand's reduction of the retirement age in 1982 from sixty-five to sixty.[28]

Balladur proposed a phased-in restructuring of the French basic and complementary pension regimes for private-sector workers, combined with an increase from 1.1 percent to 2.1 percent in the *contribution sociale généralisée* (CSG), a tax on all earnings created in 1991 by Rocard's government.[29] The government chose to use some of the funds from the increased CSG to finance old-age insurance while avoiding the job-dampening effects of increasing payroll taxes. Following the recommendations of Rocard's 1991 study of the French pension system, Balladur proposed an increase in the contribution period required for full pension vestment from thirty-seven and a half years to forty years, the indexation of pension benefits to prices rather than wages, and the extension of the reference period for benefits from the best ten to the best twenty-five years of a worker's career.

As in the case of health reform, Balladur emphasized conciliation and inclusiveness in pursuing his pension measures, inviting the unions to a conference to discuss the reforms: "In the social arena, we want to develop a new French example. . . . French society will not be reformed in preparation for the future without the cohesion, consultation, and cooperation of all."[30] By formulating reform as part of an effort to diminish social exclusion, moreover, Balladur hoped to reassure the public that he was addressing both joblessness and the crisis in social-security financing, tempering his claims of the necessity of reform with a climate of political inclusiveness and social responsibility.

Initially, the trade unions greeted the proposals with hostility. Calling for a general strike, the Confédération Générale du Travail (CGT) referred to a "calling into question of acquired rights"; the Force Ouvrière (FO) questioned the impact of the reforms on workers' economic plight; and the normally more conciliatory CFDT rejected the CSG hike as a "blank check," dangerous to employment and fundamentally unjust. Nicole Notat, leader of the CFDT, joined the other unions in mobilizing against the reform, claiming that "to do nothing would imply [our] guilt for abandoning pensions in their hour of danger."[31] Nonetheless, Balladur never wavered in his conciliatory strategy, which was not lost even on those unions that opposed the measure. Discussing an upcoming meeting with Balladur, Marc Blondel, leader of the FO, noted, "In a *soft, mild* way, the Prime Minister is trying to *impose* an austerity plan on us."[32] After the promised series of consultations, the syndicates' leaders were, if anything, even more strident. The CFDT complained of "a measure taken without any consultation"; the CGT saw the pension reform as "scandalous and antisocial"; and, most categorically, the FO asserted that Balladur's pension reform had "unilaterally put an end to consultations with unions."[33]

Despite the hostility of their leaders, however, Balladur successfully undermined mobilization among the unions' rank-and-file, which would prove instrumental to his success. The failure of the unions' membership and the public to rally around their leaders' calls to arms was attributable to both substantive and stylistic components of Balladur's strategy. First, his decision to reform benefits in the relatively non-unionized private sector helped to limit the scope of mobilization. Unions' claims to defend the working class failed to resonate with public-sector workers, who dominated the unions' rank-and-file and whose *régimes spéciaux* were not being targeted. Second, by gradually phasing in the reforms and protecting the benefits of those who had already retired, Balladur was able to create divisions within the private sector. Third, by increasing the CSG instead of payroll taxes, Balladur effectively transferred much of the cost of the reform from beneficiaries to the larger population while protecting employment, thereby promoting an image of economic responsibility while diluting the measures' impact on retirees. Fourth, by modeling his reforms after the 1991 proposals of Socialist Prime Minister Rocard, Balladur was able to avoid the appearance of a rightist attack on the constituencies of the left. Also, his creation of a *fonds de solidarité vieillesse*, which provides minimum pensions for periods of unemployment and national military service, conceded a long-standing union demand.[34] Finally, Balladur's consensual rhetoric, in part a reflection of his aspirations to the French presidency in 1995, provided a political idiom that defused unions' hostility.[35] As a result, the government's proposals passed unchanged into law, representing the first significant structural modifications to the postwar French pension system since its inception.

A Bull in a China Shop: Alain Juppé and the Perils of Welfare Bonapartism

Both the character of Balladur's approach and the results of his reform initiatives stood in stark contrast to those of his successor, Alain Juppé, who became prime minister in 1995. Juppé's confrontational and technocratic approach explicitly eschewed even the appearance of consensus and consultation, attracting rather than diffusing blame and weakening his political position. Jacques Chirac was elected to the French presidency in 1995 on a series of grand promises to cut taxes, raise wages, increase public spending, avoid health-care rationing, cut the public-sector deficit, and reduce unemployment, all made against the background of a massive social-security deficit, rising unemployment, and the impending deadline for satisfaction of the Maastricht criteria.[36] Soon after his appointment as prime minister, however, Juppé followed the lead of Chirac, who had already turned away from his election promises in favor of a program of reform. Juppé quickly made it clear that the government's agenda would be one of austerity. His pension initiatives involved applying Balladur's measures to the *régimes spéciaux* and increasing the retirement age for many public-sector workers. He also proposed extensive health reforms, including a constitutional amendment allowing Parliament to fix annual spending limits, collective penalties on doctors if they surpassed these ceilings, an increase in health contributions from retirees and the unemployed, a reduction of the annual increase in hospitals' *budget global* from 3.8 percent to 2.1 percent, an increase in the hospitals' daily patient charge, and limits on the reimbursement of certain pharmaceutical expenses.[37] Finally, he proposed the creation of a fund (the *remboursement de la dette sociale* [RDS], financed by a .5 percent tax on all revenues) to repay the rising social-security debt.

Juppé's political miscalculations were as numerous as his legislative proposals. In addition to breaking his party's election promises, Juppé simultaneously attacked many facets of the French welfare state, including the politically volatile public-sector pensions and the cherished structural independence of the sickness funds. His idiom of paternalistic arrogance, suggesting that he alone understood what reforms were necessary, concentrated blame on his government and ensured trenchant and simultaneous resistance from trade unions, doctors, and the public at large. These critical differences between his approach and Balladur's—his refusal to negotiate, his supercilious style, his immediate breaking of his party's election promises, and his pursuit of all reforms in a single package—were the principal reasons for the failure of large parts of the *plan Juppé.*

Juppé's autocratic approach had its origins in the process of the plan's formulation, which took place long before its details were made public. In a series of summer meetings cloaked in secrecy, Juppé consulted only a few select advisers, excluding even the ministers of generational solidarity and health, within whose purview the reforms ostensibly fell. Juppé's evident contempt for the perspectives of others was not limited to his treatment of members of his government, as the unions were also completely ignored. The CGT and the FO were never even contacted during the formulation process, and even the moderate CFDT, which was fast becoming the French state's *porte-parole* within the labor movement, was not informed of the details of the reforms until a few days before they were presented to Parliament. Nicole Notat, leader of the CFDT, was stunned, observing that she "had never seen a government accord so little importance to consultation."[38] Making matters worse, Chirac encouraged Juppé's insular approach, sanctioning both the secrecy of the formulation process and the implementation of the measures through rule by decree rather than through normal parliamentary debate. The lack of input from what Juppé considered "special interests" (including even members of the government) not only alienated the public; it also prevented strategic modifications that might have attenuated the ensuing political crisis while preserving core provisions. Undeterred, Juppé pressed ahead despite warnings from some of the select few involved in devising the reforms.[39]

The ensuing mobilization by public-sector workers was fueled by the low levels of complementary pension coverage for beneficiaries of the *régimes spéciaux* and the concentration of union membership in the public sector. Although the CFDT's leadership initially supported much of the plan's content and refused to participate in the protests, the CGT and the FO immediately called for a general strike. Despite these divisions among their leaders,[40] the rank-and-file of all unions supported organized resistance. In contrast to 1993, when even the militant CGT was unable to mobilize its membership, in 1995 the rank-and-file across the French labor movement lined up in opposition. Beginning in the RATP and supported by growing numbers of ordinary citizens, the protests focused initially on the pension and constitutional reforms but quickly grew into a movement against Juppé himself. Despite the prime minister's promise neither to do away with the *régimes spéciaux* nor to equalize their benefits with those of the less generous private pensions, his reforms were widely (and ironically, given the small number of beneficiaries) perceived as an attack on the core of the French welfare state.[41] As the strikes spread, it became clear that what had begun as a contest over welfare reform was quickly developing into a broader social and political crisis.[42]

Organized in reaction to the protests, Juppé's December speech to Parliament only aggravated the situation. Emphasizing his determination, Juppé famously proclaimed: "France must decide between change and decline. . . . If we withdrew [our reforms], we would go against the interests of France and the French people. . . . Maastricht or no, a country cannot endure, free and prosperous, when it is paralyzed with debt."[43] Juppé seemed almost to be courting social unrest, even explicitly refusing to cloak his reforms with the standard camouflage of EMU's fiscal constraints. In his view, the paralyzing strikes reflected a mere "misunderstanding," for which he prescribed the technocrat's explanation rather than the politician's mediation. Unsurprisingly, that same night the unions called for a new general strike, now accompanied by the CFDT, which could no longer resist its members' demands.

In the face of worsening paralysis and threats to his government's survival, Juppé rescinded the pension reform on 10 December, much to the delight of the now united unions. In the aftermath of the crisis, the *Times* of London ruefully observed, "The true lesson of the last few weeks is that France will succeed in putting its house in order when its political élite learns how to treat the French like adults."[44] The upheaval was precipitated by the widespread impression that Juppé had far overstepped the bounds of his legitimate authority.[45] His authoritarian tactics had clearly backfired, paralyzing the transportation system for a month and leaving only acrimony and questions about the integrity of French democracy.

Although his approach to health reform was similar, a combination of institutional and political factors enabled Juppé's initiatives in this area to bear fruit. As had Balladur, Juppé confronted a deeply divided profession in 1995. MG France, a signatory to the 1993 convention since January 1995 and a growing force in the medical community, supported Juppé's proposed integration of the existing nineteen regional sickness funds and the imposition of the parliamentary spending limits. Specialists were predictably hostile, with President Claude Maffioli of the CSMF remarking, "[With this reform], health professionals are confined to the role of mere executors of decisions taken [by the state]. They can intervene neither in the prioritization of spending nor in the formulation of health policies. In short, they disappear for the benefit of the state and all-powerful sickness funds."[46]

Although the liberal SML and FMF joined the protests, doctors' relatively limited numbers and their inability to unite precluded effective resistance. Juppé's support of generalists permitted him to exploit divisions among doctors, which became clear as early as October. Because generalists joined specialists in protesting the proposed collective penalty to be applied to cost overruns, however, Juppé was forced to abandon this provision,[47] demonstrating that his impositional strategy would work only where doctors were irremediably divided.

Juppé's divide-and-conquer approach to health reform was aided by a number of other factors. First, the health system's complex market logic enabled him to build the tools of division into his proposals, whereas pension reform, involving benefit cuts that are hard to nuance, represented a more salient focus for mobilization. Second, generalists' increasing power within the profession allowed Juppé to assert direct control over health spending while appearing to promote the interests of a significant part of the medical community. Finally, because the costs were to be borne largely by doctors, neither the left nor the French public was eager to fight the reforms. As in 1993, doctors were left both divided and alone, and most of Juppé's health reforms, including the controversial spending limits, were implemented.

The Enduring Challenges of French Social-Insurance Reform

Spurred by increasing alarm over rising costs and aging demographic profiles, between 1997 and 2002 the government of Socialist Prime Minister Lionel Jospin commissioned a series of studies that advanced a number of proposals for pension reform, particularly in the public sector.[48] Additional pressure on the government derived from MEDEF's Refondation Sociale, of which pension reform was one of the principal chapters. Haunted by memories of the massive unrest of 1995 and confronted with a series of strikes by public employees, however, the government avoided taking concrete action.[49] In health care, similarly, a major reform proposal in 1999 (the Johanet Plan) went nowhere, as Martine Aubry, who was focused primarily on the thirty-five-hour laws, let it die.[50]

Between 2002 and 2005, by contrast, the conservative administration of Prime Minister Raffarin took up the challenge of reform, instituting the most significant modification of the French pension system since 1993. In July 2003, after weeks of parliamentary debate and months of public outcry and protests, the government saw through a measure that aligned the more generous public-sector system with the private-sector system, gradually extending the required contribution period to forty years and further extending it to forty-one years by 2012. The law also raised contribution rates by .2 percent, indexed public pensions to prices rather than wages, introduced financial penalties for early and rewards for later retirement, created voluntary private pension funds, and liberalized restrictions on the right of workers with limited contribution histories to receive benefits while working part time.

Like Balladur, Raffarin secured the passage of his reforms by negotiating even as he proclaimed publicly that "it is not the street that governs" and expressed a determination to pursue reform despite widespread strikes. Also like Balladur, Raffarin secured the assent of the CFDT, even as the CGT and the FO led thousands of people through the streets. Proclaiming that "the path of reform is one of solidarity. The preservation of our pay-as-you-go pension system will be based upon a shared, equitable, progressive effort,"[51] Raffarin appealed to the public's attachment to the pay-as-you-go system while contrasting his self-styled social responsibility to the unions' parochial interests. Like Balladur, Raffarin also conveyed a willingness to negotiate, though he refused to accede to many of the unions' demands.[52] He adopted a similar strategy with a modest health reform in 2004.[53] The law continued the shift of health financing from payroll taxes to the CSG, instituted a mandatory €1 patient charge for all office visits, required a visit to a general practitioner (a so-called *médecin traitant*) before patients could see specialists with the right to full reimbursement, and created the Union Nationale des Caisses d'Assurance-Maladie (UNCAM) to oversee relations between doctors and the health bureaucracy.[54] This reform strengthened the state's control over expenditures without enacting a major reorganization of the system or its financing.

Reforming the volatile *régimes spéciaux* would have to await center-right President Nicolas Sarkozy and Prime Minister François Fillon, elected in May–June 2007. During the election campaign, Sarkozy promised to tackle these programs if elected, particularly those of the RATP, the SNCF, and public utilities such as Electricité de France–Gaz de France (EDF–GDF), which he condemned as both unaffordable and unjust given their greater generosity relative to the private sector. From the outset, Sarkozy's emphasis on equity resonated with those who felt that select groups of public servants had long been unjustly favored. Sarkozy also had clearly learned from Balladur's success and Juppé's failure, and he took a page from Balladur's playbook by opening high-profile negotiations with the social partners, particularly the normally intransigent CGT. Because the CGT had long been the dominant union in the public-transport sectors that make up the bulk of the *régimes spéciaux*, fostering a constructive relationship with them was important.[55] Sarkozy also cleverly proposed that each public-service enterprise negotiate independently with the government, highlighting cleavages among the unions and giving the CGT a heightened sense of responsibility. This strategy, which, like that of Balladur, compensated for the political liabilities of statism, both benefited from and reinforced an important shift in public opinion, which had become much more favorable to reform since 1995.[56] As in the case of labor-market reform, this "competitive interventionist" logic reflected both the enduring influence of the state and the political constraints that it faced in a climate of austerity. By maintaining an image of reasoned negotiation, effectively designating an influential union a favored negotiating partner, and emphasizing equity rather than raison d'état, Sarkozy and Fillon were able to succeed where Juppé had failed.

The reasons for Sarkozy's success also derived from the substance of the reform that he pursued. In particular, the government proposed instituting the harmonization between the *régimes spéciaux* and other public-sector pensions over several years and offered financial bonuses to workers who choose to retire later. In October, Labor Minister Xavier Bertrand declared that the government was willing to negotiate the details of implementation, which would be governed by firm-level negotiations, and that "we will not harmonize the pension systems overnight, nor will we introduce any brutal financial penalties."[57] The following month, however, Fillon declared that, while it had been willing to negotiate over details, the government would not compromise on the "principle of harmonization" between the *régimes spéciaux* and other public-sector pensions. The law instituted an increase in the contribution period required for full benefits from thirty-seven and a half years to forty-one years by 2012. It also created a penalty, to begin in 2010 and to increase to 5 percent by 2020, for each year of missing contributions. Benefits would henceforth be indexed to prices rather than wages and were to be calculated based on a worker's last six months of salary (a concession to the unions). The law also allowed certain opportunities for retirement before sixty, particularly for workers in strenuous occupations.[58]

As the government was declaring its intention to stand fast on the centerpieces of the reform, unions organized a series of protests designed to derail them. A major strike by public-sector workers on 18 October created massive interruptions of subway, bus, and train service throughout the country, with a record level of participation among workers in the RATP (58 percent) and the SNCF (78 percent). All major (and many minor) unions participated, with the CGT's leader, Bernard Thibault, declaring that "the reform, as it is currently constituted, will not pass. The ball is in the government's court." Bertrand and Fillon immediately offered to talk to the unions about their concerns, conveying their willingness to negotiate even as they stood firm on the reform's basic principles.[59] At the same time, however, the CGT was eager not to seem too inflexible lest it risk sacrificing the political capital that it had built in earlier negotiations.[60]

This image of reasonable dialogue allowed the government to dampen unions' resentment and calm the political waters, and it was further assisted in this regard by the continuing erosion of public support for the strike. By mid-November, just before a second major strike by the unions, 55 percent of those surveyed said that they thought that the strike was "unjustified" and that the unions were merely defending their interests rather than pursuing social justice, an increase over the 53 percent who had said so the previous month.[61] This sentiment not only strengthened the government's resolve; it also undermined the unions' mobilization by dividing them.

In late October and early November, the number of workers supporting the strike continued to decline, spurring a decision by the CGT to negotiate. The CFDT called for an end to the November strike only two days after it had begun, and the government struck a deal with the CGT on the modalities of firm-level implementation, making some concessions, such as allowing train conductors to retire without penalty at age fifty-two and a half.[62] Despite calls from the ever-intransigent FO and smaller unions such as SUD (Solidaires, Unitaires et Démocratiques), as well as some in the CGT–SNCF, to continue the strikes in December, hostile public opinion and waning support among the major unions' rank-and-file deprived union leaders of a political context that they could exploit. The reforms were finally adopted in late December and became effective in January 2008.[63] Sarkozy and Fillon seemed to have learned from Juppé's failure, repeatedly consulting the unions and yet compromising on the speed and timing of implementation.[64] Though political capital is scarce in the context of French pension reform, these experiences show that the outcome of reform depends in large measure on how and in what context such capital is deployed.[65]

Recent French social-insurance reform has involved a series of relatively ambitious initiatives, resulting in an uneven pattern of policy change. Balladur, Juppé, Raffarin, and Fillon each introduced proposals that aimed to preserve the core of pensions and health care while aligning expenditures with revenues.[66] Their success in implementing their reforms was determined not only by the content of their proposals, but also by their degree of political sophistication and ability to negotiate the treacherous relationships between the state and social partners left by the legacies of dirigisme. While Balladur, Raffarin, and Fillon were able to enact meaningful reforms, Juppé's government totally failed to reform the public-pension system and was able to see through some of its health reforms only because divisions among French doctors proved unbridgeable. The broader lesson from these episodes is that the outcomes of welfare reform are shaped not only by the institutionalized relationships between state and society, but also by authorities' ability to negotiate the opportunities and constraints that these relationships create.

The German State and the Dilemmas of Corporatist Welfare Reform

Recent German social-insurance reform has been shaped by a different set of institutional parameters from the French case. The German postwar neocorporatist model was intended to be largely self-regulating, with representatives of capital and labor given a wide range of policy responsibilities. This was no less true in the administration of social policy than in labor-market policy. Centered on funds co-managed by employers' and workers' representatives and financed through payroll taxes, the postwar German welfare state required little in the way of adjustment during the era of full employment and vibrant economic growth. Beginning in the 1980s, however, the system began to show signs of strain as a vicious circle developed between rising unemployment and increasing social-contribution rates. Following reunification in 1990, furthermore, the system proved incapable of handling the millions of additional beneficiaries who entered it. In the late 1980s and early 1990s, the government of Chancellor Helmut Kohl began to address these problems with a series of health and pension reforms. After 1998, the pace of reform accelerated, as the incoming Social Democratic administration of Gerhard Schröder enacted the most significant pension reform since the system's restructuring in 1957 and further reformed health insurance. Table 6.2 describes major German reforms since 1989.

TABLE 6.2 German Health and Pension Reforms, 1989–Present

Year	Policy Area	Proposed Reforms	Outcomes
1989	Health	Tightened regulations on prescriptions and drug prices; mandated coordination of inpatient and outpatient care; greater autonomy for *Krankenkassen*; created fee-for-service system	Doctors failed to implement reforms effectively; costs increased dramatically
1989	Pensions	Changed benefit calculation from gross to net wages; decoupled increases in payroll taxes from pension benefits; increased retirement age to sixty-five, with bonuses for later retirement; modestly increased payroll taxes; linked subsidies to contribution rates	All reforms implemented
1992	Health	Capped physicians' expenditures; instituted additional patient charges for drugs; linked payroll contributions to payments to doctors; reduced drug prices; created individual penalties for doctors who exceed cap	All reforms implemented
2000	Pensions	Reduced average benefits from 70% to 64% of gross wages; created *Ausgleichsfaktor* reducing benefits by .3% annually for those retiring after 2010; created legal right to firm-level pensions; created federal subsidies for pensions for low-income workers; instituted 20–22% cap on social-contribution rates; provided annual federal subsidies to basic pension régime; introduced mandatory, supplemental private accounts	Most reforms implemented; *Ausgleichsfaktor* abandoned; supplemental accounts made voluntary, with major financial incentives for worker uptake; commitment to maintain average benefits at 67% (including payments from private accounts)
2003	Health	Reduced health contributions; introduced patient co-payments for doctor and hospital visits; required workers to take out supplemental, private insurance to receive per diem sickness benefits; allowed patients to sign individual contracts with doctors	Most major reforms implemented; provision for individual contracts withdrawn
2006	Pensions	Gradually increased the standard retirement age for the public pension system from sixty-five to sixty-seven by 2029	Reform implemented

State Intervention and Corporatist Adjustment in German Health Insurance

The German health-insurance system revolves around 220 sickness funds (*Krankenkassen*), in which membership is mandatory for workers below a specific income ceiling but among which workers have been permitted to choose since 1996. These funds cover the vast majority of the German population, are managed by boards of union and employers' representatives, enjoy independence from the federal and *Land* governments, and compensate physicians directly. The state's role has traditionally been limited to formulating the system's legal parameters, arbitrating deadlocked negotiations, and financing hospitals' capital expenses. All physicians who practice under the sickness-fund system must join one of several regional associations, which are responsible for the oversight of care and the disbursement of physicians' fees from a pool derived from employers' and employees' contributions. The Bundesverband Deutscher Internisten (BDI), the primary specialists' organization, is the most powerful presence within the Kassenärztlichen Bundesvereinigung (KBV), which represents most physicians' associations and negotiates directly with national sickness funds. German generalists are organized within the Berufsverband der Praktischen Ärzte und Ärzte für Allgemeinmedizin Deutschlands (BPA), which, much like MG France, has traditionally occupied a weak position.[67] Since the *Kassen* distribute lump-sum payments that physicians' associations divide according to services performed, however, the generalist–specialist divide does not create the kind of cleavages that exist in France.[68]

During the 1970s and 1980s, the German health-care system was relatively successful at controlling health spending.[69] The government periodically introduced minor adjustments in health policy as part of an effort to reinforce the system's corporatist foundations and its capacity for cost control. In 1977, for example, the government of Chancellor Helmut Schmidt introduced a series of reimbursement controls and a system of "Concerted Action," coordinating *Land* and regional agreements within a national framework of physicians' organizations and sickness funds. In 1981–1982, additional co-payments and reimbursement controls were introduced. By the late 1980s, however, such piecemeal adjustments no longer sufficed, as expenditures began to rise rapidly after stabilizing or even declining earlier in the decade.[70]

In response, in 1989 the government of Chancellor Helmut Kohl passed a reform that aimed to control health costs by working within the system's corporatist foundations.[71] Doctors had to dispense available generic equivalents of prescription drugs, and fixed prices were introduced for both generic and brand-name medications. The law also aimed to reduce unnecessary hospitalization through improved coordination of inpatient and outpatient care, but the implementation of this measure was left to the sickness funds, hospitals, and doctors' associations. The funds were also given greater autonomy to experiment with cost-control measures. Finally, the law introduced a fee-for-service system, which retained the funds' role in setting compensation.[72]

In contrast to the French case, where Balladur enacted reform without the support of the political opposition by exploiting divisions among doctors, the passage of the 1989 German law was ensured by the left's willingness to cooperate with the center-right government's efforts to impose costs on the medical profession. Because the reform did not threaten the autonomy of doctors' negotiations with sickness funds, moreover, opposition was muted. Doctors also quickly realized that they could exploit the new fee-for-service system to increase their incomes. Between 1989 and 1991, certain doctors concluded a series of deals with regional and local sickness funds, thereby gradually undermining the negotiated salary and expenditure controls. As a result, health expenditures increased to a record 9.1 percent of GDP in 1990.[73] German reunification promised even greater cost spirals as the physicians, hospitals, and populations of the new *Länder* were incorporated directly into the existing system, all in the midst of a recession.[74]

In June 1992, Kohl's Health Minister Horst Seehofer tackled the implementational dilemma left unresolved by the 1989 law.[75] With the aim of saving DM 11.4 billion (€5.83 billion), Seehofer proposed a "socially balanced . . . mixture of a strict cost-saving plan and the introduction of a long-overdue structural change in compulsory health insurance."[76] Overall, DM 3.2 billion of the savings were to come from patients and DM 8.2 billion from doctors and the pharmaceutical industry. Specifically, the plan called for additional payments from patients of DM 3–DM 10 for medications, a linkage between contributions to sickness funds and payments to doctors, a binding global cap on physicians' expenditures, a 5 percent reduction in drug prices, and individual penalties for doctors who overspent.

The success of the reforms depended both on the SPD's support and on placating a medical profession whose influence within the liberal Freie Demokratische Partei (FDP), one of the CDU's coalition partners, posed a potential threat. By shifting burdens away from patients and onto doctors, Seehofer hoped to muffle unions' objections and avoid the inflationary wage hikes resulting from increases in payroll taxes, which would raise non-wage labor costs and contribute to unemployment, thereby further undermining the system's financing basis. Both the SPD and doctors opposed aspects of the proposals. For the SPD, the major sticking points were the new patient co-payments and the government's resistance to restructuring the *Kassen* to equalize risk and strengthen state control over payments to doctors.[77] Doctors resented the proposed cap on fees, which would force them to engage in a zero-sum game, with an increase in the compensation of one group of doctors coming at others' expense.

Because both doctors and the SPD opposed parts of the plan, Seehofer was forced to walk a fine line. Early on, he sheltered negotiations from public view to avoid anticipated pressures from doctors and the FDP. Once the plan's details had been worked out, however, Seehofer proposed a series of more inclusive talks in the city of Lahnstein among the SPD, the KBV, the sickness funds, and representatives of the pharmaceutical industry, ostensibly to negotiate details of implementation. Actually, the most important outcome of the talks was Seehofer's concession to the SPD's primary demand—the regionalization of sickness funds—in exchange for its pledge to support the plan in the Bundesrat, where it enjoyed a blocking majority.[78] This deal rendered doctors and the FDP politically irrelevant and presented them with a fait accompli.

During the ensuing parliamentary debate, the KBV presented a list of counterproposals (called the "Lahnstein" proposals), including certain exceptions to the annual expenditure cap, the fiscal separation of specialists and generalists within the sickness funds, and the replacement of the proposed penalties with a voluntary system of prescription control. Because the passage of the plan had already been assured, however, Seehofer could make only minor concessions and retain the controversial expenditure cap, which was critical to the reform's effectiveness. Doctors' sense of marginalization was expressed by the president of the KBV, who complained, "Our margin of action is really nil. At Lahnstein, everything was so firmly etched in stone that at best we can change a 'U' to a 'Ü.'"[79] As expected, the Bundesrat adopted the bill by an overwhelming margin on 18 December; it had passed the Bundestag the previous week. By cutting a deal with the SPD and marginalizing physicians and their FDP representatives, Seehofer could bypass corporatism and secure the reforms' passage and successful implementation.

The Limits of Consensus and Conflictual Corporatism in German Pension Reform

Restructured by Chancellor Konrad Adenauer in 1957, the German pension system showed remarkable stability until the 1980s. Designed to share the wealth of the *Wirtschaftswunder* with the retirees who had contributed to it during their working lives,[80] Adenauer replaced Bismarck's system of residual antipoverty benefits with payments linked to individuals' past wages and to rising aggregate wage levels. Whereas Bismarck's pensions were financed through state tax revenues, moreover, the new system funded workers' retirement through equally shared employer and employee contributions calculated as a percentage of gross wages. This "pay-as-you-go" system, which financed benefits (at a statistical norm of 70 percent of previous wages) out of current receipts, worked quite well during the 1950s and 1960s, supported by a growing economy and rising wages. The basic, earnings-based public pension system was constructed around separate, quasi-public regional funds managed by representatives of beneficiaries and employers, though some occupational groups were covered separately. Contributions, collected by the *Krankenkassen* on salaries up to a fixed ceiling, were transferred to the pension funds for distribution, and the federal government covered benefits for non-contributory periods during education and childrearing. In contrast to the French case, supplemental pensions in the private sector were voluntary, organized by firms, and subject to sectoral negotiations and were mandatory only for public-sector white-collar employees.[81]

During the postwar boom, bounding economic growth and negligible unemployment rates meant that neither the negative effects of social contributions on employment nor the financial balance of the pension system was much cause for concern. At 36.5 percent of GDP in 1970, social expenditures were relatively high by European standards but were balanced by rising tax receipts and social contributions. Even in 1970, after nearly two decades of rising benefits, total social contributions (which also financed other programs, such as unemployment insurance) represented only 13 percent of gross wages.[82]

In the 1980s, however, rising unemployment, slowing growth, an aging population, and rising contribution rates began to put significant pressure on the system. Kohl's CDU/CSU-led coalition, under the guidance of Labor Minister Norbert Blüm, responded with a limited reform in 1989, vaunted with the misleading (or cynical) proclamation: "The Pension System Is Safe!" The reform failed to address either the vicious circle between unemployment and the system's finances or the long-term effects of demographic change. The impetus for the measure was the "discovery" that pension expenditures would grow to nearly 20 percent of GDP in 2035 while contributions would range between 7 percent and 8 percent.[83] The sense of urgency was reinforced by the state's ultimate obligations for the pension system's finances and its responsibility for supplementing low levels of coverage among the poor.

Despite these ill omens, the 1989 reform was quite modest, resulting in the system's subsequent utter inability to cope with the pressures arising from German reunification in 1990. One of Blüm's aims was to curb reliance on early retirement (long encouraged by the government as a means of combating unemployment), which had steadily increased public pension obligations.[84] To spread burdens among workers, employers, and the state, the law provided for a change in the basis of benefit calculation from gross to net wage levels, thereby connecting payroll-tax levels to benefits. It also instituted a gradual increase in the retirement age to sixty-five for both men and women (from sixty for women and sixty-three for men), with a .5 percent per year penalty for retirement before sixty-five but a .5 percent increase in benefits for each month worked beyond that age; a modest, gradual increase in payroll taxes; a link between subsidies to the system and contribution rates; and a slightly altered benefit formula.[85]

The SPD's assent was critical, due to both its control of the Bundesrat and its representation of Germany's trade unions, whose vigorous opposition was widely expected. There were several reasons that the party decided to support the measure. First, daunted by the impending demographic pressures on the system and rapid increases in benefits since the 1970s, it felt that a one-time adjustment was necessary to ensure the system's long-term viability. Second, the SPD's support was facilitated by several concessions on the part of the government, including the removal of disincentives to early retirement and linkage of state subsidies to contribution rates, which would limit increases in payroll taxes. In addition, the continuing expansion of private-sector pensions, long supported by the SPD, promised to lessen the overall reductions in workers' retirement incomes resulting from the law. Finally, the reform's gradual implementation and limited scope was consistent with the SPD's prioritization of blue-collar workers' benefits.[86] It also did not threaten the wage-based calculation of benefits and left average benefits untouched, preserved the pay-as-you-go structure and the SPD-cherished separate fund for blue-collar workers, and compensated for the increased retirement age with the monthly percentage bonus for those retiring after sixty-five.

Predictably, given these limitations, the reform was not effective at controlling pension expenditures, which rose to 11.1 percent of GDP with an alarming 14.9 percent of the population age sixty-five or older in 1996.[87] In 1997, these pressures led Kohl to adopt a more ambitious reform, which accelerated the increase in the retirement age, reduced the percentage of wages used to calculate benefits, increased the federal government's financing burden to limit non-wage labor costs, changed the calculation formula so as to disfavor retirees under age 63, and linked annual indexation of benefits to increasing life expectancy. In contrast to the 1989 measure, however, the passage of the reform was characterized by confrontation rather than consensus. The government and the opposition differed on almost all substantive parts of the law, leading one SPD spokesman to declare that inter-party consensus on pension reform was at an end.[88] The SPD's objections fell largely on deaf ears, however, as the opposition was powerless to use its majority in the Bundesrat to block the reform, since the law as formulated did not require the upper house's approval.[89]

This pattern of relatively insular formulation of pension policy continued with the election in 1998 of the SPD–Green coalition led by Chancellor Gerhard Schröder. Soon after the election, Schröder and Labor Minister Walter Riester quashed Kohl's reform and introduced their own proposal, whose content mirrored many aspects of the CDU's 1997 law. Schröder had declared that, if elected, his government would "combine innovation in the most profound sense with social justice" and render pensions "as secure as possible" (thus subtly altering Blüm's earlier, failed promise).[90] The government's initial proposal incorporated but went beyond Kohl's earlier measures. It envisioned a reduction in total average benefits from 70 percent to 64 percent and reduced annual benefits by an additional .3 percent for those retiring in or after 2011 (the controversial *Ausgleichsfaktor,* or equivalence factor).[91] The government also proposed the creation of a legal right to firm-level pensions, federal subsidies for low-income workers' pensions, and a cap on contribution rates at 20 percent until 2020 and at 22 percent between 2020 and 2030. The reform's centerpiece and most controversial provision, however, was the introduction of mandatory supplemental private retirement accounts, into which each worker would deposit up to 4 percent of his annual income (beginning with .5 percent in 2001 and increasing by .5 percent annually until 2008) while receiving subsidies and tax exemptions from the federal government.[92] In addition, the government agreed to pay an annual supplement to the system that would increase from DM 8.1 billion (€4.2 billion) in 2001 to DM 43.7 billion (€22.3 billion) by 2030.[93] This partial privatization was unprecedented, as was the departure from parity-based financing represented by exempting employers from the obligation of matching workers' deposits.

Groups across Germany demanded major changes in the proposal, with the unions decrying a wholesale "privatization of social risk."[94] Unions demanded the maintenance of total average benefits at 67 percent (to be financed by an additional increase in social contributions), the quashing of the *Ausgleichsfaktor* (which was said to disadvantage younger workers), increased support for firm pensions, and the abandonment of the private accounts. This last demand was central, as unions suspected that employers' exemption represented the beginning of the end for parity financing and would jeopardize social cohesion and their members' financial interests.

The government embarked on an aggressive campaign to win support for the reform, often eliciting sharp protests that were intensified by its exclusionary approach. During a congress of the public-service Gewerkschaft Öffentliche Dienste, Transport und Verkehr (Union of Public Services, Shipping, and Transport; ÖTV), Schröder famously declared, in response to heckling from the audience, "It is necessary, and we are going to do it. Basta."[95] Protests were not limited to the unions. Women's groups, pensioners' associations, and the left of his own party (with one SPD member of the Bundestag complaining of "upward redistribution") were among broad swathes of German society voicing their opposition. Employers were relatively pleased with the general direction represented by the measure (in particular, the creation of a pension benefit that relied entirely on employee and state funds rather than on parity financing), but they felt it did not go nearly far enough.[96] As a result, they made no active effort to support the government's cause, preferring to watch from the sidelines as Schröder and Riester were caught in the crossfire.

Of greater concern than objections from the left was the opposition of the CDU/CSU,[97] at least some of whose votes in the Bundesrat would be required to pass the law on private accounts. The CDU's objections focused on the *Ausgleichsfaktor,* which, it said, would undermine "generational justice," the law's lack of consideration for families with children, its insufficient reduction in expenditures, and its use of federal money to subsidize low-income pensioners. In part, the incoherence of these objections reflected competition among various CDU constituencies (middle-aged workers fearful of future benefit reductions and others more concerned with imbalances in pension financing, for example), but it also mirrored the party's disorganization resulting from a major party financing scandal that broke in 1999.[98] Seeking to sharpen its profile, the opposition was almost desperate to profit from the pension controversy, leading it to resist some measures, such as the *Ausgleichsfaktor,* which had been contained in its own 1997 law. This political disorganization also led to poor strategic decisions, such as the party's release of a poster retracted after public outcry, that portrayed Schröder as a criminal in a police line-up and called for an "end to the series of pension swindles."[99] Despite his need for CDU votes, such amateurishness and incoherent leadership within the opposition gave Schröder little incentive to make major concessions.[100]

Declaring itself willing to discuss "the details, but not the principle" of the reform, the government adopted a multi-pronged strategy to secure the law's passage with the fewest possible modifications. The first component of this approach involved separating the reform into two laws. The first measure, which provided for the changes in the basic pension regime, did not need Bundesrat approval, since the German Constitution makes the federal government responsible for guaranteeing social protection and because the basic pension scheme does not affect the distribution of financial burdens between the federal government and the *Länder.*[101] The law on private accounts, to which the CDU agreed in principle but to which unions objected, was to be steered separately through Parliament.

In November, the government approved both laws, setting the stage for Bundestag debates in late 2000 and early 2001. During the debate over the first law, the unions held a national "pension summit" designed to place pressure on the government and remind it "who elected them." Supported by the left wing of the SPD, unions repeated their demands for the preservation of "guaranteed benefits" at a minimum of 67 percent, for an additional 2 percent of income to be paid by employers to firm-level pensions, and for employers to share equally the burden of financing the new private accounts. In response, the government made a series of minor concessions, "promising" to maintain total benefits at 67 percent, committing state funds for the development of firm-level pensions (rather than state *and* employer funds, as the unions had demanded), abandoning the *Ausgleichsfaktor* (the only measure opposed by both the CDU and the unions), and making the private accounts optional rather than mandatory, relying on generous tax incentives and state subsidies to draw workers into the new system.

The government, however, refused to budge on parity financing of supplemental accounts, the unions' central demand. Publicly, the unions claimed victory, pointing to the (illusory) "guarantee" of benefits at 67 percent and state support for firm-level pensions. Privately, however, union leaders admitted that the reduction in basic benefits to 64 percent and the "partial privatization of social risk" constituted an important defeat.[102] Adopted by the Bundestag on 26 January 2001 over the opposition of the CDU/CSU, the measure was heralded by Riester as "the greatest social reform of the postwar era."[103]

By contrast, the need for Bundesrat approval forced the government to enter into more substantive negotiations over the second law. Early in the debate, the CDU/CSU rejected both laws, declaring discussions with the government at an end and asserting that "consensus is not an end in and of itself."[104] Because the first law did not require Bundesrat approval, the CDU's objections to it were largely ignored. By contrast, the second law, which required a majority in both houses, presented the government with a formidable challenge, forcing it to negotiate over one of the keystones of the reform. In addition to the *Länder* ruled by the SPD or by SPD–Green coalitions, the government needed the critical Bundesrat votes of Berlin and Brandenburg, both of which were governed by SPD–CDU "grand coalitions," which traditionally abstain from votes on controversial legislation. It negotiated, however, in a way that preserved the law's core provisions, using state resources and the logic of German federalism to secure the required support. It agreed to delay the application of the law from 2001 until 2002 to relieve some of the costs of implementation to the *Länder,* at an additional expense of DM 1 billion.[105] This federal money and the administrative jobs that would be created in these economically strapped regions prompted these two critical *Länder* to vote for the measure. Although the CDU leadership promised to oppose the law in the upper house, it did not wish to repeat its politically embarrassing failure to block the government's 2000 tax reform and did not make the vote an unconditional loyalty test.[106]

This combination of careful political strategy and federal largesse permitted the government to see the law through the Bundesrat, following a close 295–252 vote in the Bundestag (with four abstentions). In all, the final version of the law provided for DM 21 billion to cover administrative costs and subsidies to participating workers. The CDU leadership (like 75 percent of the German population) continued to object to the measure, calling it a "ruin of reform" and the project of "social thieves." Even in the face of such opposition, the combination of the penury of two eastern *Länder,* chaos and division within the political opposition, and a clever navigation of the legislative process had allowed the government to enact the first major pension reform since 1957.

More recent reforms of the German pension system, though less dramatic than the 2001 measure, have likewise reflected departures from the traditionally consensual, gradualist approach. The SPD–CDU grand coalition, led by Chancellor Angela Merkel, has not had to contend with a meaningful political opposition. Though there have been some very sharp internal debates over pension reform,[107] the measures adopted have been relatively modest. The most notable was a 2006 law, led by SPD Labor Minister Franz Müntefering, which provides for a gradually phased-in increase in the standard retirement age from sixty-five to sixty-seven by 2029. The Greens and the liberal FDP objected to the government's failure to improve labor-market chances for older workers, while members of the new Left Party, led by the renegade former SPD leader Oskar Lafontaine,[108] decried a brutal "pension cut" pursued under the pretense of adapting to longer career trajectories. Such objections intensified and fueled major union protests in the run-up to the reform's adoption in March 2007. In late 2006 and early 2007, unions staged demonstrations over a law that they said amounts to forcing workers to "work until they collapse."[109] Though a bit overblown, such rhetoric reflected the unions' frustration with their exclusion from the law's formulation. The law was adopted in 2007, with union officials reduced to complaining from the sidelines about the government's abandonment of workers' interests.[110]

Institutional Adjustment and the Enduring Dilemmas of Corporatist Welfare Reform

The 2000 German pension reform provides several lessons about the changing character of German social-policy making. First and most important, the traditionally consensual, gradual policymaking paradigm that reigned during the *Wirtschaftswunder* has given way to a context of growing state intervention. Beginning under the Kohl administration with the 1997 pension reform, this trend gained considerable momentum under Schröder, as mounting funding crises and continued economic stagnation placed increasing pressure on policymakers. At the same time, however, governments have been limited in their insularity by the structure of the centrist party system and the threat of veto in the Bundesrat. In marked contrast to the French case, these factors tend to favor inter-party concertation over tripartite negotiations with the social partners, and successful strategies have tended to involve imposing change on organized interest groups. That said, German inter-party concertation sometimes assumes nontraditional forms, as in the case of Schröder's garnering the support of CDU-SPD-controlled *Länder* in negotiations over the 2000 pension reform.

These changes in the politics of reform are not unqualified, however, as other recent episodes reflect the more traditional pattern of concertation among national party leaders. In April 2003, for example, a commission chaired by the social-policy expert Bert Rürup and modeled after the Hartz Commission on labor-market restructuring issued a series of recommendations for further health reforms, which were incorporated under the rubric of the Agenda 2010 campaign.[111] In contrast to the 2000 pension reform, this measure was passed *with* the support of the national CDU/CSU after a series of negotiations between Health Minister Ulla Schmidt and the opposition, led by the venerable Seehofer. In this case, CDU/CSU support in the Bundesrat was readily forthcoming, largely because both parties had made reducing social contributions a central tenet of their health-policy platform. To finance a reduction in health contributions between 2003 and 2006 from 14.4 percent to 12.15 percent of gross wages while controlling the exploding deficits of the *Krankenkassen*, the measure introduced patient co-payments of €10 for visits to generalists, specialists, and hospitals while providing for the gradual implementation of a requirement that beneficiaries take out supplemental insurance to receive per diem sickness payments.[112] Despite her aggressive lobbying, however, Schmidt was unable to sell her more ambitious proposal to end the monopoly of *Kassen* physicians through a provision permitting patients to bypass the sickness funds by signing individual contracts with specialists. Although the reform was far from insignificant, it was more limited in scope than Seehofer's 1992 measure, reflecting prior points of agreement between the government and the opposition rather than the active negotiation of a new policy consensus.

Since the late 1980s, German social-insurance reform has been shaped by national-level institutional factors and shifting political dynamics, as well as by policymakers' increasing willingness to exploit available political resources and room for maneuver within existing institutional constraints. In the case of the 1992 health reform, Seehofer was able to buy off the opposition SPD to isolate physicians and limit their autonomy over the allocation of resources. In pensions, Schröder largely disregarded the concerns of unions and the CDU in the Bundestag, relying instead on negotiations with CDU *Länder* representatives in the Bundesrat. In both health and pension reform, as in labor-market reform, success has increasingly depended on a degree of state intervention that departs from traditional understandings of German "negotiated adjustment." If the lesson of recent French experience is that the political complexities of welfare reform often result in a disconnect between state autonomy and state capacity, in the German case the message seems to be that reform in neocorporatist systems often *requires* state intervention. Both the French and German stories, however, bear witness to the importance of careful and astute political bargaining in ways that are consistent with institutional incentives and constraints, as well as the fact that the dynamics of bargaining can evolve considerably within stable formal institutional structures.

Conclusion: Welfare Reform in an Age of Austerity

As in the case of labor-market reform, the past decade has witnessed a series of major developments in the French and German social-insurance systems. In both health care and pensions, authorities have responded to growing fiscal and demographic pressures by limiting the generosity of benefits and increasing the burdens of workers and patients. While trying to align expenditures with revenues, recent reforms have reduced non-wage labor costs, thereby shifting sources of income toward the labor market.

That said, in both countries successful reform has depended on authorities' capacity to create and exploit political windows of opportunity through a careful reading and a partial renegotiation of national political-economic institutions. In France, where the state has traditionally been the sole locus of policymaking, the pattern of competitive interventionism has involved unions' and employers' assertion of greater influence, and reform has generally depended on a government's willingness to negotiate with the social partners. While some governments have been able to see through reforms by carefully navigating France's often treacherous political system, others have failed as a result of political strategies that do not account for unions' and employers' ability to channel public fears.

Similarly, in Germany the dynamics of social-insurance reform have undergone significant changes since the early 1990s, paralleling broader changes in the character of German politics. Whereas German political culture until the 1980s was characterized by incremental change and consensual relationships between governments and both the political opposition and the organized interest groups, the past decade and a half has seen an increasingly aggressive and assertive state formulate and implement a number of major reforms with little regard for these actors' concerns. As pressures on the German economy and welfare state have worsened, and as corporatism has increasingly proved unable to respond, authorities have sought support from the political opposition to impose reforms on the social partners—in particular, doctors' organizations and trade unions.

France's and Germany's experiences with health and pension reform since 1990 have also raised significant questions about workers' ultimate economic recourse in the face of mass unemployment, welfare cuts, and generalizing economic precariousness. In Bismarckian systems such as those of France and Germany, high levels of employment have been the sine qua non not only of economic security, but also of the welfare state's financial health. As these arrangements have been altered, workers have had good reason to wonder what protection will be available if they lose their jobs, retire, or become ill. In response, French and German policymakers have acted differently to support incomes and social stability in a climate of austerity. In France, the past decade and a half has witnessed a major expansion in income policies, while the German pattern has entailed more incremental adjustments to inherited benefit structures and experimentation with new forms of income support. As is discussed in the next chapter, outcomes in this area of social protection, as with social and labor-market policy, have been shaped by both changing economic circumstances and the assets and constraints offered by political-economic institutions. In both France and Germany, however, the specters of poverty and economic exclusion have become both important economic dilemmas and, increasingly, major political challenges.

7

New Social Rights in France and Germany

As we have seen, the past two decades have witnessed a series of important adjustments in French and German social and labor-market policy. Successive governments have reformed the two countries' pension and health-care systems, working to preserve the core of their welfare states while reconciling benefits with strained economic circumstances. Benefits have been trimmed; eligibility rules have been tightened; and dysfunctional arrangements, such as the traditional reliance on early retirement, have been scaled back, all with a view to reducing unemployment and aligning expenditures with social contributions. In labor-market policy, the degree of change has been no less significant, as authorities have extended job-search requirements for unemployment insurance, liberalized regulations, introduced financial incentives for employers to create jobs, and worked to boost employment directly through a variety of new policy instruments. Reforms in these two major areas of social protection constitute co-equal parts of a broader reform strategy of "managed austerity," entailing the promotion of workers' access to income through employment, addressing the vicious circle between unemployment and Bismarckian social policies, and shoring up benefits designed to limit social and economic exclusion.

While hardly neoliberal, these trajectories of reform have led to concerns about increasing economic precariousness for vulnerable groups of workers. As social-insurance benefits have been scaled back and pressures on workers to find jobs have intensified, authorities have cast about for alternative ways to support low-income workers and ensure social peace. As during the 1980s and early 1990s, when the abandonment of French dirigisme and German reunification created demands for welfare-state expansion, since the early 1990s French and German governments have devised new ways to limit economic vulnerability. As opposed to the United States and Britain, in both countries neoliberalism is a marginal political discourse. Consequently, governments have had to temper claims of the necessity of reform with an emphasis on the state's continuing social and economic responsibilities. The emphasis on these responsibilities has been strengthened by the recent chaos in international financial markets and the global economic downturn.

One obvious possible response involves expanding means-tested policies of income support. These programs have the advantage of being financed through direct taxation rather than social contributions, and they therefore do not create the same kinds of labor-market pressures that contribute to unemployment and undermine welfare financing. Furthermore, because they are means-tested rather than wage-related, such income-support policies are unlikely to lead to the exploding costs and wage spirals to which payroll-tax-based benefits are subject. Such policies also enjoy a number of political advantages. First, welfare-state expansion is unlikely to produce the kinds of recrimination and social conflicts that derive from retrenchment, even if the tax increases that tend to accompany it may do so in certain contexts. Second, the meager benefits create limited disincentives to work and are therefore relatively immune to demands for cuts.

Although French and German authorities have shared incentives to turn to policies of income support, policymaking in this area has differed in the two countries, shaped by distinct institutional arrangements. In France, where these policies are the province of the central state, authorities have been able to expand them unfettered by competing centers of political power. Beginning in the early 1980s, French elites embarked on a period of significant expansion of antipoverty benefits, thereby plugging gaps in the coverage provided by their employment-based, Bismarckian welfare state. Although the expansion of these benefits tended to be undertaken by the left, once in place they have remained relatively uncontested by either governments of the right or employers. As French authorities have introduced a wide variety of reforms in social insurance and labor-market policies, they have also, by degrees, created an extensive social safety net that protects workers from the worst extremes of poverty and economic vulnerability.

In Germany, by contrast, the story has been more mixed and the expansion of antipoverty benefits more constrained. Unlike the case in France, where devising, implementing, and funding these benefits are the tasks of the central state, in Germany they generally lie within the administrative purview of the *Länder* and municipalities. The principal German antipoverty program, *Sozialhilfe* (social assistance), created in 1961, provides for both cost-of-living assistance and aid to those in "special circumstances" (such as physical disability). It represented a significant extension and consolidation of earlier income policies under a single system. At the same time, it was assumed that social assistance, passed during the heyday of the Economic Miracle, would remain a small-scale, residual benefit—a way for workers to bridge short-term breaks in income streams.[1] With the economic slowdown of the 1970s, and particularly since reunification in 1990, rates of inequality increased to levels unanticipated by architects of the postwar Social Market Economy. Between 1979 and 2000, for example, the Gini coefficient, as measured by gross wages, increased from 28.5 to 34.6, an average annual increase of .32.[2] Moreover, the steady increase in unemployment, coupled with rising social contribution rates, placed pressure on real wages, which remained almost unchanged between 1992 and 1998, with the ratio between wages in the top 10 percent and the bottom 90 percent of the wage scale growing significantly during the early to mid-1990s.[3]

Although, as we shall see, there have been some recent changes to the law, the original conception of market-generated income and distributive outcomes remains largely in place. German *Sozialhilfe* has not benefited from the kind of activism that has characterized French policymaking. The fact that the program is governed primarily by the *Länder* and financed largely by the municipalities has meant that the federal government's ability to expand the program has been constrained, and significant regional and local disparities in benefit levels have persisted. Furthermore, fiscal crises on the municipal and *Länder* levels have limited the capacity of these authorities to respond. This relative policy stagnation becomes clear when one compares the effects of social assistance on income inequality in Germany with those in other countries. Between 1984 and 1994, social assistance resulted in an aggregate reduction in income inequality of only .12 percent in Germany, compared with 1.82 percent in France and 4.24 percent in Norway. The effect of antipoverty benefits in Germany has been even smaller than in the United States, where it was .45 percent between 1986 and 1994.[4]

The difficulties associated with developing stepped-up antipoverty benefits have led policymakers to adopt alternative strategies for sheltering workers from economic precariousness. As is discussed in Chapters 4 and 5, recent governments have focused on subsidizing job-training and job-creation programs, which are designed to enable workers to compete more effectively in the job market. More recently, under the grand coalition led by CDU Chancellor Angela Merkel, authorities have begun to experiment with the creation of a minimum wage. Though it flies in the face of the principle of *Tarifautonomie,* which has long reserved wage setting to the social partners, the controversy surrounding the Hartz labor-market reforms and Agenda 2010, along with the rise of an aggressive far-left party, has intensified political pressures for the government to respond. Though far from universal, the sectoral minimum wage adopted in the summer of 2007 lays the groundwork for future extensions into additional sectors and for an increasingly aggressive federal role in supporting incomes at the bottom of the wage scale.

These divergent national trajectories have been governed by important institutional differences and by evolving relationships between the state and social partners. Below, I explore recent trends in French and German income-support policies, with a particular focus on the institutional and political contexts that have driven recent developments in this area. I begin with the French case, where successive governments since the 1980s have created a series of benefits, both general and targeted, aimed at protecting citizens from the economic vulnerability that has resulted from the enduring climate of economic austerity.

Weaving the Safety Net: The Expansion of French Income-Support Policies

In the wake of the economic crises of the 1970s, France confronted a number of social and economic problems unprecedented in the postwar era. Rising unemployment, growing poverty, and increasingly precarious employment placed the plight of workers in stark relief and called into question the credo that the rising tide of economic prosperity created during the *trente glorieuses* would continue to lift all boats. Although the near-revolution of May 1968 had raised significant concerns about the social costs of economic inequities, it was the aftermath of the first OPEC oil shock in 1973 that converted poverty from a relatively marginal issue into a central concern.[5] The ensuing period of slowed growth and rising joblessness highlighted the weaknesses of the postwar Bismarckian social-insurance system, whose equation of "workers" and "citizens" had been predicated on an assumption of full employment. When these conditions began to erode, a growing number of French citizens could no longer rely on employment-linked benefits. If the expansion of the postwar French welfare state between the late 1940s and the mid-1960s was a testament to the unprecedented prosperity of the era, the end of the boom forced a rethinking of the system that had both supported and relied on rapid economic growth.[6]

In response, during the 1970s, the center-right governments of the time began to take tentative steps toward the erection of a network of means-tested antipoverty benefits managed and funded by the state. At the time, the only existing such benefit was the *minimum vieillesse,* instituted in 1956 to provide basic pension benefits to elderly citizens whose inadequate contribution histories left them without coverage from the basic or complementary regimes.[7] In the mid-1970s, governments under President Valéry Giscard d'Estaing created additional income-support programs in response to concerns about rising unemployment. In 1975, for example, the government instituted the *allocation pour adulte handicapé* (AAH), which provided an income for disabled workers equal to that furnished by the *minimum vieillesse.* In 1976, the government passed a law creating the *allocation de parent isolé* (API), which provided a means-tested benefit to single parents, usually mothers, until their children reached the age of three. Although such measures reflected a growing recognition of the need for state-sponsored income-support programs, their purview was rather limited and left many groups unprotected.[8]

It was with Socialist President François Mitterrand's abandonment of dirigisme in 1983 that the expansion of French antipoverty benefits truly began to accelerate. As the government struggled to cope with the spike in unemployment attendant to the repudiation of redistributive Keynesianism, it embarked on a broad expansion of the welfare state designed to compensate for the sudden absence of industrial policies as a means of economic redistribution. As is discussed in Chapter 3, this period of welfare expansion was designed to maintain political stability and social peace in the wake of the embrace of liberalization. In 1984, the government instituted the *allocation de solidarité spécifique* (ASS), which provided benefits for unemployed workers who had exhausted their rights to unemployment insurance. In the same year, the government created the *allocation d'insertion,* a short-term benefit for people in periods of transition into the labor market, such as newly arrived refugees, French citizens returning from abroad, and applicants for political asylum.[9] As the government turned from state to market as the organizing force in the political economy, it paradoxically accelerated its move toward state-managed antipoverty programs as the income guarantors of last resort.

The post-1983 expansion of income policies found perhaps its clearest expression in 1988, with the creation of the *revenu minimum d'insertion* (RMI) by the government of Socialist Prime Minister Michel Rocard. During his election campaign of the same year, President Mitterrand had issued an open letter to the French population, proclaiming that "a means of living, or, rather, of surviving, must be guaranteed to those who have nothing, who are unable to do anything, who are nothing. This is the condition of their reinsertion into society."[10] The president's explicit linkage of the proposed antipoverty benefit and "social reinsertion" pointed to the measure's dual character. On the one hand, all French residents older than twenty-five whose income was below a fixed ceiling (adjusted for the number of family members) would be entitled to a flat-rate monthly benefit, calculated as the difference between a family's income ceiling for eligibility and existing income.[11] Recipients were also entitled to other forms of social assistance, including increased housing benefits, assistance with medical expenses, and exemption from the residence tax. The amount of the RMI averaged FFr 1889 in 1995, and by 2004 the maximum benefit had increased to €417.88 (FFr 2741) for a single person with no dependents.[12] The law's second component was an ensemble of professional-support and job-placement services, which were organized on the level of the *département.*[13] The RMI thus represented a kind of precursor to the PARE (discussed in Chapter 5), for, though it did not make receipt of benefits contingent on an active job search, it explicitly linked antipoverty measures to labor-market activation.[14]

This connection of social assistance with employment reflected the social and economic preoccupations of the time. As unemployment began to rise in the 1970s, there first appeared in the French lexicon the concept of *exclusion,* which is an untranslatable term used to refer to a panoply of societal ills, including long-term unemployment, poverty, and mental or physical illness.[15] With the demise of dirigisme in the early 1980s, unemployment rose dramatically, from 8.3 percent in 1983 to 10.5 percent in 1987, and poverty and homelessness became endemic.[16] By the late 1980s, the notion of *exclusion* had become a central preoccupation of policymakers and was the subject of a growing number of scholarly works, such as Joseph Wresinski's *Great Poverty and Economic and Social Precariousness.*[17] Such concerns reflected the deteriorating social situation in many parts of the country, particularly in the poor suburbs of Paris and in recently deindustrialized areas, many of which had substantial immigrant populations living side by side with disaffected whites. Tensions in such areas fueled concerns about the rise of the far-right Front National, which tended to do best in poor areas and those with significant immigrant communities.[18] The RMI was conceived as a partial response to such tensions, leading to its unanimous approval by Parliament. The explosion in the number of beneficiaries following its creation reflected pent-up demand for such a measure, which replaced the earlier, spotty system of locally administered benefits.[19] The annual rate of increase in the number of recipients was 14.2 percent in 1991, 15.3 percent in 1992, and 21.2 percent in 1993, and, by the end of 2003, the number of beneficiaries had risen to 1.1 million, with a total of 2.1 million people covered, including family members and dependent children.[20]

More recently, the Socialist administration of Lionel Jospin (1997–2002) further expanded the network of antipoverty benefits. In 2001, for example, the government raised the national minimum wage, the *salaire minimum interprofessionel de croissance* (SMIC) by more than 4 percent, an increase well above mandatory cost-of-living adjustments.[21] This measure, which set the SMIC at €6.66 per hour, boosted the incomes of all low-wage workers, particularly those younger than twenty-six, who made up a third of all workers earning the minimum wage, and women, whose incidence among minimum-wage workers was twice that of men.[22]

Such efforts to "make work pay" informed another of the Jospin government's major antipoverty initiatives: the 2001 *prime pour l'emploi* (employment bonus). The *prime* is essentially an income-tax break for low-wage workers (similar to the American Earned Income Tax Credit) that grants an annual payment to all workers earning between .3 and 1.4 times the SMIC but below a fixed income ceiling.[23] The benefit, which has increased steadily to €961 in

2008 for a single worker with no dependents whose wages are equal to the SMIC, increases with income starting at .3 times the SMIC, peaks at the SMIC, and then decreases to zero at 1.4 times the minimum wage.[24] Although the requirement that a person be employed to receive the benefit was controversial, since it echoed the Anglo-American emphasis on increasing incentives to work, it dovetailed nicely with the government's other initiatives aimed at reducing unemployment,[25] such as intensified job-search requirements for unemployment benefits. It was also consistent with the RMI's connection between work and social assistance. Despite some controversy, the measure garnered enough support to ensure passage, although the Greens (who preferred a universal, flat-rate benefit) and the center-right (who argued that the measure provided insufficient work incentives) abstained.[26]

The government continued to pursue its antipoverty agenda in 2001 and 2002.[27] In March 2001, Labor Minister Elisabeth Guigou introduced a proposal for a new benefit for the elderly poor, called the *allocation personnalisée d'autonomie* (APA). This measure, whose initial annual cost was projected at between €2.29 million and €2.59 million, to rise to about €3.51 million by 2003, was to be financed in part by a .1 percent increase in the CSG, a general tax on all revenue. By 2004, the benefit was providing support to more than 800,000 elderly (older than sixty) who had lost some or all of their ability to care for themselves and who earned less than €914.69 per month.[28] Unlike the *prestation spécifique dépendance* (PSD) passed by Juppé in 1997, which had benefited only 135,000 people, the APA's looser income requirements and its calculation of benefits with reference to both resources and the extent of handicap allowed nearly five times as many individuals to receive it. The amount of the benefit is adjusted upward with increasing degrees of disability, ranging in 2004 from €482.39 to €1125.59 per month.[29] Guigou heralded the measure as the government's "fourth great social law" after the thirty-five-hour work week, the *emploi-jeunes,* and the CMU (discussed later), celebrating it as "a new right, integrally connected with national solidarity, which defines the loss of personal autonomy as a new social risk from which people must be protected."[30]

Even more highly fêted by the government was a new program of universal health insurance, the *couverture maladie universelle* (CMU), which took effect in 2000. The CMU created a universal right to health insurance, irrespective of one's contribution history and subject only to an income ceiling. The law made affiliation with the *régime général* mandatory for all French citizens, offering free health insurance to all those who earned less than FFr 3,500 (€533.60) per month. Even more important in terms of the resulting number of beneficiaries, the CMU offered complementary health insurance to those who already had rights under the basic system but who could not afford secondary coverage. Like the basic benefit, this complementary coverage is financed largely by the state, which pays premiums to sickness funds or to private insurance companies.[31] The measure was financed in part through an increase of 1 percentage point in the CSG. In 2007, about 1.5 million people received the benefit as their basic health insurance (subject to a residency requirement), and 4.8 million received complementary coverage through the program.[32]

The politics of the CMU have been relatively uncontroversial. When a similar shift in the financing of a portion of French health insurance to the CSG was proposed by the center-right Juppé administration in 1996, it was fiercely opposed by the FO and the CGT, which feared that the initiative reflected a transfer of authority from the social partners to the state.[33] When Jospin proposed the CMU, however, union opposition was muted. Others were more distrustful, including the CNAMTS, whose president complained that the government's approach to health insurance was "Law, law, and more law" and that the state's role in health insurance should be limited to guaranteeing the right to benefits rather than acting as a "manager."[34] Despite such concerns and the opposition of the center-right, the measure's popularity ensured its passage through Parliament, supported by a large majority on the left.[35]

The record of the Jospin administration was one of steadily expanding benefits; that of his center-right successor Jean-Pierre Raffarin was more mixed. When Raffarin took power in 2002, his primary agenda in social and labor-market policy was to reform the previous administration's laws on the thirty-five-hour work week and to devise a major reform of the French pension system. Once those dossiers had been dealt with, however, the government turned to a series of income-policy measures which reflected a more market-embracing orientation. In 2003, for example, the government created the *revenu minimum d'activité,* a complementary antipoverty benefit paid to those who had received the RMI for a year or more. The benefit, equal to a weekly minimum of twenty times the hourly SMIC, obliged recipients to agree to work at least twenty hours per week for a maximum of eighteen months.[36] Although the measure did not limit eligibility for the RMI, it expanded the underdeveloped "reinsertion" half of the benefit.

In a more liberal move, in September 2003 the government announced a reform of the ASS that introduced a two-year limit on eligibility for future recipients and a three-year maximum for current beneficiaries, except for those age fifty-five or older. At the time, nearly 400,000 workers were receiving the ASS, many for several years. Accordingly, nearly 110,000 people stood to lose their benefits in 2004, and even more in 2005,[37] resulting in estimated savings of €150 million in 2004, €500 million in 2005, and €800 million per year "on a forward-looking basis." The government's aims were not merely to save money, however; the proposal was also consistent with its broader effort to reduce unemployment by limiting disincentives to work. The proposal elicited vigorous opposition, not only from the left but also from members of the center-right majority. Despite such opposition, however, Prime Minister François Fillon secured enough support to pass the measure, making only the minor concession of delaying its effective date by three months.[38]

Not all recent antipoverty reforms have had a liberal, marketizing tenor, however, as recent governments have also undertaken initiatives to increase support for the poor. For example, in June 2003 the government announced an unusually generous 5.3 percent nominal increase in the SMIC, representing a 3.7 percent rise in real terms. Although for some, such as minimum-wage workers affected by the thirty-five-hour week, the increase would be less, the measure significantly boosted incomes, with more than 1 million workers (47 percent of those earning the minimum wage) standing to receive the maximum increase.[39] Similarly, in March 2003 the government passed a measure providing an additional €400 million to French departments to finance the APA, whose cost had well exceeded initial estimates.[40] Equally important, the government left in place the bulk of the antipoverty measures adopted under previous administrations, in marked contrast to its attack on other aspects of Jospin's agenda, such as the thirty-five-hour work week. Although Raffarin enacted some cuts in antipoverty benefits, most notably the reform of the ASS, he matched such measures with increases in payments in other areas and left the basic fabric of the expanded French antipoverty safety net intact.

This strategy of "buttressed liberalization," involving a combination of labor-market activation and increased support for the poor, has continued under the government of President Nicolas Sarkozy. In late 2007, the government introduced a new benefit, the *revenu de solidarité active* (RSA), at first experimentally in select *départements* but extended nationwide in June 2009. The benefit aims to reduce disincentives to work arising from the fact that taking a job ends eligibility for antipoverty benefits such as the RMI and API.[41] Workers older than twenty-five with low-paying jobs can continue to work while receiving the RSA, which tops up their income to equal the level of the RMI or API, depending on which is applicable. If the person is unemployed, the RSA will equal either the RMI or the API. It is to be financed through a transfer of resources currently dedicated to the RMI and API, with an additional €1 billion to €1.5 billion provided by the state.[42] This benefit is consistent with the "welfare through work" strategy, with labor-market activation as the top priority and other benefits designed to support workers' return to employment.[43]

Over the past twenty-five years, a series of governments has thus presided over the creation of an extensive network of antipoverty benefits (see Table 7.1). Initially a response to rising unemployment in the 1970s and the social and economic effects of post-1983 liberalization, the extension of social rights gained significant momentum in the late 1980s, culminating in a series of benefits created by Lionel Jospin's Socialist administration between 1997 and 2002. Beginning under the center-left governments of Socialist President François Mitterrand in the early to mid-1980s, the development was most extensive

TABLE 7.1 French Antipoverty Benefits, 1956–Present

Program/Law	Year	Provisions
Minimum vieillesse	1956	Basic pension to the elderly poor without entitlements to other pension benefits
Salaire minimum inter-professionnel de croissance (SMIC)	1970	Statutory minimum wage; revalued periodically
Allocation pour adulte handicapé (AAH)	1975	Payment (equal to *minimum vieillesse*) to disabled workers
Allocation de parent isolé (API)	1976	Means-tested benefit to single parents with young children
Allocation de solidarité spécifique (ASS)	1984	Means-tested benefit to unemployed workers having exhausted eligibility for unemployment insurance; restrictions introduced in 2003
Allocation d'insertion (AI)	1984	Short-term support for those in periods of transition into the labor market
Revenu minimum d'insertion (RMI)	1988	Means-tested, flat-rate benefit for all adults older than twenty-five, adjusted for number of family members
Prestation spécifique dépendance (PSD)	1997	Limited benefit to dependent elderly; replaced by APA
Couverture maladie universelle (CMU)	1999	Universal, means-tested health insurance provided to those without other coverage
Prime pour l'emploi (PPE)	2001	Tax benefit for low-wage workers; provides annual payments to workers earning .3–1.4 times the SMIC; adjusted for number of dependents
Allocation personnalisée d'autonomie (APA)	2001	Partially means-tested benefit to dependent elderly, adjusted for degree of handicap
Revenu minimum d'activité (RMA)	2003	Supplemental antipoverty benefit for those receiving RMI for more than one year; entails maximum eighteen-month work requirement
Revenu de solidarité active (RSA)	2007–2008	Experimental benefit administered by départements, expanded nationwide in 2009; provides supplemental income for low-wage workers, up to level of the RMI; benefit equal to the RMI for the unemployed poor

under Socialist administrations—first, that of Rocard in the late 1980s, and then that of Jospin in the late 1990s and early 2000s.

That said, the expansion of social rights has not been an entirely partisan affair. Not only did the creation of the RMI in 1988 enjoy unanimous support by left and right, but governments of the right have themselves devised new income policies, such as the PSD created by Prime Minister Alain Juppé. What is more, increases in the real value of the minimum wage have tended to be as generous under the right as under the left. Further, the right has refrained from rolling back most of the benefits created by the left, reflecting both a broad political consensus about the need for such measures and their popularity among voters.[44] As successive governments have used state power to extend antipoverty policies, they have furthered, although much later and under a different guise than he might have imagined, the realization of Pierre Laroque's dream of a universalistic French welfare state.[45]

Rediscovering Germany's Poor: Income Policies and the Challenges of Corporatism and Federalism

In contrast to the steady increase in the generosity of French income policies, the development of German antipoverty measures has been more constrained and has displayed a wider array of policy approaches. Beginning in the 1970s, as economic growth slowed and unemployment began to rise, an increasing number of German citizens confronted strained economic circumstances. Despite this disquieting trend, the network of German antipoverty benefits remained more or less unchanged, and the real value of benefits actually began to decline in the 1980s. This stagnation of German income policies was the result of a confluence of factors, including the federal administration of social assistance, which reserves to the *Länder* and municipalities the authority to set benefit levels, and a worsening fiscal crisis confronted by the *Länder* and local governments. It also derived from the institutional predicates of neocorporatism and the Social Market Economy, which reserved wage setting and income policies to the social partners. While French officials have used state authority to expand the network of antipoverty benefits, such constraints have left German authorities with fewer means with which to do so. If the trajectory of antipoverty benefits in France has amounted to steady expansion, the story in Germany, until quite recently, has been one of semi-benign neglect.

Postwar German antipoverty benefits were established by the 1962 Federal Social Assistance Law, or *Bundessozialhilfegesetz* (BSHG). The measure represented a tacit admission that the proceeds of the German Economic Miracle and the expanded postwar Bismarckian welfare state had not fulfilled the constitutional guarantee of a dignified life free from poverty. That said, the law's content was shaped by assumptions that the fruit of the Economic Miracle would benefit all but the most marginalized members of society. Accordingly, the law was intended to create "a small-scale residual benefit" rather than an extensive network of antipoverty benefits and to provide short-term payments to workers to enable them to cope with short-term economic contingencies.[46] This residual character was reinforced by the principle of subsidiarity, which held that social assistance would come into play only if a person was unable to secure support from other means, including family, employment, and employment-based social benefits.[47]

The other major principle that informed the BSHG was that of "individualization," meaning that it should provide benefits based on "the specific features of the individual case, particularly toward the person of the social assistance recipient, his type of needs and the local conditions."[48] This original conception of social assistance is reflected in the federal character of the system, which delegates to municipalities and the *Länder* the primary responsibility for both assessing recipients' needs and distributing payments. The task of regulating social assistance falls to the *Länder,* and the municipalities finance the bulk of payments through their share of tax revenue and from occasional transfers from the federal government or from richer *Länder* and municipalities.[49] Although such a system seems a reasonable means of accounting for regional and local differences in economic conditions, the fiscal crises confronted by the states and municipalities since the 1980s have left them poorly equipped to respond, particularly in economically struggling areas in the former GDR.[50]

As with the regulatory system of *Sozialhilfe,* the structure of the benefits is heavily colored by the principles of subsidiarity and individualization. The first benefit is cost-of-living assistance, designed to pay for food, utilities, housing, and other basic needs. Although the federal government sets the basket of goods and services with respect to which the benefits are defined, the *Länder* themselves set the *levels* of benefits, revised each July, with reference to a "basic standard rate" and variations in needs among particular socioeconomic and demographic categories (children, single-parent households, and so on). Cost-of-living benefits for individuals range from 50 percent to 100 percent of the basic standard rate and are broadly similar across the *Länder.*[51] Citizens are also eligible for a 20 percent supplementary benefit if they fall into categories with specific additional needs, including pregnant women and certain elderly people with physical disabilities. Some are also eligible for one-time payments for particular contingencies, such as urgently needed home repair and expensive consumer durables. The other major category of assistance involves payments to people in "special circumstances." These include a wide range of targeted benefits that provide money for the blind and handicapped, expectant and new mothers, those who are sick but lack health insurance through the statutory system, and those in need of preventive health care. These programs, the need for which is assessed independently of cost-of-living assistance, can be temporary or longer-term, depending on the duration of the "special circumstance" and the degree of financial need.

This system has remained almost unchanged since its inception in 1961, though expenditure levels have climbed considerably, reflecting an increasing degree of need for assistance and the expansion of poverty. In 1963, two years after the system's inception, total expenditures were a mere DM 1.86 billion (€.95 billion). By 1973 this figure had more than tripled, to DM 5.66 billion, and by 1983 total outlays had risen to DM 17.6 billion, a more than threefold increase over the 1973 figure. By 1998, total *Sozialhilfe* expenditures, including those in the new Eastern *Länder,* were DM 45 billion (DM 39.4 billion in former West Germany), after peaking at DM 52 billion in 1995.[52] This steady increase in the cost of German social assistance reflects the effects of the advent of economic stagnation in the 1970s and unemployment in the 1980s and, later, the massive economic problems associated with reunification. These figures, however, somewhat overstate the extent of antipoverty benefits. Although the percentage of the total German population receiving benefits increased from 1 percent in 1963 to 3.5 percent in 1997, the generosity of benefits barely grew in real terms. In fact, in the 1990s, when economic need was most pronounced, the real value of the standard rate actually declined.[53] Even as the number of people requiring social assistance has steadily grown, in other words, the benefits that they receive have become less effective at protecting them.[54]

This failure of the German social-assistance system to respond to mounting economic precariousness has been reflected in increases in the poverty rate. Although income inequality increased only modestly between the mid-1980s and the mid-1990s, the percentage of German citizens living in poverty increased sharply between 1981 and 2000.[55] After being significantly upgraded in 1970, moreover, the consumer-goods basket that defines the standard rate for *Sozialhilfe* was left untouched during the 1970s and 1980s, resulting in a widening gap between real wages and social-assistance benefits and an erosion of the purchasing power of recipients.[56] Against this background of policy inactivity, rising unemployment and recent labor-market reforms have led to an alarming increase in poverty rates. Between 1997 and 2008, the percentage of German workers in poverty, defined as earnings below two-thirds of the median wage, increased from 15 percent to 22.2 percent.[57]

An important exception to this lack of development was the creation of a long-term-care benefit for the elderly in 1994.[58] Financed through social contributions with periodic supplements from the federal government, this program provided benefits to the dependent elderly, whether they are cared for in hospices, in other long-term-care facilities, or at home by family members.[59] In addition to plugging an important gap in the social-protection system, this policy aimed to relieve some of the financing burden on the *Länder* and local authorities.[60] This goal was achieved, at least in the short run: Once the provision came into effect in 1996, social-assistance expenditures on long-term care dropped from DM 17.7 billion in 1994 to DM 6.8 billion in 1997, although they began to rise once again in 1998.[61] Some changes to the policy followed a decision by the Constitutional Court in 2001 that the absence of benefit supplements for the number of children in a family was unconstitutional, although the court upheld the program's basic structure.[62]

While the introduction of long-term-care insurance demonstrated that the federal government can overcome obstacles to expanding antipoverty protection, recent years have witnessed few similar initiatives. In fact, the most recent debates over antipoverty benefits have centered on *reducing* levels of income support, which is increasingly seen as discouraging the unemployed from finding a job. These discussions echoed the prevailing discourse of "rights and obligations" under the government of SPD Chancellor Gerhard Schröder between 1998 and 2005. For example, in 2001, Roland Koch, the CDU minister-president of Hesse and an aspirant to the chancellor's office, advanced a series of proposals for reforms of the German system of income support. Inspired by the example of Wisconsin, where in the 1990s welfare benefits were made contingent on recipients' active search for work, Koch instituted a similar program in his *Land* and campaigned aggressively for such a policy to be adopted on the national level.[63]

Despite such pressures to curtail social assistance, recent governments have begun to take the challenge of combating poverty more seriously.[64] Until the early 2000s, German governments worked in piecemeal fashion within existing policy frameworks—for example, increasing the size of benefits for children or increasing subsidies to university students.[65] Such efforts paralleled expansions in more traditional labor-market instruments, such as job-creation and retraining programs, particularly in the former GDR. Since the Agenda 2010 reforms, however, this pattern has begun to change. If the recent labor-market reforms have resulted in a more flexible labor market, they have also exposed a growing number of Germans to economic vulnerability. Between 1989 and 2000, the German Gini coefficient increased from .257 to .275, while the 90–10 income-inequality index increased by 13 percent, from 2.990 to 3.366.[66] Despite the partial economic recovery of the late 1990s, the rate of poverty (defined as disposable income less than 50 percent of the median) grew from 9.1 percent in the mid-1990s to 9.8 percent in 2000.[67] By 2004, 16 percent of Germans had post-transfer disposable income below 60 percent of the median, a major increase relative to 2000.[68] Clearly, the Social Market Economy was no longer fulfilling Erhard's promise of "prosperity for all," as a growing share of the population was falling into poverty and the incomes of the poor were shrinking, even as the economy grew and unemployment declined. As continuing protests against the reforms, the SPD's loss in the 2005 elections, and the (related) rise of Die Linke, a far-left party with an explicitly redistributive agenda, have all made clear, poverty and economic inequality have become sensitive political issues that the government can no longer afford to ignore.

In the summer of 2007, the grand coalition debated introducing a statutory minimum wage that would apply to all sectors of the German economy. Such a move would represent the first time in the postwar era that the state has engaged in serious regulation of wage setting, an area in which the social partners' monopoly has long been assumed. Initially, the SPD pushed for a comprehensive law covering all sectors, but the CDU (and initially the unions) rejected the measure as an impermissible attack on *Tarifautonomie*. After much public debate, particularly between Merkel and Labor Minister Franz Müntefering of the SPD, in June 2007 the SPD and the CDU reached a compromise. There would be no global minimum wage, but in sectors in which at least half of the workforce is covered by a binding wage contract, the *Arbeitnehmer-Entsendegesetz* (Employee Assignment Law) of 1996, which gives the Labor Ministry the power to set working conditions in particular sectors, would be extended to provide for the negotiation of a minimum-wage agreement. Initial estimates projected that the measure would result in agreements for at least 4 million workers,[69] beginning with the national postal service, which struck a deal in late 2007. This awkward compromise represented a substantive victory for the SPD, though the CDU was quick to frame the scuttling of a global measure as a victory for the principle of *Tarifautonomie*. Not only did the SPD succeed in creating the necessary conditions for minimum-wage agreements in wide swathes of the German economy, but it could also use the CDU's intransigence as a campaign issue in the 2009 elections.

Given the increasingly vocal presence of the newly constituted Linke, or Left Party, led by the renegade Social Democrat Oskar Lafontaine, such positions may be quite important to the SPD's electoral fortunes. Though unions privately grumbled about the erosion of their authority in the wage-setting process, they publicly supported the law as "the best they could get" and as a boost in economic security for many workers.[70] More important, the measure set an important precedent for future state intervention in this area and for additional measures to support workers who have failed to benefit from the labor-market recovery of 2004–2007.[71] If Germany has not yet adopted an activist approach to antipoverty initiatives in the French fashion, neither are authorities willing to leave such questions entirely to the labor market. Germany has begun to accept that, in an age of austerity, both political necessity and economic equity require some adjustment of distributive outcomes through public policy.

Conclusion: Income Support and the Changing Dynamics of Social-Protection Reform

The past twenty years have witnessed distinct trajectories in the development of income-support policies in France and Germany. In France, following the abandonment of dirigisme, governments have significantly expanded the network of antipoverty benefits, thereby filling gaps in the postwar, employment-based system of social protection. As unemployment continued to rise in the late 1980s and early 1990s, this new ensemble of policies increased in political and economic significance as a growing number of French citizens were forced to rely on them. Although the expansion of income support has been pursued with greater vigor by governments of the left, administrations of the center-right have also participated and, equally important, have left in place most benefits instituted by the left. The centralization of political authority in France has thus enabled governments to develop an extensive and relatively coherent social safety net.

In Germany, by contrast, mounting fiscal crises faced by the *Länder* and municipalities, coupled with recent reductions in the generosity of unemployment insurance, resulted in a long period of stagnation of benefits. Though authorities responded sluggishly to increasing poverty until the early 2000s, the development of new labor-market programs, as well as the current debate over the desirable scope of minimum-wage statutes, reflects real changes in the German policymaking climate. That said, neither the institutional structures of the German political system nor the financial circumstances faced by the authorities responsible for income support have been propitious for an ambitious expansion of German antipoverty benefits in the French fashion.

Comparing these contrasting national experiences in the realm of income policies with the policy outcomes explored in Chapters 5 and 6 reveals that both trajectories of reform and the institutional and political-economic contexts that shape them have changed significantly since the 1970s. In labor-market policy, for example, evolving relationships between the state and social partners have determined authorities' degree of success in resolving the dilemma of "welfare without work." Because the social partners enjoy extensive institutionalized authority over labor-market programs, reforms of these programs require delicate, and often contentious, negotiations among state authorities, unions, and employers' associations. Similarly, in pensions and health care, inherited institutional differences and distinctive historical relationships between the state and social partners have presented French and German governments with unique reform challenges and led to important changes in bargaining dynamics.

In the realm of income policies, by contrast, the structure of the state itself has been most influential. Because the expansion of income policies is less politically contested than labor-market or social-insurance reforms, relationships among political parties or between the state and social partners play a less significant role in shaping reform trajectories than in other areas of the welfare state. Whereas the French state's ample authority in this area has enabled it to expand antipoverty programs consistently during the past two decades, federalism and corporatism have deprived the German government of either the authority or the political legitimacy to adopt a similar strategy. With few exceptions, policies designed to support German workers' incomes have tended to come in other areas, such as subsidies for university students and long-term-care patients, or to be developed through existing corporatist institutions. An important lesson of a comparative study of French and German social protection is thus that policy-specific institutional contexts that connect the welfare state and the broader political economy, rather than the structure of the state or welfare state alone, define the dynamics and extent of policy change. In the book's conclusion, I explore these theoretical issues, situating them within a broader discussion of the development of the French and German political economies, the politics of economic austerity, and the dynamics of political-economic change.

Conclusion

French and German Welfare-Capitalist Adjustment in Historical and Comparative Perspective

This book's account of political and economic change in France and Germany sheds light on the much broader question of the dynamics of welfare capitalism in advanced industrial countries. Since the late 1940s, as one phase of adjustment has given way to another, new economic challenges have reshaped the political relationships through which adjustment has been negotiated. From the postwar period of rapid economic growth supported by expanded welfare states to dramatic processes of liberalization and marketization supported by further welfare-state expansion during the 1980s and early 1990s and the contemporary period of social-protection reform and labor-market activation, France and Germany have continued to respond creatively to shifting political-economic challenges of both domestic and international vintage. As the prevailing economic context has evolved from prosperity in the 1950s and 1960s to austerity in the post-1973 period, the two countries have reformed major components of their political economies in ways that have been shaped, but not rigidly defined, by their social and political histories. In stark contrast to common portraits of "frozen" continental European political economies, France and Germany have continued to adjust, often leading to quite surprising results. If Shonfield's world of comfortable postwar prosperity is gone, and with it the dominance of the "public power" that he emphasized, public authorities have nonetheless played critically important roles in facilitating adjustment at each of these historical junctures. If governments are no longer calling all of the shots in an age of austerity, in other words, neither are they the mere handmaidens of rampant neoliberalism. The current international economic crisis has brought the importance of politics and the role of public authorities in managing economic adjustment into even starker relief.

At each stage of France's and Germany's development, no less today than during the postwar boom, developments in the welfare state have been intimately tied to changes in the broader political economy. In a major departure from the narrower focus of much of the welfare-state and comparative-political-economy literatures, this book shows that analyses of economic adjustment must be cast broadly, with careful attention to parallel processes of change across policy and institutional domains. This is the spirit in which I have chosen the concept of "welfare capitalism" invoked in the book's title. Though I am far from the first to use the term, it has usually been employed in more limited contexts. Gøsta Esping-Andersen's "three worlds of welfare capitalism," for example, are really distinct worlds of *welfare states.*[1] Here, the term is used in a quite different sense, invoking the broad ensemble of social and economic policies and institutions that govern how capitalist economies develop over time. In this way, the book thus calls for bridging the gap between the literatures on the welfare state and comparative political economy that, despite some nods of mutual recognition, have remained largely distinct, ultimately to the cost of both.[2] In contrast to this somewhat Balkanized character of most existing studies of capitalist adjustment, this book shows that capturing its substance and dynamics requires an extension of analytical focus beyond particular domains such as the welfare *state* or firms to a more encompassing and dynamic notion of welfare *capitalism,* entailing linked processes of adjustment across the political economy.

Equally important, this book demonstrates that economic adjustment is driven by shifting political dynamics, coalitions, and bargaining structures that vary from one political-economic context to another. Each period of adjustment in French and German welfare capitalism has been governed by a distinctive policymaking model arising from changes in the incentives and opportunities facing key political actors. These changes in incentives, coupled with actors' evolving interpretations of their interests and the policy opportunities represented by existing bargaining structures and institutions, have redefined battles over reform even as they have reshaped the political coalitions that govern them. That said, the political change that comes with the advent of economic austerity cannot be reduced to a mere shift in economic incentives, as many more rationalist accounts would suggest. Rather, it derives from the complex but identifiable interaction of changes in economic interests and the prevailing interpretations of those interests by key political actors, as well as their evolving understandings of the interests and strategies of their interlocutors and opponents. An important lesson to be drawn from more than three decades of French and German reform is thus that economic crisis creates new power relations and may act as the impetus behind the emergence of a new politics, even in the absence of major changes in a country's formal political institutions. Actors are not mere pawns or mechanistic cogs in the reform process, exerting their formal resources of power in pursuit of defined and static economic interests. Instead, they continually reinterpret both the substance of their interests and the strategies most likely to serve them. If Peter Gourevitch is surely right to argue that "policy requires politics,"[3] then, so, too, does politics reshape the meaning and significance of policy for both the actors themselves and the political economy as a whole.

This book has developed these theoretical arguments through an analysis of adjustment in French and German politics and social and economic policy across three major historical periods. The first of these was the postwar era of *welfare-capitalist expansion,* the "golden age" of rapid growth accompanied and supported by major expansions of the welfare state. In France, the reconstituted postwar dirigiste system transformed a stagnant agrarian society into a vibrant, internationally competitive industrial economy in the space of two decades. During the same period, German authorities laid the institutional foundations of the Social Market Economy that underpinned Germany's evolution from a political pariah and economic wasteland into an exemplar of economic success, democratic politics, and social stability. The politics of this period were governed by France's and Germany's distinctive institutional models and related distributions of political authority. In France, the state generally called the shots, while in Germany it negotiated reform with empowered non-state actors.

The second period, beginning with the advent of economic austerity in the 1970s and extending into the early 1990s, is what I term the era of *socialized marketization,* entailing dramatic turns toward the market supported by major expansions of the welfare state. As the postwar era of prosperity gave way to an era of slowed growth and rising unemployment, France and Germany struggled to adjust their welfare states and political economies and were forced to rethink cherished assumptions about how the economy worked and its relationship to the political system. In France, beginning in the early 1980s, authorities completely dismantled the state-led growth model, embarking on a period of ambitious market creation and liberalization. During this period, the French welfare state was significantly expanded in an attempt to cope with the economic and social dislocation that liberalization left in its wake. Similarly, following reunification in 1990 German authorities re-created the postwar Social Market Economy in the former GDR from the ground up. This monumental task not only involved the transfer of the West German social and economic models to the East; it also entailed a significant expansion of the social-protection system to support the integration of millions of destitute Easterners who were ill-prepared for the competitive pressures of life under advanced capitalism. Like the first stage, this second phase of adjustment also witnessed a transformation of the French and German political models. In France, the dirigiste system was beginning to cede power to previously marginalized actors such as small business and trade unions; in Germany, the "semi-sovereign state" gained influence and legitimacy in the wake of the social partners' failures to respond to the challenges of economic austerity.[4]

The most recent stage of French and German adjustment is the contemporary era of *managed austerity,* which involves the recalibration of social policy and a prioritization of labor-market activation. During the past decade and a half, French and German policymakers have turned their attention to the tasks of labor-market and welfare reform. Though welfare-state expansion had been essential to the preceding process of liberalization and stabilization of the French and German economies, the resulting arrangements came under increasing fiscal and competitive pressure as the 1990s wore on. In this context, governments needed to re-create the capacity for economic growth before they could undertake welfare reform without fatally undermining political stability or the system's legitimacy. Even as they continued to extend the reach of market forces to develop a sustainable model of economic growth, they also developed a new approach to labor-market policies designed to unleash the economy's productive capacity while curtailing the financial burdens created by their employment-based, "Bismarckian" welfare states. French and German governments have worked to alleviate their respective "welfare-without-work" syndromes, subsidizing job creation by limiting employers' social-contribution burdens, increasing incentives for the unemployed to find jobs, trimming unemployment benefits to reduce the attractiveness of long-term unemployment, cutting dysfunctional early-retirement programs, and liberalizing a range of labor-market regulations. In France, such measures have been accompanied by reductions in annual work time, generous subsidies designed to encourage firms to create jobs, and stepped-up pressure on the unemployed to seek out and accept available positions. In Germany, policymakers have enacted a series of job-creation and training measures aimed at vulnerable populations such as the young, older workers, and the long-term unemployed while also increasing pressure on the unemployed to find work.

The French and German social-insurance systems likewise have witnessed significant reforms during the past twenty years, involving efforts to balance social-security funds in the face of sluggish growth and increasingly unfavorable demographic profiles. French authorities have cut pension replacement rates and increased required contribution periods, first in the private sector in 1993 and then in the public sector in 2003 and 2008. In health care, they have reduced reimbursement rates, increased patients' co-payments, limited hospital budgets, and created parliamentary spending caps designed to control expenditures. In Germany, similar measures have been accompanied by limitations on health-contribution rates and drug prices, as well as the introduction of competition among doctors and sickness funds. Reforms in the German pension system have been more ambitious, involving increases in the retirement age, altered benefit-calculation formulas, reductions in benefit levels, and caps on contribution rates. In 2001, the introduction of supplemental, private retirement accounts was subsidized by significant state funds and generous tax breaks. Then in 2007, the grand coalition of the CDU and the SPD raised the standard retirement age for the public pension system to sixty-seven, much to the displeasure of Germany's trade unions and the left.

Unlike the cases of labor-market policy and social insurance, where reform trajectories have been broadly similar in the two countries, outcomes in the realm of antipoverty benefits have diverged. In France, authorities have responded to generalizing economic precariousness by expanding the network of means-tested income-maintenance programs. Since the late 1980s, French governments of both the left and the right have created benefits aimed at supporting the incomes of specific populations (such as the elderly poor), as well as others, such as the RMI and RSA, designed to protect the poor irrespective of personal circumstances. The result has been an extensive system of state-funded programs that has filled significant gaps in the country's Bismarckian social-insurance system. In Germany, by contrast, a federal division of political authority and fiscal crises on the *Länder* and local levels have stymied the development of such benefits and encouraged other approaches to combating poverty. Particularly in the wake of the Hartz and Agenda 2010 reforms described in Chapter 5, German authorities have prioritized active labor-market policies, which are designed to improve workers' labor-market competitiveness rather than to provide direct cash benefits. In 2007, however, in a major departure from the principle of *Tarifautonomie,* and amid significant political controversy, officials also introduced a modified minimum wage in some sectors of the economy and continue to debate its extension to others. I present an overview of major policy outcomes in these areas in Tables C.1 and C.2.

Both the substantive goals and the practical strategies of French and German social- and economic-policy reforms have thus shifted significantly since World War II. During the postwar boom, the prevailing challenge was preserving social stability and political legitimacy during the process of economic expansion and political reconstruction and, in France, the shift from an agrarian to an industrial economy. Rapid economic growth and supportive social policies were complementary components of this strategy for postwar growth and adjustment. With the advent of economic austerity in the 1970s, however, France and Germany began a period of liberalization and marketization supported by expansion of the welfare state. Since the early 1990s, both countries have confronted uneven growth and intensifying demographic pressures by rationalizing their social-protection systems and making them more market-conforming while supporting social peace and governability by expanding income-support programs and subsidizing job creation. At each of these three historical moments, both the welfare state and the broader political economy changed in ways that were interconnected and mutually constitutive. But the political dynamics that drove these reforms were not invariant; nor were they

TABLE C.1 Major French Social-Protection Reforms, 1988–Present

Policy Area and Program/Law	Year	Key Provisions
LABOR MARKET		
Five-Year Law on Employment	1993	Subsidized employers who reduced work time; prioritized firm-level bargaining; annualized work time
Aubry Laws	1998, 2000	Introduced thirty-five-hour work week; subsidized firms who reduced work time and created jobs; created annual work-time and overtime limits; increased flexibility
Plan d'aide et de retour à l'emploi (PARE)	2000	Made unemployment insurance conditional on a contract with the national employment office
Loi sur la rénovation de la démocratie sociale et réforme du temps de travail	2008	Increased the number of allowable workdays and redefined the rights of union representation
Loi sur les droits et les devoirs des demandeurs d'emploi	2008	Tightened rules for unemployment insurance; required acceptance of "reasonable job offers"
PENSIONS		
Balladur reforms	1993	Increased contribution periods in the private sector; increased CSG; altered benefit indexation
Raffarin reforms	2003	Aligned rules for public-sector and private-sector pensions; increased contribution period and rates; limited incentives for early retirement; created voluntary private pension accounts
Sarkozy–Fillon reforms	2008	Aligned *régimes spéciaux* with 2003 rules for other public-sector pensions; increased contribution period to forty-one years
HEALTH		
Balladur reforms	1993	Introduced spending constraints on doctors, reimbursement limits, and increases in co-payments
Juppé reforms	1995	Established parliamentary spending caps; raised co-payments; cut reimbursement rates and hospital budgets
ANTIPOVERTY		
SMIC	Periodic	Real increases in statutory minimum wage
RMI	1988	Means-tested, flat-rate benefit for adults over age twenty-five
CMU	1999	Universal, means-tested health insurance
Prime pour l'emploi	2001	Tax break for low-wage workers
RSA	2007–2008	Provides supplemental income for low-wage workers

TABLE C.2 Major German Social-Protection Reforms, 1989–Present

Policy Area and Program/Law	Year	Key Provisions
LABOR MARKET		
Reform of Employment Promotion Act	1993	Introduced federal wage subsidies; allowed wages below those provided for by sectoral contracts
JUMP	1998	Created job services for younger workers and wage subsidies for firms hiring unemployed youth
JOB-AQTIV Gesetz	2002	Linked unemployment benefits to contract with BA; created retraining and job-creation programs
Agenda 2010 reforms	2003–2005	Equalized unemployment assistance with basic income support
PENSIONS		
Blüm reforms	1989 (1992)	Changed benefit calculation from gross to net wages; increased retirement age to sixty-five; modestly increased payroll taxes; linked subsidies to contribution rates
Riester reforms	2000	Reduced benefits; created legal right to firm pensions; set caps on social contributions; provided subsidies to basic pension regime; created supplemental private accounts
Müntefering reform	2006	Increased the standard retirement age from sixty-five to sixty-seven
HEALTH		
Seehofer reforms	1992	Introduced caps on physicians' expenditures; linked social contributions to doctors' compensation; reduced drug prices; introduced penalties for doctors
Schmidt reforms	2003	Reduced health contributions; created new patient co-payments; required supplemental, private insurance
ANTIPOVERTY		
Mindestlohn (minimum wage)	2007–2008	Introduced provisions for negotiating minimum wages in certain sectors

always consistent with the power relations suggested by formal, constitutionally based distributions of authority among actors and institutions. Instead, they displayed remarkable fluidity as new political dynamics in each country laid the groundwork for new and often surprising policy outcomes. The result has been that the models of French and German welfare capitalism have been recast, with respect to the content and modalities of social and economic policies, the relationships between the two, and the political coalitions and bargaining dynamics that drive and sustain them.

The Politics of Austerity and the Dynamics of Welfare-Capitalist Adjustment in Advanced Industrial Democracies

The perspective adopted in this book differs in three important ways from prevailing approaches to the comparative study of advanced capitalism. First, it offers a broad theoretical framework for understanding how advanced industrial countries *as ensembles of policies and institutions* respond to economic austerity rather than focusing on particular policy areas, such as the welfare state, or limiting analysis to ad hoc descriptions of reform in particular countries. It shows that national models of welfare capitalism tend to respond to austerity in two separate stages, which may overlap but remain substantively distinct. In the first stage, countries engage in liberalization and market creation, assigning the market a central role in guiding economic development. As governments engage in economic liberalization and expand market forces, older developmental strategies, such as sectoral industrial policies, state ownership of strategic enterprises, and selective credit allocation are replaced by a focus on labor-market activation, corporate profitability, and international competitiveness. In contradistinction to neoliberal claims of convergence on an Anglo-American model, however, this process of liberalization does not involve the gutting or dismantling of the state. Instead, governments remain critically important actors, expanding the network of social protection to buffer workers from the pain of economic adjustment and to maintain social and political stability in its wake.[5] The process of "socialized marketization" thus involves the parallel expansion of market forces *and* the welfare state, along with a reorientation of the goals and strategies of public policy rather than an abdication or narrowing of the state's responsibilities. In such contexts, expanded welfare spending becomes a *means* of reform, not an alternative to it.

The second phase of adjustment, which I call "managed austerity," involves the reform and recalibration of the expanded networks of social protection that had previously facilitated marketization and liberalization. Though essential for the earlier stage of market making, expanded welfare states confronted the challenges of high rates of unemployment, sluggish economic growth, and aging populations. As the French and German economies struggled in the 1980s and 1990s, authorities came under increasing pressure to boost economic growth, reduce unemployment, and bring revenues and social expenditures into balance. Governments responded by reducing payroll taxes and non-wage labor costs, limiting workers' reliance on the welfare state through strategies of labor-market activation, subsidizing job creation, limiting employers' share of social contributions, and promoting job-generating small and medium-sized enterprises. Welfare reform has been a critical component of this phase of adjustment, but reform has not meant outright retrenchment or, still less, the dismantling of systems of social protection. Instead, it has involved restructuring and rationalizing the welfare state to encourage market participation while sheltering workers from economic precariousness. Just as the period of socialized marketization required an expanded welfare state, the period of managed austerity has required both the preservation of social protection and new policy approaches that support the market's capacity to sustain prosperity and political and social stability.

This book also allows for a more complete and nuanced account of political and economic change than that offered by much of the prevailing literature. By adopting a multidimensional and dynamic conception of reform that considers developments across a wide array of policy and institutional domains, rather than just the formal welfare state or isolated areas of economic policy, the "welfare-capitalist" approach employed here generates insight into how change across policy and institutional arenas interrelates. This framework corrects misleading accounts of the recent history of advanced capitalist countries. In the early 1990s, for example, the absence of significant reform in the German welfare state, coupled with rapidly rising social expenditures, led many observers to conclude that the country was failing to adjust economically. This conclusion, however, failed to consider the epochal process of marketization that followed German reunification and the integral role of welfare-state expansion in facilitating this transformation. Similarly, following the demise of dirigisme in the 1980s, many students of French economic policy proclaimed the outright failure of the French postwar model and predicted an embrace of an Anglo-American liberal variant. But this conclusion ignored the expansion of the French welfare state that enabled the country's population to adjust to marketization and liberalization. Some recent literature has begun to employ a broader conception of economic adjustment.[6] However, "Welfare regimes are still by and large neglected as potential factors of variance in economic performance and economic governance of contemporary capitalism."[7] This book aims to help fill that gap.

This book's conception of welfare-capitalist adjustment also provides a more coherent and consistent vision of economic adjustment than is offered by existing scholarship. Much of this work, such as scholarship on "frozen" European welfare states prevalent in the 1990s, tends to equate the *conjunctural* fortunes of a political economy with that system's *structural* (in)capacity to adjust, thereby reifying current empirical trends into a priori analytical categories. Just as the postwar boom yielded images of France and Germany as paragons of economic dynamism, the 1990s and early 2000s produced portraits of the two countries as sclerotic and hopelessly maladaptive. In the early to mid-2000s, French and German economic recovery led some observers to suggest that the two countries may have something to teach Americans about their own struggling economy, and the advent of the current global economic crisis and recession is likely to shift such perceived lessons once again. Particularly in such volatile times, it is important to emphasize that economic adjustment is not merely a matter of the short-term fortunes of a single policy or institutional domain and that the proclamation of eternal verities based on single cases can lead to profoundly misleading or distorted conclusions unsupported by the consideration of a wider range of evidence. The dynamics of economic adjustment and the adaptability of particular models of capitalism are defined by complex and evolving relationships between the welfare state and the broader political economy, and these dynamics cannot be understood without the use of cross-national comparisons or a careful consideration of the effects of the prevailing economic context on a wide range of policy and institutional domains.

Just as this book provides a more inclusive conception of economic adjustment, it also offers a more dynamic understanding of the political drivers behind it. Existing literature on "national models" or "varieties" of capitalism tends to privilege continuity over change and generally fails to provide adequate tools for understanding how the politics of adjustment evolve over time.[8] By contrast, this book shows that the political drivers of adjustment, and the political coalitions and relationships on which they rest, operate differently during periods of austerity than they do during times of prosperity. At each historical moment, politics is played out according to a different set of rules and governed by an evolving set of relationships between key political and economic actors. As a result, the capacity of governments and interest groups to influence policy also changes, often in ways that formal institutional structures would not lead one to expect. Rather than following predictably from the formal distribution of authority, these dynamics vary over time, even when formal institutional arrangements remain relatively stable. Political function, in other words, does not necessarily follow institutional form. Instead, trajectories of economic adjustment are shaped not only by existing formal institutional arrangements, but also by changes in the prevailing interests, strategies, and interpretations of governments and interest groups. To recall Mark Blyth's observation invoked in Chapter 1, austerity thus brings not only changed policy imperatives, but also new ideas that "allow agents to . . . propose a particular solution to a moment of crisis, and empower[s] agents to resolve that crisis by constructing new institutions in line with [them]."[9]

In both France and Germany, these new political dynamics represent major departures from the politics of the postwar boom. In France, where policymaking was long dominated by the state, the new pattern of *competitive interventionism* has involved an increasing influence by the social partners over policy outcomes and the reform agenda. In Germany, by contrast, the traditionally non-interventionist state has begun to punch its weight, yielding a new dynamic of *conflictual corporatism*. In response to constitutional prohibitions against state intervention in collective bargaining and the social partners' failure to promote the adjustment of the labor market, the state has exercised increasing authority and become a leading force for reform in many areas.

The fact that France and Germany, with such different political and institutional legacies, should demonstrate similarly phased processes of adjustment and shifting political dynamics reflects a broader dynamic that governs adjustment in advanced industrial countries. To the extent that it can generate broad claims about such patterns of adjustment cross-nationally, this book's analysis can help to dispel prevailing misinterpretations of the significance of political and economic change in an age of austerity. For example, many neoclassical economists would expect successful liberalization to accompany the dismantling of existing social-policy arrangements, which they tend to see as impediments to market-based adjustment. Such perspectives would not treat social-policy expansion in the wake of liberalization as an instance of successful reform; rather, they would see it as evidence of failed adjustment. Similarly, dominant approaches to welfare reform and comparative capitalism would lead one to believe that, with rare exceptions in the advanced industrial world, the past two decades have witnessed little fundamental change in the welfare state or the institutional predicates of the political economy. This book has shown the limitations of both assumptions; relatedly, it suggests the need to rethink both our metric of reform and its degree of success and our understanding of how and why it takes place. Such lessons are particularly important today as the world confronts a grave and probably prolonged economic crisis, and the solutions of the past—such as heavy-handed state intervention and neoliberal strategies of extensive liberalization and deregulation—are clearly inadequate to the task of surmounting it.

The Dynamics of Welfare-Capitalist Adjustment in the Advanced Industrial World and Avenues for Future Research

Across Western Europe, the 1980s and early 1990s witnessed extensive marketization and liberalization, supported in some instances by significant social-policy expansion. The following decade and a half has been marked by ambitious efforts to reform the welfare state and activate labor markets. In both periods, economic adjustment has been driven by distinctive political dynamics that are markedly different from those that characterized the postwar boom during the 1950s and 1960s. Although the modalities of the recent period of reform have varied from country to country, the entire advanced industrial world has seen policymakers endeavor to cope with the social pressures and economic dislocation that liberalization has produced. This book's exploration of more than three decades of reform in France and Germany shows that a dynamic, inclusive conception of economic adjustment is essential for understanding processes of economic adjustment in advanced capitalism. It also shows that such developments cannot be understood in merely economic terms. Instead, we must remain receptive to how the politics of reform changes with shifting economic circumstances and how these changing politics govern the degree and sustainability of those reforms that are attempted.

Clearly, a rigorous assessment of the applicability of such an analytical perspective to other national contexts (particularly in the countries of the developing world, where dramatically different political, social, and economic conditions prevail) would require the same sort of close, multidimensional, comparative analysis of policy and institutional developments that I have applied here to the French and German cases. Nonetheless, the expanded conception of welfare capitalism developed here represents a promising point of departure for such inquiry. As the countries of both the advanced and developing worlds confront the present economic crisis, their success or failure to adjust will be determined by their favored policy responses as well as by the politics that make such reform achievable or impossible. In this sense, now as ever, economic change is ultimately a political process.

The experience of France and of Germany thus provides important lessons for scholars and policymakers. First, it shows that ideologically neoliberal approaches to reform are unlikely to succeed in terms either of generating sustainable economic outcomes or of maintaining social peace and political support for reform in the long term. A brief glance at the current international economic turmoil, a meltdown in which American regulatory failures and a related hollowing out of the state over the past three decades have played no small part, drives home the fact that liberalization without supportive social and economic policies and regulatory institutions is shortsighted, at best. This book also shows that historical patterns of politics provide unreliable guides for how the bargaining process that underpins adjustment will evolve in the wake of new economic pressures; new coalitions among governments and interest groups will likely determine both the kinds of reforms that each country eventually pursues and their chances of success. Just as adjusting to austerity has required new kinds of policy strategies—in France and Germany, as elsewhere—it has produced new political dynamics and reshaped existing political relationships and discourses. A final lesson to be drawn from the French and German experience is that robust social protection and liberal economic reform can be complementary rather than oppositional. The implications of this insight go beyond narrow policy concerns; they underscore the broader theoretical point that welfare states are integral parts of market economies rather than mere footnotes or, as some would assert, impediments to them. If adjustment to austerity must involve a serious confrontation of the economic imperatives of reform, then, it must also be sustained by social-protection systems and regulatory frameworks and institutions that make successful reform possible.

Notes

INTRODUCTION

1. Paul Pierson, "Coping with Permanent Austerity: Welfare State Restructuring in Affluent Democracies," in *The New Politics of the Welfare State*, ed. Paul Pierson (Oxford: Oxford University Press, 2001), esp. 425–427.

2. Some recent scholarship has worked to bridge this gulf between the comparative-political-economy and welfare-state literatures. See, e.g., Bernhard Ebbinghaus and Philip Manow, eds., *Comparing Welfare Capitalism: Social Policy and Political Economy in Europe, Japan and the USA* (London: Routledge, 2001); Wolfgang Streeck and Kozo Yamamura, "Introduction: Convergence or Diversity? Stability and Change in German and Japanese Capitalism," in *The End of Diversity? Prospects for German and Japanese Capitalism*, ed. Wolfgang Streeck and Kozo Yamamura (Ithaca, N.Y.: Cornell University Press, 2003).

3. Andrew Shonfield, *Modern Capitalism: The Changing Balance of Public and Private Power* (London: Oxford University Press, 1969 [1965]).

4. Peter A. Hall, *Governing the Economy: The Politics of State Intervention in Britain and France* (New York: Oxford University Press, 1986); John Zysman, *Governments, Markets, and Growth: Financial Systems and the Politics of Industrial Change* (Ithaca, N.Y.: Cornell University Press, 1983).

5. Shonfield, *Modern Capitalism*, 131.

6. Peter Katzenstein's notion of the "semi-sovereign state" is consistent with an extensive literature on the incremental and consensual character of German politics: see, e.g., Peter Katzenstein, *Policy and Politics in West Germany: The Growth of a Semisovereign State* (Philadelphia: Temple University Press, 1987); Philip Manow and Eric Seils, "Adjusting Badly: The German Welfare State, Structural Change, and the Open Economy," in *Welfare and Work in the Open Economy, Volume 2: Diverse Responses to Common*

Challenges, ed. Fritz W. Scharpf and Vivien A. Schmidt (Oxford: Oxford University Press, 2000); Kees van Kersbergen, *Social Capitalism: A Study of Christian Democracy and the Welfare State* (London: Routledge, 1995). For more skeptical interpretations of the notion of "semi-sovereignty," see Mark I. Vail, "Rethinking Corporatism and Consensus: The Dilemmas of German Social-Protection Reform," *West European Politics* 26, no. 3 (July 2003): 41–66; Simon Green and William E. Paterson, eds., *Governance in Contemporary Germany: The Semisovereign State Revisited* (Cambridge: Cambridge University Press, 2005).

7. The "new institutionalism" of scholars such as Kathleen Thelen, Stephen Skowronek, and James March and Johan Olsen represented a significant modification to prevailing understandings of the relationship between institutions and political dynamics. Whereas the neo-Weberian "old institutionalism" of earlier decades tended to view political life as governed by formal, constitutionally based distributions of authority, the "new" variant allowed more space for alternative avenues of political influence. For formulations of the "new institutionalism," see James March and Johan Olsen, "The New Institutionalism: Organizational Factors in Political Life," *American Political Science Review* 78 (September 1984): 734–749; Stephen Skowronek, *Building a New American State: The Expansion of National Administrative Capacities, 1877–1920* (Cambridge: Cambridge University Press, 1982); Kathleen Thelen, *Union of Parts: Labor Politics in Postwar Germany* (Ithaca, N.Y.: Cornell University Press, 1991). For the classic overview of "new institutionalism," see Peter A. Hall and Rosemary Taylor, "Political Science and the Three New Institutionalisms," *Political Studies* 44 (December 1996): 936–957.

8. Peter Gourevitch, *Politics in Hard Times: Comparative Responses to International Economic Crises* (Ithaca, N.Y.: Cornell University Press, 1986).

9. For an analysis of recent political change in France and Germany and its significance for the study of political institutions, see Mark I. Vail, "Bending the Rules: Institutional Analysis, Political Change and Labor-Market Reform in Advanced Industrial Societies," *Comparative Politics* 42, no. 1 (October 2009), forthcoming.

10. Gøsta Esping-Andersen, *The Three Worlds of Welfare Capitalism* (Princeton, N.J.: Princeton University Press, 1990).

11. Prominent examples include Thomas Friedman, *The Lexus and the Olive Tree* (New York: Farrar, Straus and Giroux, 1999); Kenichi Ohmae, *The Borderless World: Power and Strategy in the Interlinked Economy* (Cambridge, Mass.: MIT Press, 1991).

12. See, e.g., Andre Sapir, "Globalization and the Reform of European Social Models," *Journal of Common Market Studies* 44, no. 2 (June 2006): 369–390.

13. Peter A. Hall and David Soskice, "An Introduction to Varieties of Capitalism," in *Varieties of Capitalism: The Institutional Foundations of Comparative Advantage*, ed. Peter A. Hall and David Soskice (Oxford: Oxford University Press, 2001), 1, 6, 13.

14. In this respect, the Varieties of Capitalism approach shares concerns with other works of comparative political economy that aim to dispel the twin myths of national convergence and hegemonic neoliberalism: see, e.g., the chapters in Suzanne Berger and Ronald Dore, eds., *National Diversity and Global Capitalism* (Ithaca, N.Y.: Cornell University Press, 1996).

15. For an analysis of the weaknesses of the Varieties of Capitalism approach, see Chris Howell, "Varieties of Capitalism: And Then There Was One?" *Comparative Politics* 36, no. 1 (October 2003): 106–124.

16. Though they aim to address criticisms of the approach, the contributions in a recent collection retain the same firm-centered, relatively apolitical perspective that char-

acterized the original *Varieties of Capitalism* volume: see Bob Hancké, Martin Rhodes, and Mark Thatcher, eds., *Beyond Varieties of Capitalism: Conflict, Contradiction, and Complementarities in the European Economy* (Oxford: Oxford University Press, 2007).

17. Paul Pierson, *Politics in Time: History, Institutions, and Social Analysis* (Princeton, N.J.: Princeton University Press, 2004), introduction, esp. 10–11, and 42–44.

18. Paul Pierson, *Dismantling the Welfare State? Reagan, Thatcher, and the Politics of Retrenchment* (Cambridge: Cambridge University Press, 1994); idem, "New Politics of the Welfare State," *World Politics* 48, no. 2 (1996): 143–179.

19. For the classic treatment of the "welfare-without-work" syndrome, see Gøsta Esping-Andersen, "Welfare States without Work: The Impasse of Labour Shedding and Familialism in Continental European Social Policy," in *Welfare States in Transition,* ed. Gøsta Esping-Andersen (London: Sage, 1996). See also idem, *The Three Worlds of Welfare Capitalism,* esp. 226–228; idem, *Social Foundations of Postindustrial Economies* (Oxford: Oxford University Press, 1999), 153.

20. Though, as I show in Chapter 5, the Hartz IV reforms in Germany and recent labor-market liberalization in France represent fundamental departures from past practice, most observers have continued to dismiss such reforms as "glimmerings of a response" or as "diluted" or "half-hearted": see, e.g., Barry Eichengreen, *The European Economy since 1945: Coordinated Capitalism and Beyond* (Princeton, N.J.: Princeton University Press, 2007), 417; Wolfgang Streeck and Christina Trampusch, "Economic Reform and the Political Economy of the German Welfare State," *German Politics* 14, no. 2 (June 2005): 185; "Attali the Hun," *Economist,* 26 January–1 February 2008, 51.

21. Ellen M. Immergut, *Health Politics: Interests and Institutions in Western Europe* (Cambridge: Cambridge University Press, 1992), 8, 26.

22. Manow and Seils, "Adjusting Badly," 265.

23. Katzenstein, *Policy and Politics in West Germany.*

24. On Germany's "externalization" strategy, see Manow and Seils, "Adjusting Badly."

25. Martin Rhodes, "Southern European Welfare States: Identity, Problems and Prospects for Reform," in *Southern European Welfare States: Between Crisis and Reform,* ed. Martin Rhodes (Portland, Ore.: Frank Cass, 1997), 16.

26. See, e.g., Vivien A. Schmidt, "Values and Discourse in Adjustment" in *Welfare and Work in the Open Economy, Volume 1: From Vulnerability to Competitiveness,* ed. Fritz W. Scharpf and Vivien A. Schmidt (Oxford: Oxford University Press, 2000), 293–298.

27. Colin Crouch, "Welfare State Regimes and Industrial Relations Systems: The Questionable Role of Path Dependency Theory," in Ebbinghaus and Manow, *Comparing Welfare Capitalism,* 117.

28. Typical examples include Maurizio Ferrera and Martin Rhodes, "Recasting European Welfare States: An Introduction," in *Recasting European Welfare States,* ed. Maurizio Ferrera and Martin Rhodes (Portland, Ore.: Frank Cass, 2000); Fritz W. Scharpf and Vivien A. Schmidt, "Introduction," in *Welfare and Work in the Open Economy,* vol. 2, 11–13; Gøsta Esping-Andersen, "After the Golden Age? Welfare State Dilemmas in a Global Economy," in Esping-Andersen, *Welfare States in Transition*; Paul Pierson, "Coping with Permanent Austerity," in Pierson, *New Politics of the Welfare State,* 448. Though Europe's recent economic recovery and the lowest unemployment rates in two decades have resulted in a somewhat more charitable view of France's and Germany's capacity for

adjustment, such images of sclerosis persist: see "Squaring the Circle," *Economist,* 11–17 February 2006, 8; Jonas Pontusson, *Inequality and Prosperity: Social Europe versus Liberal America* (Ithaca, N.Y.: Cornell University Press, 2005), 69–77, 120–121; Herbert Kitschelt and Wolfgang Streeck, "From Stability to Stagnation: Germany at the Beginning of the Twenty-First Century," in *Germany: Beyond the Stable State,* ed. Herbert Kitschelt and Wolfgang Streeck (London: Frank Cass, 2003); Isabella Mares, *Taxation, Wage Bargaining, and Unemployment* (Cambridge: Cambridge University Press, 2006), 167–173.

29. For a description of France's and Germany's postwar boom, see Andrew Glyn et al., "The Rise and Fall of the Golden Age," in *The Golden Age of Capitalism: Reinterpreting the Postwar Experience,* ed. Stephen A. Marglin and Juliet B. Schor (Oxford: Clarendon, 1990), 39–125.

30. For a discussion of the conservatism of the Third Republic, see Stanley Hoffmann, "Paradoxes of the French Political Community," in *In Search of France,* ed. Stanley Hoffmann (New York: Harper, 1963), chap. 1.

31. For the contours of the postwar German model, see Shonfield, *Modern Capitalism,* chap. 11; Gary Herrigel, *Industrial Constructions: The Sources of German Industrial Power* (New York: Cambridge University Press, 1996).

32. Thelen, *Union of Parts.* See also Wolfgang Streeck and Norbert Kluge, eds., *Mitbestimmung in Deutschland: Tradition und Effizienz: Expertenberichte für die Kommission Mitbestimmung* (Frankfurt: Campus, 1999); van Kersbergen, *Social Capitalism.*

33. The political stakes were particularly high for France and Germany, where the legacies of collaboration and Nazism required a vindication of the notion that the two countries could combine democratic politics and economic prosperity.

34. For a detailed discussion, see Jonah D. Levy, *Tocqueville's Revenge: State, Society, and Economy in Contemporary France* (Cambridge, Mass.: Harvard University Press, 1999).

35. This pattern is consistent with Karl Polanyi's insight that market making both is heavily governed by politics and generates demands for social protection: Karl Polanyi, *The Great Transformation: The Political and Economic Origins of Our Time* (Boston: Beacon Press, 1957 [1944]).

36. See Wolfgang Streeck and Kathleen Thelen, "Introduction: Institutional Change in Advanced Political Economies," in *Beyond Continuity: Institutional Change in Advanced Political Economies,* ed. Wolfgang Streeck and Kathleen Thelen (Oxford: Oxford University Press, 2005); Kathleen Thelen, *How Institutions Evolve: The Political Economy of Skills in Germany, Britain, the United States, and Japan* (Cambridge: Cambridge University Press, 2004).

CHAPTER 1

1. Andrew Shonfield, *Modern Capitalism: The Changing Balance of Public and Private Power* (London: Oxford University Press, 1965), 3.

2. Peter Gourevitch, *Politics in Hard Times: Comparative Responses to International Economic Crises* (Ithaca, N.Y.: Cornell University Press, 1986), 17.

3. Mark Blyth, *Great Transformations: Economic Ideas and Institutional Change in the Twentieth Century* (Cambridge: Cambridge University Press, 2002), 10, n. 20.

4. Ibid., 11.

5. This argument dovetails with the literature on "social pacts" in its emphasis on the coalitional foundations of economic reform. It differs, however, by accounting for a wider range of political change, seeing reform as the product of both imposition and consensus, and emphasizing long-term political trajectories and historical legacies: see, e.g., Martin Rhodes, "The Political Economy of Social Pacts: 'Competitive Corporatism' and European Welfare Reform," in *The New Politics of the Welfare State,* ed. Paul Pierson (Oxford: Oxford University Press, 2001); Giuseppe Fajertag and Philippe Pochet, eds., *Social Pacts in Europe* (Brussels: European Trade Union Institute, 2000).

6. Peter A. Hall, *Governing the Economy: The Politics of State Intervention in Britain and France* (Oxford: Oxford University Press, 1986), 1; Shonfield, *Modern Capitalism,* 64.

7. Stephen A. Marglin, "Lessons from the Golden Age: An Overview," in *The Golden Age of Capitalism: Reinterpreting the Postwar Experience,* ed. Stephen A. Marglin and Juliet B. Schor (Oxford: Clarendon Press, 1990), 16.

8. Between 1950 and 1973, real growth averaged 4.1 percent in France and 5 percent in Germany, with unemployment averaging 1.7 percent and 2.7 percent between 1952 and 1964 in France and Germany, respectively: Andrew Glyn et al., "The Rise and Fall of the Golden Age," in Marglin and Schor, *The Golden Age of Capitalism,* 47.

9. Barry Eichengreen, *The European Economy since 1945: Coordinated Capitalism and Beyond* (Princeton, N.J.: Princeton University Press, 2007), 253–256.

10. For a detailed discussion, see Glyn et al., "Rise and Fall of the Golden Age," 72–88.

11. Jonah D. Levy, "The State Also Rises: The Roots of Contemporary State Activism," in *The State after Statism: New State Activities in the Age of Liberalization,* ed. Jonah D. Levy (Cambridge, Mass.: Harvard University Press, 2006), 7.

12. See, e.g., Michel Crozier, Samuel P. Huntington, and Joji Watanuki, *The Crisis of Democracy: Report on the Governability of Democracies to the Trilateral Commission* (New York: New York University Press, 1975).

13. Paul Pierson, *Dismantling the Welfare State? Reagan, Thatcher, and the Politics of Retrenchment* (Cambridge: Cambridge University Press, 1994), 18. For a succinct formulation of Pierson's argument, see idem, "New Politics of the Welfare State," *World Politics* 48, no. 2 (1996): 143–179.

14. One recent attempt to do so is Vivien Schmidt, *The Futures of European Capitalism* (Oxford: Oxford University Press, 2002). Though admirable in its emphasis on the importance of ideas (or "discourse," to use Schmidt's preferred term), the book largely endorses, rather than challenges, two decades of historical institutionalist work on national models and "varieties" of capitalism, with the result that it underestimates the degree of change experienced by these models. To the extent that it does acknowledge change, it overstates the influence of putative "Europeanization" at the expense of a fine-grained analysis of shifts in domestic politics.

15. Wolfgang Streeck and Kathleen Thelen, "Introduction: Institutional Change in Advanced Political Economies," in *Beyond Continuity: Institutional Change in Advanced Political Economies,* ed. Wolfgang Streeck and Kathleen Thelen (Oxford: Oxford University Press, 2005), 1, 9; Kathleen Thelen, *How Institutions Evolve: The Political Economy of Skills in Germany, Britain, the United States, and Japan* (Cambridge: Cambridge University Press, 2004), 35. For a more dynamic perspective on German political-economic adjustment, see Wolfgang Streeck, "Introduction: Explorations into the Origins of Nonliberal Capitalism in Germany and Japan," in *The Origins of Nonliberal Capitalism:*

Germany and Japan in Comparison, ed. Wolfgang Streeck and Kozo Yamamura (Ithaca, N.Y.: Cornell University Press, 2001), esp. 34–38.

16. Peter A. Hall and David Soskice, "An Introduction to Varieties of Capitalism," in *Varieties of Capitalism: The Institutional Foundations of Comparative Advantage,* ed. Peter A. Hall and David Soskice (Oxford: Oxford University Press, 2001); Michel Goyer, "Varieties of Institutional Investors and National Models of Capitalism: The Transformation of Corporate Governance in France and Germany," *Politics and Society* 34, no. 3 (September 2006): 402.

17. Thelen, *How Institutions Evolve,* 36.

18. Streeck and Thelen, "Introduction," 22–24. For Eric Schickler's discussion of "layering," see his *Disjointed Pluralism: Institutional Innovation and the Development of the U.S. Congress* (Princeton, N.J.: Princeton University Press, 2001).

19. Jacob S. Hacker, "Policy Drift: The Hidden Politics of U.S. Welfare Retrenchment," in Streeck and Thelen, *Beyond Continuity,* 42.

20. Hall, *Governing the Economy,* 19, quoted in Richard Deeg, "Change from Within: German and Italian Finance in the 1990s," in Streeck and Thelen, *Beyond Continuity,* 172; Streeck and Thelen, "Introduction," 13–14.

21. An illustrative recent example is Sabina Avdagic, "One Path or Several? Understanding the Varied Development of Tripartism in New European Capitalisms," Max-Planck-Institut für Gesellschaftsforschung Discussion Paper 06/5 (Cologne: Max-Planck-Institut für Gesellschaftsforschung, 2006).

22. Gretchen Helmke and Steve Levitsky, "Introduction," in *Informal Institutions and Democracy: Lessons from Latin America,* ed. Gretchen Helmke and Steve Levitsky (Baltimore: Johns Hopkins University Press, 2006), 5. The contributions to this volume explore how informal institutions and social and political relationships have governed adjustment across a range of Latin American countries. See also idem, "Informal Institutions and Comparative Politics: A Research Agenda," *Perspectives on Politics* 2, no. 4 (December 2004): 725–740.

23. There are some exceptions to the prevailing, relatively formalistic analyses of institutions and politics. Two important examples are Peter Swenson, *Fair Shares: Unions, Pay, and Politics in Sweden and West Germany* (Ithaca, N.Y.: Cornell University Press, 1989); Richard M. Locke and Kathleen Thelen, "Apples and Oranges Revisited: Contextualized Comparisons and the Study of Comparative Labor Politics," *Politics and Society* 23, no. 3 (September 1995): 337–367. See also Helmke and Levitsky, "Conclusion," in Helmke and Levitsky, *Informal Institutions and Democracy,* 274.

24. For a more quantitatively oriented application of similar insights to the role of trust in Latin American politics, see Matthew R. Cleary and Susan C. Stokes, *Democracy and the Culture of Skepticism: Political Trust in Argentina and Mexico* (New York: Russell Sage, 2006).

25. See Robert Boyer, *The Regulation School: A Critical Introduction* (New York: Columbia University Press, 1990), for an overview.

26. Chris Howell, *Regulating Labor: The State and Industrial Relations Reform in Postwar France* (Princeton, N.J.: Princeton University Press), 9–10.

27. Such an analytical framework departs from traditional historical institutionalist approaches, according to which a country's "distinctive institutional structure" leads to "predictable patterns of policy and strategy." This book shows that such patterns are determined by both the formal distribution of political authority in a political economy

and how shifts in economic context affect how that authority is exercised. For an example of the older perspective, see John Zysman, "How Institutions Create Historically Rooted Trajectories of Growth," *Industrial and Corporate Change* 3, no. 1 (1994): 279.

28. Pepper D. Culpepper, "Institutional Change in Contemporary Capitalism: Coordinated Financial Systems since 1990," *World Politics* 57, no. 2 (January 2005): 176; idem, "The Politics of Common Knowledge: Ideas and Institutional Change in Wage Bargaining," *International Organization* 62, no. 1 (January 2008): 1–33.

Though relatively neglected in the comparative-politics literature, this emphasis on the importance of shifting interpretations of interests has become influential in some strands of political theory: see, e.g., the chapters in Robert Adcock, Mark Bevir, and Shannon C. Stimson, eds., *Modern Political Science: Anglo-American Exchanges since 1880* (Princeton, N.J.: Princeton University Press, 2007).

29. One of the most influential attempts is Peter A. Hall, ed., *The Political Power of Economic Ideas: Keynesianism across Nations* (Princeton, N.J.: Princeton University Press, 1989).

30. Karl Polanyi, *The Great Transformation: The Political and Economic Origins of Our Time* (Boston: Beacon Press, 1957 [1944]), esp. chaps. 12 and 14.

31. See Horst Siebert, "Labor Market Rigidities: At the Root of Unemployment in Europe," *Journal of Economic Perspectives* 11, no. 3 (Summer 1997): 37–54; Organization for Economic Cooperation and Development, *OECD Employment Outlook: Boosting Jobs and Incomes* (Paris: OECD, 2006), esp. chap. 3.

32. Jonah D. Levy, *Tocqueville's Revenge: State, Society, and Economy in Contemporary France* (Cambridge, Mass.: Harvard University Press, 1999), esp. chap. 1.

33. For an analysis of the German reliance on the welfare state to finance reunification, see Philip Manow and Eric Seils, "Adjusting Badly: The German Welfare State, Structural Change, and the Open Economy," in *Welfare and Work in the Open Economy, Volume 2: Diverse Responses to Common Challenges,* ed. Fritz W. Scharpf and Vivien A. Schmidt (Oxford: Oxford University Press, 2000); Gerhard A. Ritter, *Der Preis der deutschen Einheit: Die Wiedervereinigung und die Krise des Sozialstaates* (Munich: Verlag C. H. Beck, 2006).

34. Gøsta Esping-Andersen, "Welfare States without Work: The Impasse of Labour Shedding and Familialism in Continental European Social Policy," in *Welfare States in Transition: National Adaptations in Global Economies,* ed. Gøsta Esping-Andersen (London: Sage, 1996); idem, *The Three Worlds of Welfare Capitalism* (Princeton, N.J.: Princeton University Press, 1990), esp. 226–228.

35. This two-stage process of adjustment tends to characterize continental, Bismarckian systems such France, Germany, and Italy, where decentralized welfare-state institutions present a distinctive set of political challenges under austerity. In more centralized systems such as Britain and Sweden, by contrast, governments can initiate simultaneous economic liberalization and welfare reform more easily, but the centralization of social-policy administration may lead to a political backlash that can limit the scope of welfare reform when it is pursued as part of an aggressive neoliberal agenda.

36. Levy, "The State Also Rises," 2.

37. Pierson, "New Politics of the Welfare State."

38. Shonfield, *Modern Capitalism,* 131.

39. Klaus Hinrich Hennings, "West Germany," in *The European Economy: Growth and Crisis,* ed. Andrea Boltho (Oxford: Oxford University Press, 1982), 475.

40. For an analysis of the state's failure to empower allies for reform, see Levy, *Tocqueville's Revenge*.

41. Herbert Kitschelt and Wolfgang Streeck, "From Stability to Stagnation: Germany at the Beginning of the Twenty-First Century," in *Germany: Beyond the Stable State*, ed. Herbert Kitschelt and Wolfgang Streeck (London: Frank Cass, 2004), 28.

42. For a discussion, see John T. S. Keeler, "Corporatist Decentralization and Commercial Modernization in France: The Royer Law's Impact on Shopkeepers, Supermarkets, and the State," in *Socialism, the State, and Public Policy in France*, ed. Philip Cerny and Martin Schain (London: Frances Pinter, 1985); Levy, *Tocqueville's Revenge*, 61–62.

43. Though the image of a gradualist, consensual postwar Germany has been dominant, there have been strands of skepticism about the system's degree of "consensus": see Wolfgang Streeck, "Neo-Corporatist Industrial Relations and the Economic Crisis in West Germany," in *Order and Conflict in Contemporary Capitalism*, ed. John H. Goldthorpe (Oxford: Clarendon Press, 1984); Andrei S. Markovits, *The Politics of West German Trade Unions: Strategies of Class and Interest Representation in Growth and Crisis* (Cambridge: Cambridge University Press, 1986). I am indebted to Peter Hall for emphasizing this point.

44. The seminal work is Esping-Andersen, *The Three Worlds of Welfare Capitalism*. For modifications of Esping-Andersen's typology, see Giuliano Bonoli, "Classifying Welfare States: A Two-Dimension Approach," *Journal of Social Policy* 26, no. 3 (1997): 351–372; Maurizio Ferrera, "The 'Southern Model' of Welfare in Social Europe," *Journal of European Social Policy* 6, no. 1 (1996): 17–37; Francis G. Castles and Deborah Mitchell, "Worlds of Welfare and Families of Nations," in *Families of Nations: Patterns of Public Policy in Western Democracies*, ed. Francis G. Castles (Brookfield, Vt.: Dartmouth University Press, 1993).

For more recent attempts to bridge the divide between comparative political economy and studies of the welfare state, see Bernhard Ebbinghaus and Philip Manow, eds., *Comparing Welfare Capitalism: Social Policy and Political Economy in Europe, Japan and the USA* (London: Routledge, 2001); Wolfgang Streeck and Kozo Yamamura, "Introduction: Convergence or Diversity? Stability and Change in German and Japanese Capitalism," in *The End of Diversity? Prospects for German and Japanese Capitalism*, ed. Wolfgang Streeck and Kozo Yamamura (Ithaca, N.Y.: Cornell University Press, 2003).

CHAPTER 2

1. The best account of the Vichy years is Robert O. Paxton, *Vichy France: Old Guard and New Order, 1940–1944* (New York: Columbia University Press, 2001 [1972]). The work has been translated as *La France de Vichy, 1940–1944* (Paris: Seuil, 1997). For an account of the retributions of the immediate postwar period, see Henry Rousso, *The Vichy Syndrome: History and Memory in France since 1944*, trans. Arthur Goldhammer (Cambridge, Mass.: Harvard University Press, 1991), chap. 1.

2. Between 1953 and 1973, annual economic growth averaged 5.3 percent in France and 5.5 percent in Germany. Annual productivity growth during the same period was equally impressive, averaging between 4 percent and 5 percent in both countries: see Andrea Boltho, "Growth," in *The European Economy: Growth and Crisis*, ed. Andrea Boltho (Oxford: Oxford University Press, 1982), 10, 22.

3. Quoted in Gordon Wright, *France in Modern Times: From the Enlightenment to the Present*, 5th ed. (New York: W. W. Norton, 1995), 411–412.

4. Stanley Hoffmann, "Paradoxes of the French Political Community," in *In Search of France,* ed. Stanley Hoffmann (New York: Harper, 1963), chap. 1.

5. Henry C. Galant, *Histoire politique de la sécurité sociale française, 1945–1952* (Paris: Armand Colin, 1955), chaps. 2–4.

6. Andrew Shonfield, *Modern Capitalism: The Changing Balance of Public and Private Power* (London: Oxford University Press, 1965), 66–67. Although German policymakers never fully embraced the Keynesian ideas prevalent elsewhere, the state nonetheless played an instrumental role in restructuring the postwar German political economy.

7. Ibid., 63–67.

8. Ibid., 74–80.

9. Tom Kemp, *Industrialization in Nineteenth-Century Europe* (London: Longman, 1985 [1969]), 96–100. As Gerald Feldman argues, the banks became particularly important once industrialization had gained significant momentum; in its initial stages, the process was supported more by the state than by the financial sector: see Gerald Feldman, "Responses to Banking Concentration in Germany, 1900–33," in *A Century of Banking Consolidation in Europe: The History and Archives of Mergers and Acquisitions,* ed. Manfred Pohl, Teresa Tortella, and Hermann van der Wee (Aldershot: Ashgate, 2001).

10. Jonah D. Levy, *Tocqueville's Revenge: State, Society, and Economy in Contemporary France* (Cambridge, Mass.: Harvard University Press, 1999), 36–37.

11. Ibid., 7. For the classic discussion of the continuities in the post-Revolutionary state, see Alexis de Tocqueville, *L'ancien régime et la Révolution,* 3rd ed. (Paris: Gallimard, 1857). In Tocqueville's formulation, "If centralization survived the Revolution unscathed, it is because it provided the Revolution with both its impetus and defining characteristic" (Tocqueville, *L'ancien régime et la Révolution,* 115). For a discussion of statist economic policy under Vichy, see Paxton, *Vichy France,* 210–220.

12. Levy, *Tocqueville's Revenge,* 7, 31; Jean-Jacques Rousseau, *The Social Contract,* trans. Maurice Cranston (London: Penguin, 1968 [1762]), 63–64.

13. Hoffmann, "Paradoxes of the French Political Community." One of the starkest indications of the extent of this transformation was the precipitous decline in agricultural employment, which shrank by more than 3 million, or 60 percent, between 1954 and 1975: William James Adams, *Restructuring the French Economy: Government and the Rise of Market Competition since World War II* (Washington, D.C.: Brookings Institution, 1989), 21.

14. Levy, *Tocqueville's Revenge,* 18.

15. Shonfield, *Modern Capitalism,* 126.

16. Ibid., 131; Richard F. Kuisel, *Capitalism and the State in Modern France: Renovation and Economic Management in the Twentieth Century* (Cambridge: Cambridge University Press, 1981), 17.

17. Ibid., 224.

18. Peter A. Hall, *Governing the Economy: The Politics of State Intervention in Britain and France* (New York: Oxford University Press, 1986), 141–142.

19. Ibid., 143.

20. Shonfield, *Modern Capitalism,* 126–127.

21. Kuisel, *Capitalism and the State in Modern France,* 252–259. Kuisel points out that this shift was reinforced by the activist ethos of the Ecole Nationale d'Administration (ENA) and its inculcation of a preference among the French elite for economic affairs.

The seminal study of the postwar French bureaucratic elite is Ezra Suleiman, *Politics, Power, and Bureaucracy in France: The Administrative Elite* (Princeton, N.J.: Princeton University Press, 1974).

22. Shonfield, *Modern Capitalism,* 148–150; Levy, *Tocqueville's Revenge,* 28.

23. John Zysman, *Governments, Markets, and Growth: Financial Systems and the Politics of Industrial Change* (Ithaca, N.Y.: Cornell University Press, 1983), chap. 3.

24. Ibid., 114.

25. Levy, *Tocqueville's Revenge,* 18.

26. Suzanne Berger, "Lame Ducks and National Champions: Industrial Policy in the Fifth Republic," in *The Fifth Republic at Twenty,* ed. William G. Andrews and Stanley Hoffmann (Albany: State University of New York Press, 1981), 294–295.

27. Galant, *Histoire politique de la sécurité sociale française,* 9–11.

28. Exceptions to this pattern of fragmentary and residual coverage emerged in major industrial centers, such as the coal-mining areas of Le Creusot and Montceau-les-Mines. There, employers established more comprehensive institutions of social protection and used company towns as a means of ensuring a stable labor pool.

29. As Bruno Palier points out, the Third Republic did witness some limited attempts to establish an obligatory, national system of social protection, including laws in 1889 (on abandoned or abused children), 1898 (on workplace accidents), 1910 (on pensions), and 1932 (on family assistance). These laws partially supplanted an earlier mixture of charity and locally based institutions: see Bruno Palier, *Gouverner la sécurité sociale: Les réformes du système français de protection sociale depuis 1945* (Paris: Presses Universitaires de France, 2002), 65–71.

30. Only in 1898 did the state recognize the mutual societies' legal right to exist and to elect their own representatives. For a detailed discussion of the pre-1940 antecedents of the French welfare state, see Galant, *Histoire politique de la sécurité sociale française,* chap. 1.

31. Palier, *Gouverner la sécurité sociale,* 73–74.

32. Marie-Thérèse Join-Lambert et al., eds., *Politiques sociales,* 2nd ed. (Paris: Presses de Sciences Po et Dalloz, 1997), 37–38.

33. Palier, *Gouverner la sécurité sociale,* 72.

34. Ibid., 75.

35. Peter Baldwin, *The Politics of Social Solidarity: Class Bases of the European Welfare State, 1875–1975* (Cambridge: Cambridge University Press, 1990), 163–186.

36. This performance was particularly remarkable when compared with earlier periods. Even during the relatively dynamic decade of the 1920s, for example, France's GDP grew by a "mere" 57 percent. While prewar growth was uneven on a year-to-year basis, furthermore, the economy grew in every year between 1958 and 1973: Adams, *Restructuring the French Economy,* 4–5.

37. Boltho, "Growth," 22, 34.

38. Christian Sautter, "France," in Boltho, *The European Economy,* 458. Following the 1958 devaluation, real wage growth plummeted from 9.9 percent in 1957 to negative 1.8 percent in 1958. Thereafter, the rate of increase grew once again, to 2.7 percent in 1960 and 6.8 percent in 1961, but then fell to 4.7 percent in 1962: Chris Howell, *Regulating Labor: The State and Industrial Relations Reform in Postwar France* (Princeton, N.J.: Princeton University Press, 1992), 57.

39. Sautter, "France," 449.

40. The degree of welfare-state expansion during this period is reflected in social-spending levels, which rose from 6.9 percent of GDP in 1950 to 14.3 percent in 1970, compared with a mere .9 percent in 1938: Join-Lambert et al., *Politiques sociales,* 41.

41. At 25 percent in 1955, the share of national income earned by the most prosperous 10 percent increased to about 27 percent in 1960 and 28 percent in 1968, then declined steadily over the following decade, reaching a level of about 25 percent in the late 1970s. Over the same ten-year period (1968–1978), the share of income going to the richest 5 percent declined from about 19 percent to about 17 percent: Tony Atkinson, Michel Glaude, and Lucile Olier, eds., *Inégalités économiques,* Rapport du Conseil d'Analyse Économique (Paris: La Documentation Française, 2001), 154–155.

42. Before 1933, Adenauer was a leader of the Catholic Zentrum Party and spent much of the war either in prison or on the run from the Gestapo.

43. Gerhard Lehmbruch, "The Institutional Embedding of Market Economies: The German 'Model' and Its Impact on Japan," in *The Origins of Nonliberal Capitalism: Germany and Japan in Comparison,* ed. Wolfgang Streeck and Kozo Yamamura (Ithaca, N.Y.: Cornell University Press, 2001), 80–81.

44. Quoted in ibid., 80.

45. Also called "Christian Socialists," social Catholics saw full employment and economic redistribution as desirable goals of public policy and emphasized the political and social responsibilities of all social and economic groups: ibid., 84–85.

46. Zysman, *Governments, Markets, and Growth,* 253. As Razeen Sally points out, such an expansive conception of state intervention in the pursuit of social welfare was not originally part of the Ordoliberal creed, which stressed self-help and individual responsibility rather than a developed welfare state: Razeen Sally, "The Social Market and Liberal Order," *Government and Opposition* 29 (Fall 1994): 461–476.

47. Peter Gourevitch, *Politics in Hard Times: Comparative Responses to International Economic Crises* (Ithaca, N.Y.: Cornell University Press, 1986), 171.

48. The political-economic institutions that emerged during this period were far from self-regulating, contrary to what many have suggested. Rather, they were the products of a significant degree of state intervention with respect to both their original construction and their subsequent development.

49. As many observers have pointed out, there are important differences between more purely corporatist systems and the German variant—notably, the existence of sectoral rather than peak-level wage bargaining. Accordingly, I use the terms "neocorporatism" and, more generally, "corporatism," loosely in the German context to refer to the country's relatively diffuse distribution of authority among political-economic actors.

50. Peter J. Katzenstein, *Policy and Politics in West Germany: The Growth of a Semi-Sovereign State* (Philadelphia: Temple University Press, 1987), chaps. 1, 3, 4.

51. These councils emerged from firm–worker alliances against Allied occupation forces, who wished to dismantle a number of large German companies.

52. For a full discussion, see Kathleen Thelen, *Union of Parts: Labor Politics in Postwar Germany* (Ithaca, N.Y.: Cornell University Press 1991), chap. 3.

53. Ibid., 81–83.

54. Kemp, *Industrialization in Nineteenth-Century Europe,* 96–100.

55. Richard Deeg, *Finance Capitalism Unveiled: Banks and the German Political Economy* (Ann Arbor: University of Michigan Press, 1999), 46–47.

56. Shonfield, *Modern Capitalism,* chap. 11.

57. Ibid., 249.

58. Philip Manow, "Welfare State Building and Coordinated Capitalism in Japan and Germany," in Streeck and Yamamura, *Origins of Nonliberal Capitalism,* 119.

59. Many of Bismarck's social policies were devised explicitly to preserve social peace in the wake of the depression of 1873–1878: ibid., 112.

60. These discrepancies in the treatment of blue-collar and white-collar workers reinforced the emerging self-definition of the latter as a coherent class: Jürgen Kocka, "Class Formation, Interest Articulation, and Public Policy: The Origins of the German White-Collar Class in the Late Nineteenth and Early Twentieth Centuries," in *Organizing Interests in Western Europe: Pluralism, Corporatism, and the Transformation of Politics,* ed. Suzanne Berger (Cambridge: Cambridge University Press, 1981).

61. Katzenstein, *Policy and Politics in West Germany,* 177.

62. Baldwin, *The Politics of Social Solidarity,* 273–275. The resulting coalition among liberals, the *Mittelstand* (SMEs that are often family-owned and traditionally have been an engine of economic and employment growth), trade unions, and the center-right enabled the government to pass the law over the objections of the SPD, which continued to clamor for a more universalistic system.

63. This system functioned quite smoothly during the 1950s and 1960s, when a growing economy (and rising wage levels) allowed increases in social contributions to remain modest. With average annual rates of economic growth at 4.4 percent and unemployment rates of a mere 1.1 percent, neither the effect of social contributions on job creation nor the financial balance of the pension system was much cause for concern: Fritz W. Scharpf, "Economic and Institutional Constraints of Full-Employment Strategies: Sweden, Austria, and West Germany, 1973–1982," in *Order and Conflict in Contemporary Capitalism,* ed. John H. Goldthorpe (Oxford: Clarendon Press, 1984), 258.

64. Katzenstein, *Policy and Politics in West Germany,* 178. This original conception has remained largely unchanged and is reflected in the Health and Social Security Ministry's official description: "Social assistance (*Sozialhilfe*) is there to ensure that anyone in need in the Federal Republic can still live a decent life. It is not some kind of charity." See Bundesministerium für Gesundheit und Soziale Sicherung, "German Social Security at a Glance" (Bonn: Bundesministerium für Gesundheit und Soziale Sicherung, 2003), 124.

65. Philip Manow and Eric Seils, "Adjusting Badly: The German Welfare State, Structural Change, and the Open Economy," in *Welfare and Work in the Open Economy, Volume 2: Diverse Responses to Common Challenges,* ed. Fritz W. Scharpf and Vivien A. Schmidt (Oxford: Oxford University Press, 2000), 270.

66. Andrew Glyn et al., "The Rise and Fall of the Golden Age," in *The Golden Age of Capitalism: Reinterpreting the Postwar Experience,* ed. Stephen A. Marglin and Juliet B. Schor (Oxford: Clarendon Press, 1990), 47.

67. Ibid., 43, 47.

68. Gerald A. Epstein and Juliet B. Schor, "Macropolicy in the Rise and Fall of the Golden Age," in Marglin and Schor, *The Golden Age of Capitalism,* 136. Philip Manow, "Social Insurance and the German Political Economy," Max-Planck-Institut für Gesellschaftsforschung Discussion Paper 97/2, November 1997, 40.

69. Thelen, *Union of Parts,* 32–33.

70. Glyn et al., "The Rise and Fall of the Golden Age," 73–87.

71. Michael J. Piore and Charles F. Sabel, *The Second Industrial Divide: Possibilities for Prosperity* (New York: Basic Books, 1984), chap. 6, esp. 184–187.

72. See, e.g., Epstein and Schor, "Macropolicy."

73. Glyn et al., "The Rise and Fall of the Golden Age," 42.

74. John Bispham and Andrea Boltho, "Demand Management," in Boltho, *The European Economy,* 313.

75. Christopher Allsopp, "Inflation," in Boltho, *The European Economy,* 73.

76. Howell, *Regulating Labor,* 61–73.

77. Levy, *Tocqueville's Revenge,* 39.

78. Ibid., 41–43. For a discussion of a policies designed to placate "dangerous" social groups, see John T. S. Keeler, "Corporatist Decentralization and Commercial Modernization in France: The Royer Law's Impact on Shopkeepers, Supermarkets, and the State," in *Socialism, the State, and Public Policy in France,* ed. Philip Cerny and Martin Schain (London: Frances Pinter, 1985).

79. Cited in Hall, *Governing the Economy,* 188.

80. CIASI was the heir to the Délégation à l'Aménagement du Territoire et à l'Action Régionale (DATAR), created in the 1960s to promote regional economic development: Levy, *Tocqueville's Revenge,* 42.

81. Berger, "Lame Ducks and National Champions," 300–306.

82. Levy, *Tocqueville's Revenge,* 19, 43–46.

83. Katzenstein, *Policy and Politics in West Germany,* 90–92.

84. Scharpf, "Economic and Institutional Constraints," 280–281.

85. These developments are described in detail in Deeg, *Finance Capitalism Unveiled,* chap. 5.

86. Wolfgang Streeck, "On the Institutional Conditions of Diversified Quality Production," in *Beyond Keynesianism: The Socio-Economics of Production and Full Employment,* ed. Egon Matzner and Wolfgang Streeck (Worcester: Edward Elgar, 1991), 21–61. Perhaps the most prominent of such works was Michel Albert, *Capitalisme contre capitalisme* (Paris: Seuil, 1991), which held Germany up as a model for French renewal.

87. In 1990, real GDP grew by an annual 5.7 percent (compared with 2.5 percent in France and 2.1 percent in the United Kingdom), inflation was a modest 2.7 percent (compared with 3.4 percent in France and 9.5 percent in Britain), and unemployment was 6.2 percent (compared with 9.4 percent in France and 5.9 percent in the United Kingdom). Germany was also relatively successful at controlling social expenditures, which in 1990 accounted for 23.2 percent of GDP, compared with 26.7 percent in France: Fritz W. Scharpf and Vivien A. Schmidt, "Statistical Appendix," in *Welfare and Work in the Open Economy, Volume 1: From Vulnerability to Competitiveness,* ed. Fritz W. Scharpf and Vivien A. Schmidt (Oxford: Oxford University Press, 2000), 338–341, 364.

88. By 1982, as the world entered a major recession, French government spending had increased by 27.6 percent, and policymakers were finding it increasingly difficult to maintain their spending commitments while containing exploding budget and trade deficits.

CHAPTER 3

1. Jonah D. Levy, *Tocqueville's Revenge: State, Society, and Economy in Contemporary France* (Cambridge, Mass.: Harvard University Press, 1999), 43.

2. Pierre Favier and Michel Martin-Roland, *La décennie Mitterrand, Volume 1: Les ruptures (1981–1984)* (Paris: Seuil, 1990), 25.

3. Ibid., 39.

4. Mark Kesselman, "The French Left and the Transformation of French Society: Sisyphus Revisited," in *The Fifth Republic at Twenty,* ed. William G. Andrews and Stanley Hoffmann (Albany: State University of New York Press, 1981), 197–200.

5. Levy, *Tocqueville's Revenge,* 40.

6. Favier and Martin-Roland, *La décennie Mitterrand,* 1:107.

7. Levy, *Tocqueville's Revenge,* 19.

8. The term "redistributive Keynesianism" is Peter Hall's, in *Governing the Economy: The Politics of State Intervention in Britain and France* (New York: Oxford University Press, 1986), 193–195.

9. Elie Cohen, *L'Etat brancardier: Politiques du déclin industriel (1974–1984)* (Paris: Calmann-Lévy, 1989), 309.

10. Levy, *Tocqueville's Revenge,* 260.

11. Jonah D. Levy, "France: Directing Adjustment?" in *Welfare and Work in the Open Economy, Volume II: Diverse Responses to Common Challenges,* ed. Fritz W. Scharpf and Vivien A. Schmidt (Oxford: Oxford University Press, 2000), 326.

12. Hall, *Governing the Economy,* 204.

13. Favier and Martin-Roland, *La décennie Mitterrand,* 1:131.

14. Cited in ibid., 132–133.

15. Levy, *Tocqueville's Revenge,* 44.

16. Levy, "France: Directing Adjustment?" 321. Peter A. Hall, "The State and the Market," in *Developments in French Politics,* ed. Peter A. Hall, Jack Hayward, and Howard Machin (London: Macmillan, 1994), 177.

17. Favier and Martin-Roland, *La décennie Mitterrand,* 1:111.

18. Ibid., 115.

19. Fritz W. Scharpf and Vivien A. Schmidt, "Statistical Appendix," in *Welfare and Work in the Open Economy, Volume 1: From Vulnerability to Competitiveness,* ed. Fritz W. Scharpf and Vivien A. Schmidt (Oxford: Oxford University Press, 2000), 359.

20. Michael Loriaux, *France after Hegemony: International Change and Financial Reform* (Ithaca, N.Y.: Cornell University Press, 1991), 215.

21. Favier and Martin-Roland, *La décennie Mitterrand,* 1:75.

22. Marc de Montalembert, ed., *La protection sociale en France,* 3rd ed. (Paris: La Documentation Française, 2001), 45.

23. Presaging more dramatic expansions later in the decade, the number of participants in various early-retirement schemes exploded from 213,000 in 1980 to 695,000 in 1983: ibid., 46.

24. Favier and Martin-Roland, *La décennie Mitterrand,* 1:117–119.

25. By 1982, the budget deficit had risen to 3 percent of GDP.

26. Inflation was 12.5 percent in 1981, 11.0 percent in 1982, and 9.3 percent in 1983, despite the advent of the international recession: Loriaux, *After Hegemony,* 216.

27. Hall, *Governing the Economy,* 198. In 1982, the volume of French exports declined by 1.7 percent while the volume of imports rose by 5.8 percent: Peter A. Hall, "The Evolution of Economic Policy under Mitterrand," in *The Mitterrand Experiment: Continuity and Change in Modern France,* ed. George Ross, Stanley Hoffmann, and Sylvia Malzacher (Oxford: Polity Press, 1987), 61.

28. The 1982 budget was based on predictions of a rate of GDP growth of 3.3 percent; actual growth was only 2.3 percent: Favier and Martin-Roland, *La décennie Mitterrand,* 1:405.

29. Levy, *Tocqueville's Revenge,* 46.

30. The value of the franc fell from 5.35 to the dollar in April 1981 to 8.60 in 1984: Hall, *Governing the Economy,* 199.

31. Levy, *Tocqueville's Revenge,* 46.

32. Loriaux, *After Hegemony,* 218.

33. Favier and Martin-Roland, *La décennie Mitterrand,* 1:427.

34. Ibid., 461.

35. For a discussion of the emergence of this dysfunctional economic strategy in the 1970s, see Suzanne Berger, "Lame Ducks and National Champions: Industrial Policy in the Fifth Republic," in *The Fifth Republic at Twenty,* ed. William G. Andrews and Stanley Hoffmann (Albany: State University of New York Press, 1981).

36. Levy, *Tocqueville's Revenge,* 47–48.

37. Cited in Favier and Martin-Roland, *La décennie Mitterrand,* 1:401. The translation into English is mine.

38. This account draws from Levy, *Tocqueville's Revenge,* 48–51, 55.

39. The erosion of support for the government was reflected in the 1982 regional elections, in which both the PS and PCF lost a number of seats to parties of the center-right: Favier and Martin-Roland, *La décennie Mitterrand,* 1:411–412.

In April 1981, 60 percent of the French public had a favorable opinion of the PS, compared with 30 percent unfavorable (the remaining 10 did not respond or had no opinion). By October 1985, the figures were 41 percent favorable and 47 percent unfavorable (11 percent did not respond or had no opinion): Alain Lancelot and Marie-Thérèse Lancelot, "The Evolution of the French Electorate: 1981–86," in Ross et al., *The Mitterrand Experiment,* 96.

40. Levy, *Tocqueville's Revenge,* 55.

41. Ibid., 63.

42. Pierre Favier and Michel Martin-Roland, *La décennie Mitterrand, Volume 2: Les épreuves (1984–1988)* (Paris: Seuil, 1991), 506–507.

43. Scharpf and Schmidt, "Statistical Appendix," 361; Organization for Economic Cooperation and Development (OECD), *Tax Ratios: A Critical Survey,* Tax Policy Studies, no. 5 (Paris: OECD, 2001), 67.

44. Levy, *Tocqueville's Revenge,* 63–64.

45. Scharpf and Schmidt, "Statistical Appendix," 359.

46. The franc stabilized after 1987 at about 3.4 francs to the mark, a level that it would maintain for the next six years: Jacques E. Le Cacheux, "The *Franc Fort* Strategy and the EMU," in *Remaking the Hexagon: The New France in the New Europe,* ed. Gregory Flynn (Boulder, Colo.: Westview Press, 1995), 74.

47. These moves and the development of the *franc fort* strategy are discussed in detail in David Ross Cameron, "From Barre to Balladur: Economic Policy in the Era of EMS," in Flynn, *Remaking the Hexagon,* 136–140. This shift in fiscal policy also reflected an altered conception of the sources of French competitiveness. Rather than easing pressures on exports through devaluation, which reduced the relative prices of French goods abroad, the nascent regime of "competitive disinflation" opted to promote competitiveness by reducing supply costs and promoting product innovation by French firms.

48. Levy, *Tocqueville's Revenge,* 64–65.

49. Ibid., 65, 334.

50. Favier and Martin-Roland, *La décennie Mitterrand,* 2:512.

51. Ibid., 2:510; Scharpf and Schmidt, "Statistical Appendix," 341.

52. As Levy points out, the limited results of the government's reforms were due partly to Chirac's reticence to be perceived as a sort of French Thatcher in the run-up to the 1988 presidential election, in which he planned to stand: Levy, *Tocqueville's Revenge,* 67–68.

53. After conservative Prime Minister Edouard Balladur took office in 1993, his administration picked up the program of privatization where Chirac had left off, selling off large portions of a broad array of companies, including state-owned banks, financial concerns, and steel and automobile manufacturers. Peter A. Hall, "The Evolution of Economic Policy," in *Developments in French Politics 2,* ed. Alain Guyomarch et al. (Houndmills, Basingstoke: Palgrave, 2001), 177.

54. In 1972, the *garantie de ressources licenciement* (GRL) was introduced as a complement to the FNE, which since 1963 had funded early-retirement benefits for dismissed workers. In addition to the GRL, which provided early retirees with 70 percent of their most recent salary, a number of additional measures were targeted at specific categories of employees, such as older female manual workers, who were considered particularly vulnerable: Conseil d'Orientation des Retraites, *Retraites: Renouveler le contrat social entre les générations* (Paris: La Documentation Française, 2002), 35–36.

55. Levy, "France: Directing Adjustment?" 327.

56. Dominique Taddei, ed., *Retraites choisies et progressives,* Rapport du Conseil d'Analyse Économique (Paris: La Documentation Française, 2000), 101.

57. Bernhard Ebbinghaus, "Any Way Out of 'Exit from Work'? Reversing the Entrenched Pathways of Early Retirement," in Scharpf and Schmidt, *Welfare and Work in the Open Economy,* 2:526.

58. Scharpf and Schmidt, "Statistical Appendix," 341.

59. Favier and Martin-Roland, *La décennie Mitterrand,* 2:68–69.

60. Conseil d'Orientation des Retraites, *Retraites: Renouveler le contrat social entre les générations,* 36.

61. Some of these schemes were managed by the state and some by UNEDIC. In 1984, the state assumed control over the FNE. Thereafter, both the state and UNEDIC undertook parallel expansions of the early-retirement system: see Taddei, *Retraites choisies et progressives,* 102; Marie-Thérèse Join-Lambert et al., eds., *Politiques sociales,* 2nd ed. (Paris: Presses de Sciences Po et Dalloz, 1997), 229–230.

62. Join-Lambert et al., *Politiques sociales,* 228. With unemployment still high, these schemes remained popular in the 1990s, when the number of participants began to increase once again. At about five hundred thousand in 1993, the total number of beneficiaries grew to nearly five hundred fifty thousand by 2001: Taddei, *Retraites choisies et progressives,* 100; Conseil d'Orientation des Retraites, *Retraites: Renouveler le contrat social entre les générations,* 38.

63. Taddei, *Retraites choisies et progressives,* 105.

64. This figure was among the lowest levels in the OECD. In 1990, for example, the activity rate for workers in this category was 67.8 percent in Britain, 70.4 percent in Sweden, and 54.5 percent in Germany: Join-Lambert et al., *Politiques sociales,* 230.

65. Ibid., 231.

66. Levy, *Tocqueville's Revenge,* 194–195.

67. Ibid., 195.

68. Scharpf and Schmidt, "Statistical Appendix," 341.

69. Bruno Palier, *Gouverner la sécurité sociale: Les réformes du système français de protection sociale depuis 1945* (Paris: Presses Universitaires de France, 2002), 283–287. For a trenchant critique of the French welfare state's inability to cope with the spread of economic precariousness in the 1980s and 1990s, see Pierre Rosanvallon, *La nouvelle question sociale: Repenser l'Etat-providence* (Paris: Seuil, 1995).

70. Favier and Martin-Roland, *La décennie Mitterrand,* 1:47–48. In 1983, government officials held a series of "reflective seminars" at which they debated how to proceed with industrial restructuring and compensatory social-protection measures.

71. Rocard became prime minister after the Socialists won the presidential and parliamentary elections in 1988. The development of French incomes policies experienced a hiatus during the neoliberal Chirac administration but resumed with the left's return to power.

72. De Montalembert, *La protection sociale en France,* 146.

73. Ibid., 147.

CHAPTER 4

1. The literature on the diplomacy of German reunification is vast: see Dennis L. Bark and David R. Gress, *A History of West Germany, Volume 2: Democracy and Its Discontents,* 2nd ed. (Oxford: Blackwell, 1993), part 13, chap. 1; Timothy Garton Ash, *In Europe's Name: Germany and the Divided Continent* (New York: Random House, 1993). The best full-length scholarly study of reunification is Charles S. Maier, *Dissolution: The Crisis of Communism and the End of East Germany* (Princeton, N.J.: Princeton University Press, 1997).

2. Gerald Opie, "Views of the *Wende,*" in *The New Germany: Social, Political and Cultural Challenges of Unification,* ed. Derek Lewis and John R. P. McKenzie (Exeter: University of Exeter Press, 1995), 48–49.

3. Wade Jacoby, *Imitation and Politics: Redesigning Modern Germany* (Ithaca, N.Y.: Cornell University Press, 2000), 131.

4. Gerhard A. Ritter, *Der Preis der deutschen Einheit* (Munich: Verlag C. H. Beck, 2006), 14.

5. Bark and Gress, *A History of West Germany,* 756.

6. Lowell Turner, *Fighting for Partnership: Labor and Politics in Unified Germany* (Ithaca, N.Y.: Cornell University Press, 1998); Jacoby, *Imitation and Politics,* chap. 5.

7. The revamping of the postal and telecommunications systems each cost DM 100 billion over the 1990s: Christopher Flockton, "Policy Agendas and the Economy in Germany and Europe," in *The New Germany in the East: Policy Agendas and Social Developments since Unification,* ed. Christopher Flockton, Eva Kolinsky, and Rosalind Pritchard (London: Frank Cass, 2000), 65.

8. Matthias Knuth, "Active Labor Market Policy and German Unification: The Role of Employment and Training Companies," in *Negotiating the New Germany: Can Social Partnership Survive?* ed. Lowell Turner (Ithaca, N.Y.: Cornell University Press, 1997), 72.

9. Philip Manow and Eric Seils, "Adjusting Badly: The German Welfare State, Structural Change, and the Open Economy," in *Welfare and Work in the Open Economy, Volume 2: Diverse Responses to Common Challenges,* ed. Fritz W. Scharpf and Vivien A. Schmidt (Oxford: Oxford University Press, 2000), 292–293.

10. At the end of 2003, the BA was renamed the Bundesagentur für Arbeit (Federal Labor Agency), reflecting semantically the prioritization of policies of labor-market activation.

11. Such accounts were particularly prevalent on the political left. Illustrative examples include the contributions in Hanna Behrend, ed., *German Unification: The Destruction of an Economy* (London: Pluto Press, 1995).

12. The uncompetitiveness of Eastern industry was significantly exacerbated by the terms of the currency union, which resulted in real wages that outstripped Eastern productivity rates and accelerated deindustrialization.

13. An estimate in June 1991 set the total cost of reunification at about DM 500 billion for the period up to 1994. This included DM 90 billion for social-insurance payments and infrastructure investments; DM 115 billion for the German Unity Fund; DM 50 billion for the repayment of East German debts to the Soviet Union; and DM 110 billion to cover the debts of East German firms: Bark and Gress, *A History of West Germany,* 759–760.

14. Kenneth Dyson, "The Economic Order—Still *Modell Deutschland*?" in *Developments in German Politics 2,* ed. Gordon Smith, William E. Paterson, and Stephen Padgett (Durham, N.C.: Duke University Press, 1996), 204–205; Karl Koch, "The German Economy: Decline or Stability?" in Lewis and McKenzie, *The New Germany,* 136–137.

15. Jürgen A. K. Thomaneck, "From Euphoria to Reality: Social Problems of Post-Unification," in Lewis and McKenzie, *The New Germany,* 8. Given the scale of environmental devastation in the East and the depth of its economic problems, such a landscape was unlikely either literally or metaphorically. In 1990, 92.6 percent of the population of Leipzig suffered from some sort of sulfur-dioxide-related health problem, and wastewater from factories was so dirty that 45 percent could not be made drinkable through any known process: Jeremy Cherfas, "East Germany Struggles to Clean Its Air and Water," *Science,* vol. 248, 20 April 1990, 295–296.

16. In the first five years after reunification, net transfers from West to East amounted to 5 percent of German GDP and 40 percent of the value added in the Eastern economy: Dyson, "The Economic Order," 205.

17. Knuth, "Active Labor Market Policy and German Unification," 69.

18. Christopher Flockton, "Economic Management and the Challenge of Reunification," in Smith et al., *Developments in German Politics 2,* 216.

19. Ibid., 219.

20. Manow and Seils, "Adjusting Badly," 289.

21. Henning Klodt, "Public Transfers and Industrial Restructuring in Eastern Germany," in *Ten Years of German Unification: Transfer, Transformation, Incorporation?* ed. Jörn Leonhard and Lothar Funk (Birmingham: Birmingham University Press, 2002), 216.

22. Flockton, "Policy Agendas and the Economy in Germany and Europe," 65.

23. The redefinition of lines of property ownership was rendered more complex by the need to identify rightful owners. After 1933, many holdings, disproportionately owned by Jews, were expropriated by the Nazis. After the war, many of these properties located in the Soviet zone of occupation became holdings of the East German state, and the records identifying lines of ownership either disappeared entirely or were very poorly maintained. As a result, after 1990 it became quite difficult—and sometimes impossible—to identify the rightful owners.

24. Roland Czada, "The German Political Economy in Flux," in Leonhard and Funk, *Ten Years of German Unification,* 157.

25. Flockton, "Economic Management and the Challenge of Reunification," 225.

26. Bark and Gress, *A History of West Germany,* 744.

27. The Treuhand's privatization strategy elicited a number of criticisms. Some argued that the agency adopted a "scorched earth" approach, selling off assets as quickly as possible rather than working to save viable enterprises and limit the negative effects of privatization on employment. Such contentions, however, are difficult to square with the Treuhand's substantial efforts to minimize job losses resulting from restructuring and privatization. For examples of such critiques, see Christopher S. Allen, "Institutions Challenged: German Unification, Policy Errors, and the 'Siren Song' of Deregulation," in Turner, *Negotiating the New Germany,* 149–150; Horst Kern and Charles F. Sabel, "Trade Unions and Decentralized Production: A Sketch of Strategic Problems in the West German Labor Movement," *Politics and Society* 194 (December 1991): 373–402.

28. Ritter, *Der Preis der deutschen Einheit,* 13.

29. That said, the banks' subsequent extent of investment in Eastern firms was disappointing. Although they were prepared to make long-term loans to troubled enterprises, banks were reluctant to purchase equity in them or to assist firms' restructuring efforts: Richard Deeg, *Finance Capitalism Unveiled: Banks and the German Political Economy* (Ann Arbor: University of Michigan Press, 1999), 190–199.

30. Flockton, "Economic Management and the Challenge of Reunification," 225–226.

31. Ibid., 227.

32. Ibid.

33. Czada, "The German Political Economy in Flux," 159.

34. Flockton, "Economic Management and the Challenge of Reunification," 225.

35. Flockton, "Policy Agendas and the Economy in Germany and Europe," 67.

36. This policy shift was formalized with the 1993 Solidarity Pact, adopted under union pressure, in which the government committed to long-term industrial policies in the East: Turner, *Fighting for Partnership,* 45.

37. That said, the government also undertook a number of efforts to promote the growth of SMEs, which, it was hoped, would be able to take advantage of lower labor costs in the East and hire many unemployed industrial workers. A prime example was the Kreditanstalt für Wiederaufbau, an agency that offered low-interest loans to promote the growth of the small-business sector: Flockton, "Policy Agendas and the Economy in Germany and Europe," 65, 69.

38. Klodt, "Public Transfers and Industrial Restructuring in Eastern Germany," 217.

39. Gary Herrigel, "The Limits of German Manufacturing Flexibility," in Turner, *Negotiating the New Germany,* 186. Elsewhere, Herrigel shows that this collapse accelerated a broader decline in the German machine-tool industry that had begun in the 1980s: Gary Herrigel, *Industrial Constructions: The Sources of German Industrial Power* (Cambridge: Cambridge University Press, 1996), 194–199. See also J. Nicholas Ziegler, *Governing Ideas: Strategies for Innovation in France and Germany* (Ithaca, N.Y.: Cornell University Press, 1997), chap. 4, esp. 128–129, 152–153.

40. Mark J. Jrolf, "The Politics of Restructuring Business Enterprises in the Former GDR: The Case of EKO Stahl," in *Dimensions of German Unification: Economic, Social,*

and Legal Analyses, ed. A. Bradley Shingleton, Marian J. Gibbon, and Kathryn S. Mack (Boulder, Colo.: Westview Press, 1995), 32.

41. Klodt, "Public Transfers and Industrial Restructuring in Eastern Germany," 218, 220.

42. Flockton, "Policy Agendas and the Economy in Germany and Europe," 65.

43. Ibid., 77–78.

44. Wade Jacoby uses the concept of "institutional transfer" to characterize the implantation of West German social partnership in the former GDR, as well as a series of other cases of German institutional "imitation" since World War II: Jacoby, *Imitation and Politics,* 11–12.

45. Turner, *Fighting for Partnership,* 2.

46. Ibid., 16.

47. Kirsten S. Wever, "Renegotiating the German Model: Labor–Management Relations in the New Germany," in Turner, *Negotiating the New Germany,* 217–218.

48. Michael G. Huelshoff, "The 'Storm before the Calm': Labor Markets, Unemployment, and Standort Deutschland," in *Breakdown, Breakup, Breakthrough: Germany's Difficult Passage to Modernity,* ed. Carl Lankowski (New York: Berghahn, 1999), 117.

49. For a discussion, see Kathleen Thelen and Ikuo Kume, "The Future of Nationally Embedded Capitalism: Industrial Relations in Germany and Japan," in *The End of Diversity? Prospects for German and Japanese Capitalism,* ed. Kozo Yamamura and Wolfgang Streeck (Ithaca, N.Y.: Cornell University Press, 2003).

50. Cited in Thomaneck, "From Euphoria to Reality," 29.

51. Steen Mangen, "German Welfare and Social Citizenship," in Smith et al., *Developments in German Politics 2,* 255–256.

52. Fritz W. Scharpf and Vivien A. Schmidt, "Statistical Appendix," in Scharpf and Schmidt, *Welfare and Work in the Open Economy,* 2:359, 364.

53. Manow and Seils, "Adjusting Badly," 293; Knuth, "Active Labor Market Policy and German Unification," 72. Eastern workers enjoyed access to this provision until 1992.

54. Dominique Taddei, ed., *Retraites choisies et progressives,* Rapport du Conseil d'Analyse Economique (Paris: La Documentation Française, 2000), 213.

55. By 1997, the number of workers in the new *Länder* participating in such schemes had declined to about 362,000: Organization for Economic Cooperation and Development, *OECD Economic Surveys, 1997–1998: Germany* (Paris: OECD, 1998), 100, 102.

56. Knuth, "Active Labor Market Policy and German Unification," 71, 75.

57. Ibid., 77.

58. The difference between registered and effective unemployment (including participants in job-creation and retraining schemes) can be considerable. In 1996, for example, the registered unemployment rate in the East was 15.1 percent, while the estimated total of both official and "hidden" unemployment was 28.9 percent: OECD, *OECD Economic Surveys, 1997–1998: Germany,* 100.

59. In 1991, for example, unemployment-insurance contributions were set at their highest level ever, primarily to finance ETC-like job-creation and retraining schemes. In 1991, employment offices in the East spent a total of DM 46 billion on active and passive labor-market measures, with only DM 7.5 billion collected from Eastern workers' social contributions. The rest was provided out of surpluses in Western social contributions

(64 percent) and federal revenues (36 percent): Knuth, "Active Labor Market Policy and German Unification," 73.

60. Alan B. Krueger and Jörn-Steffen Pischke, "A Comparative Analysis of East and West German Labor Markets: Before and after Unification," NBER Working Paper 4154, National Bureau of Economic Research, Cambridge, Mass., August 1992, 26.

61. Knuth, "Active Labor Market Policy and German Unification," 72; OECD, *OECD Economic Surveys, 1997–1998: Germany,* 100.

62. Knuth, "Active Labor Market Policy and German Unification," 72; OECD, *OECD Economic Surveys, 2000–2001: Germany* (Paris: OECD, 2001), 115.

63. OECD, *OECD Economic Surveys, 2000–2001: Germany,* 115.

64. Stephen J. Silvia, "Political Adaptation to Growing Labor Market Segmentation," in Turner, *Negotiating the New Germany,* 164.

65. Stewart Wood, "Labour Market Regimes under Threat? Sources of Continuity in Germany, Britain, and Sweden," in *The New Politics of the Welfare State,* ed. Paul Pierson (Oxford: Oxford University Press, 2001), 389.

66. Silvia, "Political Adaptation to Growing Labor Market Segmentation," 164.

67. Mangen, "German Welfare and Social Citizenship," 256.

68. OECD, *OECD Employment Outlook* (Paris: OECD, 2001), 24.

69. Mary Daly, "Globalization and Bismarckian Welfare States," in *Globalization and European Welfare States: Challenges and Changes,* ed. Robert Sykes, Bruno Palier, and Pauline M. Prior (Houndmills: Palgrave, 2001), 95.

70. Interview, Ludger Loop, Gesellschaft für Innovation, Beratung und Service, IG Metall, 13 March 2001.

71. Koch, "The German Economy," 145; and OECD, *OECD Economic Surveys, 1998–1999: Germany* (Paris: OECD, 1999), 37.

72. Hans-Werner Sinn, "Germany's Economic Unification: An Assessment after Ten Years," NBER Working Paper 7586, NBER, Cambridge, Mass., March 2000, 10–11.

73. Ibid., 117.

74. In 1998, 70 percent of new contracts signed in Eastern Germany were subsidized by either the federal or *Länder* governments: Pepper D. Culpepper, "Employers, Public Policy, and the Politics of Decentralized Cooperation in Germany and France," in *Varieties of Capitalism: The Institutional Foundations of Comparative Advantage,* ed. Peter A. Hall and David Soskice (Oxford: Oxford University Press, 2001), 289. See also Peter A. Hall and David Soskice, *Creating Cooperation: How States Develop Human Capital in Europe* (Ithaca, N.Y.: Cornell University Press, 2003), chap. 4.

75. Bundesagentur für Arbeit, *Der Arbeits- und Ausbildungsmarkt in Deutschland* (Nuremberg: BA, 2008), 47–48.

76. In 1995–1996, the percentage of Easterners without basic life necessities was 15 percent, nearly double the rate in Western Germany (8 percent): Wolfgang Voges and Olaf Jürgens, "The Dynamics of Social Exclusion in Germany: Solving the East–West Dilemma?" in *The Dynamics of Social Exclusion in Europe: Comparing Austria, Germany, Greece, and the UK,* ed. Eleni Apospori and Jane Millar (Cheltenham: Edward Elgar, 2003), 73–75.

77. OECD, *OECD Economic Surveys, 2000–2001: Germany,* 107; idem, *OECD Economic Surveys, 2004: Germany* (Paris: OECD, 2004), 31

78. Flockton, "Policy Agendas and the Economy in Germany and Europe," 217–219.

CHAPTER 5

1. Andrew Shonfield, *Modern Capitalism: The Changing Balance of Public and Private Power* (Oxford: Oxford University Press, 1965), 64.

2. Progressive income taxes and expanded welfare benefits were to act as "automatic stabilizers" by supporting demand during periods of rising unemployment and increasing tax and social-contribution receipts during periods of rising inflation: see Andrea Boltho, ed., *The European Economy: Growth and Crisis* (Oxford: Oxford University Press, 1982), 170–179, 290–300.

3. Richard F. Kuisel, *Capitalism and the State in Modern France: Renovation and Economic Management in the Twentieth Century* (Cambridge: Cambridge University Press, 1985), 248–252; Jonah D. Levy, *Tocqueville's Revenge: State, Society, and Economy in Contemporary France* (Cambridge, Mass.: Harvard University Press, 1999), 18; Shonfield, *Modern Capitalism*, 148–150.

4. Andrew Glyn et al., "The Rise and Fall of the Golden Age," in *The Golden Age of Capitalism: Reinterpreting the Postwar Experience*, ed. Stephen A. Marglin and Juliet B. Schor (Oxford: Clarendon Press, 1990), 61.

The Bundesbank's tight monetary policies and the prevailing conception that the social market economy was inherently self-regulating precluded expansionary, countercyclical public spending, and high interest rates periodically drove the country into recession. Between 1967 and 1973, however, the social democrats embarked on a period of Keynesian macroeconomic policies, properly so called: see Fritz Scharpf, "Economic and Institutional Constraints of Full-Employment Strategies: Sweden, Austria, and West Germany, 1973–1982," in *Order and Conflict in Contemporary Capitalism*, ed. John H. Goldthorpe (Oxford: Clarendon Press, 1984), 274–286; Peter A. Hall, *Governing the Economy: The Politics of State Intervention in Britain and France* (New York: Oxford University Press, 1986), chap. 9.

5. By 1995, health-care costs had reached an all-time high of 9.6 percent and 9.5 percent of GDP in Germany and France, respectively. The numbers for pensions were even more alarming, at 11.1 percent of GDP in Germany, projected to rise to 18.4 percent by 2040, and 10.6 percent, to increase to 14.3 percent, in France: the health data are cited in Patrick Hassenteufel, *Les médecins face à l'Etat: Une comparaison européenne* (Paris: Presses de la Fondation Nationale des Sciences Politiques, 1997). The pension data are drawn from John Myles and Paul Pierson, "Reforming Public Pensions," paper presented at the New Politics of the Welfare State conference, Harvard University Center for European Studies, Cambridge, Mass., 5–7 December 1997.

The Maastricht criteria, later subsumed into the Stability and Growth Pact for European Economic and Monetary Union, limited budget deficits at 3 percent and national debt at 60 percent of GDP. By 1993, the budget deficit had risen to 3.5 percent of GDP in Germany and 6.1 percent in France. By the same year, social expenditures had risen to record levels (29.2 percent of GDP in Germany and 29.7 percent in France), with domestic taxation at some of the highest levels since World War II (39 percent in Germany and 43.9 percent in France): the data are from Fritz W. Scharpf and Vivien A. Schmidt, "Statistical Appendix," in *Welfare and Work in the Open Economy, Volume I: From Vulnerability to Competitiveness*, ed. Fritz W. Scharpf and Vivien A. Schmidt (Oxford: Oxford University Press, 2000), various tables.

6. Gøsta Esping-Andersen, *The Three Worlds of Welfare Capitalism* (Princeton, N.J.: Princeton University Press, 1990), esp. chap. 2. While Esping-Andersen draws heavily from Karl Polanyi's account of the limits of labor's commodification, Polanyi sees these limits as inherent products of the imposition of a market economy, whereas Esping-Andersen treats de-commodification as a deliberate achievement of social policy. As a result of this conceptual confusion, Esping-Andersen's account tends to be at once too optimistic about the capacity of social policies to promote economic independence and too pessimistic about workers' ability to achieve such within the labor market. The essence of economic vulnerability is not exposure to the labor market per se but, rather, the unavailability of stable and adequate income when workers are unable to compete successfully.

For an in-depth discussion, see Mark I. Vail, "From 'Welfare without Work' to 'Buttressed Liberalization': The Shifting Dynamics of Labor-Market Adjustment in France and Germany," *European Journal of Political Research* 47, no. 3 (May 2008): 334–358.

7. Structural unemployment is the level of unemployment below which an economy, GDP held constant, cannot be reduced without producing increases in inflation. The concept is often referred to as the non-accelerating inflation rate of unemployment (NAIRU), set by long-run growth and technological trends rather than short-term public policy. There is intense debate about the level of NAIRU and even about its existence. For a brief discussion, see Jean Pisani-Ferry, *Plein emploi,* Rapport du Conseil d'Analyse Economique (Paris: La Documentation Française, 2000), 172–173.

8. Scharpf and Schmidt, "Statistical Appendix," 341.

9. Ibid. Even according to the more restrictive OECD definitions, unemployment had reached 9.9 percent by 1997: Organization for Economic Cooperation and Development, *OECD Employment Outlook* (Paris: OECD, 2001), 208.

10. For a discussion, see Philip Manow and Eric Seils, "Adjusting Badly: The German Welfare State, Structural Change, and the Open Economy," in *Welfare and Work in the Open Economy, Volume 2: Diverse Responses to Common Challenges,* ed. Fritz W. Scharpf and Vivien A. Schmidt (Oxford: Oxford University Press, 2000).

11. Scharpf and Schmidt, "Statistical Appendix," 346.

12. In 1999, for example, the ratio of the number of temporary jobs in the goods-producing sector compared to their prevalence in the economy as a whole was .96 and .92 in France and Germany, respectively. By contrast, the same ratio for the French and German service sectors was 1.02 and 1.05: OECD, *OECD Employment Outlook,* 118, 122.

13. Ibid., 214, 218–219.

14. As in other areas of French politics, economic discontent tends to result in demands on the state for solutions, thereby raising the political stakes for policymakers. In the words of Chris Howell, "The state no longer feels able to leave labor regulation to the market. . . . Not only wage demands but the whole constellation of social relations and class struggle between capital and labor [have been] displaced upward and become focused on the state": Chris Howell, *Regulating Labor: The State and Industrial Relations Reform in Postwar France* (Princeton, N.J.: Princeton University Press, 1992), 20.

15. Interview, Stéphane Le Foll, Cabinet Director of the First Secretary, Parti Socialiste, 11 April 2002.

16. For example, in 1995 President Jacques Chirac vowed to end the French "social fracture," and in 1998, newly elected German Chancellor Gerhard Schröder pledged to reduce the number of jobless to fewer than 3.5 million in his first term in office.

17. In France, political pressures to address unemployment were exacerbated by a wave of layoffs in the early 2000s, which were increasingly seen as *licenciements boursiers*, or layoffs for the sake of short-term shareholder value.

18. For an analysis of the dilemmas of labor-market policymaking in corporatist countries, see Anton C. Hemerijck and Mark I. Vail, "The Forgotten Center: State Activism and Corporatist Adjustment in Holland and Germany," in *The State after Statism: New State Activities in the Age of Liberalization*, ed. Jonah D. Levy (Cambridge, Mass.: Harvard University Press, 2006), 57–92.

19. In 1979, for example, there were 20,000 layoffs in the French steel industry: Anthony Daley, *Steel, State, and Labor: Mobilization and Adjustment in France* (Pittsburgh: University of Pittsburgh Press, 1996), 127.

20. Marie-Thérèse Join-Lambert et al., *Politiques sociales*, 2nd ed. (Paris: Presses de Sciences Po et Dalloz, 1997), 198.

21. Jacques Bouchoux and Marc Hervelin, *A chaque état son chômage* (Paris: Hatier, 1991), 46.

22. This provision was characteristic of the French response to the near-revolution of May 1968 and the rise of unemployment after 1973. For a discussion, see Levy, *Tocqueville's Revenge*, 39–43.

23. Interview, Frédéric Bruggeman, Syndex, 15 February 2002.

24. The law also required the consultation of experts and set a mandatory three-week waiting and consultation period between the announcement and implementation of redundancies.

25. Created in 1963 as a sort of catch-all fund for a wide variety of labor-market policies, from training to supplemental unemployment benefits, the FNE was originally understood as a discretionary tool to bring labor supply and demand into equilibrium. With the advent of mass unemployment, however, the FNE became essentially a revenue source for early-retirement schemes, accounting for more than a third of their financing after 1983: Dominique Taddei, ed., *Retraites choisies et progressives*, Rapport du Conseil d'Analyse Economique (Paris: La Documentation Française, 2000), 103; Daley, *Steel, State, and Labor*, 35–36.

26. Taddei, *Retraites choisies et progressives*, 100–102.

27. Created by a convention between employers and unions in 1958, UNEDIC remained structurally bipartite until 2008 and still retains significant authority for administering and defining the parameters of unemployment insurance: Bruno Palier, *Gouverner la sécurité sociale: Les réformes du système français de protection sociale depuis 1945* (Paris: Presses Universitaires de France, 2002), esp. 356–361; Taddei, *Retraites choisies et progressives*, 101–102.

28. Although policymakers scaled back these programs somewhat in the 1990s, the accumulated effects of twenty years of reliance on these schemes left France with one of the lowest activity rates for older workers in the OECD (41.5 percent among male workers in 1995): Taddei, *Retraites choisies et progressives*, 100; Daley, *Steel, State, and Labor*, 34.

29. An illustrative episode of such political pressures was the controversy surrounding Prime Minster Edouard Balladur's introduction of an "insertion wage" for younger workers, known as the SMIC-*jeunes*. Anticipating the logic of the CPE (*contrat première embauche*) of Dominique de Villepin in 2006, the measure proposed allowing firms to hire younger workers at 80 percent of the minimum wage but was withdrawn in the face

of protests. For details, see Jonah D. Levy, "France: Directing Adjustment?" in Scharpf and Schmidt, *Welfare and Work in the Open Economy,* 2:333.

30. This increasing imbalance of union–employer power derived from the decentralization of wage bargaining, which was increasingly occurring at the firm level, and the deindustrialization of the French economy, which eroded unions' traditional power base: Howell, *Regulating Labor,* 219–220.

31. As Howell points out, the decentralization of wage bargaining was a legacy of the 1982 Auroux Laws, which privileged firm-level works councils over unions: ibid., chaps. 7–8.

32. Join-Lambert et al., *Politiques sociales,* 279, 305–307.

33. The impact of the law itself, however, was somewhat disappointing. By the end of 1995, the law had resulted in only five sectoral accords (out of 126 recognized sectors) and sixty-eight firm-level deals: ibid., 307.

34. By contrast, the 1993 law provided for only a 10 percent reduction in work time and failed to specify social-security exemptions, which were to be negotiated case by case.

35. Bernard Brunhes et al., 35 *heures: Le temps du bilan* (Paris: Desclée de Brouwer, 2001), 17–18.

36. As of 1997, part-time employment accounted for nearly 17 percent of all French jobs, a figure more than double that of the early 1980s: Levy, *Tocqueville's Revenge,* 247. For concise discussions of the *loi Robien,* see Dominique Méda, *Le partage du travail* (Paris: La Documentation Française, 1997), 53–54; Join-Lambert et al., *Politiques sociales,* 318.

37. The danger of the law's defensive wing lay in the difficulty of verifying that firms not fabricate "planned" layoffs to take advantage of the plan's generous subsidies. One mechanism for avoiding such fraud was recourse to a 1993 measure requiring any firm applying for subsidies under the *loi Robien* to present an approved *plan social.*

38. Levy, "France: Directing Adjustment?" 338.

39. The incentives to employers were broadly similar to those offered by the *loi Robien,* with an annual subsidy of FFr 9,000 (€1,372) per worker offered in exchange for a 10 percent reduction in work time against a 6 percent increase in payrolls, and a payment of FFr 14,000 (€2,134) for a 15 percent reduction in time against a 9 percent increase in the number of workers. These subsidies were to decline by FFr 1,000 (€152) per year until they reached FFr 5,000 (€762) in 2002.

40. In July 2000, these exemptions averaged FFr 21,500 (€3,278) for workers earning the minimum wage, declining as wages increased to FFr 4,000 (€610) at the ceiling of 1.8 times the minimum wage: Direction de l'Animation de la Recherche, des Etudes, et des Statistiques (DARES), "Le passage à 35 heures vu par les employeurs," *Premières Synthèses* (April 2002): 10.

41. Agence France-Presse wire service, 14 October 1997.

42. Interview, Jean Pisani-Ferry, Ecole Polytechnique and Chargé de Mission au Trésor, 20 August 2003.

43. The government would increasingly blame employers for the law's failure, a strategy that played well among the left's core constituencies and deflected blame from the government.

44. According to one Labor Ministry official, Gandois's resignation was prompted by a "misunderstanding" between Jospin and Gandois, who had met secretly before the laws

had been made public. Gandois had assumed that his demands for substantive negotiations between the government and social partners over the measures' details had been incorporated into the laws: interview, Dominique Libault, Chef de Service adjoint au Directeur, Direction de la Sécurité Sociale, Ministère de l'Emploi et de la Solidarité, 7 February 2002.

45. See Levy, *Tocqueville's Revenge,* 61–62, on Gattaz's stewardship. For a discussion of MEDEF's political strategy in the late 1990s, see Isabelle Mandraud and Caroline Monnot, "Comment le Medef organise son coup d'état permanent," *Le Monde Economie,* 3 April 2001, I.

46. Interview, Chargée de Mission, Délégation Générale à l'Emploi et à la Formation Professionnelle, Département Synthèses, Ministère de l'Emploi et de la Solidarité, 21 March 2002.

47. In the words of Denis Kessler, then second in command at MEDEF and the architect of MEDEF's reform agenda, employers' primary objection centered on the state's intrusion and the continued "atrophy of civil society": interview, Denis Kessler, president, Fédération Française des Sociétés d'Assurances, 15 May 2002.

48. The employment effects of the thirty-five-hour laws have been a subject of debate. For an overview, see Brunhes et al., *35 heures.*

49. Marc de Montalembert, ed., *La protection sociale en France,* 4th ed. (Paris: La Documentation Française, 2004), 53.

50. "The Gaullist Revolutionary," *Economist,* 12–18 May 2007, 24–26.

51. Etienne Lefebvre, "Heures supplémentaires: Vers un régime avantageux avec garde-fous," *Les Echos,* 4 June 2007, 3.

52. Jean-Francis Pécresse, "ISF, 35 heures, retraites: Vraies réformes, fausses victoires," *Les Echos,* 2 June 2008, 14.

53. These factors weakened the unions' mobilization against the reform, with fewer than 500,000 people participating in a demonstration on 17 June and François Chérèque, leader of the CFDT, reduced to declaring that "the repercussions of the reform will be felt after the summer is over, when workers will realize that they have been duped": as quoted in Derek Perrotte, "35 heures: Les mobilisations limitées confortent l'exécutif dans sa volonté de réforme," *Les Echos,* 18 June 2008, 2.

54. Etienne Lefebvre, "Représentativité: Le chef de l'Etat salue la 'position commune' des partenaires sociaux," *Les Echos,* 21 April 2008, 4.

55. Interview, Alain Petitjean, CFDT, 1 July 2008.

56. Palier, *Gouverner la sécurité sociale,* 222.

57. The data are from the website of the Ministère du Travail, des Relations Sociales et de la Solidarité, available online at http://www.travail-solidarite.gouv.fr (accessed 13 April 2009).

58. Ernest-Antoine Seillière, "Indispensable et fragile refondation sociale," *Le Monde,* 6 December 2000, 16.

59. Interview, Kessler, 15 May 2002.

60. This famous statement was made in the context of an interview on national television about the effects of and potential government reaction to Michelin's announcement of major layoffs and submission of a *plan social* to the government.

61. The other significant reform to come out of the Refondation Sociale involved modest changes to private-sector complementary pensions in 2001, which followed MEDEF's proposals to index benefits to inflation and slightly raise contribution rates and

lower replacement rates. Claiming that it would not "be responsible for the bankruptcy" of the system, MEDEF threatened to withdraw from the system's administration if its proposals were not accepted. Hoping to protect the legitimacy of the bipartite management structure in which they had a significant political stake, the CFDT and the CFTC signed the accord, which was duly approved by the government: interview, Francis Bazile, MEDEF, 19 November 2001; Conseil d'Orientation des Retraites, *Retraites: Renouveler le contrat social entre les générations* (Paris: La Documentation Française, 2001), 74.

62. This account is confirmed by accounts on all sides of the debate, from MEDEF to UNEDIC and members of the government including, but not limited to, Dominique Chertier, Directeur Général, UNEDIC, 19 November 2001; Bernard Boisson, Conseiller Social, MEDEF, 24 October 2001; and Jean-François Chadelat, inspector general, Inspection Générale des Affaires Sociales, 3 October 2001.

63. In an allusion to the *plan social* at the tire company, the government added a "Michelin amendment," which obliged firms to negotiate a thirty-five-hour work week before proceeding with layoffs.

64. "Le projet de loi sur les licenciements économiques: Un piège pour les salariés?" *Les Echos,* 24 October 2001, 56.

65. Dominique Seux, "Les députés élargissent la suspension de la loi anti-licenciements," *Les Echos,* 4 December 2002, 3; idem, "Loi sur les licenciements: Fillon résiste à la pression de l'aile libérale de la majorité," *Les Echos,* 6 December 2002, 4.

66. "Frankreich drängt Arbeitslose; Präsident Sarkozy will Zumutbarkeitsregeln verschärfen," *Frankfurter Allgemeine Zeitung,* 7 May 2007, 12.

67. "Faut-il sanctionner les chômeurs?" *Alternatives Economiques,* no. 270 (June 2008): 7.

68. Even as he has tightened restrictions on unemployment insurance, Sarkozy has introduced other measures designed to encourage the unemployed to find work and to provide basic income support. One such policy is the *revenu de solidarité active* (RSA), which, unlike the RMI, allows workers to combine income from a low-paying job and state benefits up to a certain threshold. Initially experimental on the departmental level, the benefit was extended nationwide on 1 June 2009: For a discussion, see Chapter 7 in this volume and Mireille Elbaum, *Economie politique de la protection sociale* (Paris: Presses Universitaires de France, 2008), 128–129.

69. The merger is designed to save money while offering more coherent support services to the unemployed. MEDEF strongly supported the merger, but the unions opposed a move that they saw as an effort to intensify pressure on the jobless while eroding the social partners' influence. Though the fusion will effectively end the bipartite structure of job-placement services, which will be administered by a single *Pôle emploi,* or employment center, unemployment benefits will remain the purview of unions and employers: interview, Bruno Lucas, Directeur Général Adjoint, ANPE, 4 July 2008. For a discussion, see Lucie Robequain, "Fusion ANPE-Assedic: Les sources d'économies possibles se dessinent," *Les Echos,* 4 January 2008, 3; Etienne Lefebvre, "Le gouvernement assigne des objectifs ambitieux à 'Pôle emploi'," *Les Echos,* 17 October 2008, 3; Elbaum, *Economie politique de la protection sociale,* 125–126.

70. "CFDT et FO critiques sur le projet d'offre raisonnable d'emploi," *Les Echos,* 27 May 2008, 3.

71. Interview, François-Xavier Selleret, Conseiller auprès du Ministre, Ministère du Travail, des Relations Sociales et de la Solidarité, 16 July 2008. For example, a poll

conducted in 2008 showed that 52 percent wanted the government to go further with work-time reform, despite a precipitous decline in Sarkozy's approval ratings: "The Reformist President," *Economist,* 26 July–1 August 2008, 60–61.

72. In late December 2008, the prospects of a deteriorating labor market in the wake of deepening economic recession prompted the social partners to increase such support. The accord reduced the required length of employment for workers to become eligible to receive unemployment insurance from six out of the last twenty-two months to four months out of the last twenty-eight; increased the maximum benefit period from twenty-three to twenty-four months; and set the number of days of employed contributions equal to the number of days of benefits for eligible workers. For details, see Leila de Comarmond, "Un jour d'indemnisation par jour travaillé," *Les Echos,* 26 December 2008, 3.

73. My calculations; Pisani-Ferry, *Plein emploi,* 29.

74. OECD, *OECD in Figures: Statistics on the Member Countries* (Paris: OECD, 2001), 18; Elbaum, *Economie politique de la protection sociale,* 289; OECD, *OECD Economic Surveys: France* (Paris: OECD, 2001), 32; Observatoire Français des Conjunctures Economiques, *L'économie française 2008* (Paris: La Découverte, 2007), 49.

75. That said, unemployment rates for workers age fifty-five and older increased significantly between 1994 and 2005 and remain above the OECD average: OECD, *OECD Employment Outlook* (Paris: OECD, 2006), 37.

76. Between 1975 and 1985, during the height of France's use of early retirement, activity rates for this group fell from 67.1 percent to 46.7 percent. In the ensuing decade, by contrast, the rate declined from 46.7 percent to 38.7 percent. In 2005, the activity rate for workers age fifty-five to fifty-nine had declined to 54.5 percent and was 13.0 percent for workers age sixty to sixty-four: Taddei, *Retraites choisies et progressives,* 132; Elbaum, *Economie politique de la protection sociale,* 295.

77. Observatoire Français des Conjunctures Economiques, *L'économie française: 2002* (Paris: La Découverte, 2002), 59.

78. "Le chômage recule grâce aux emplois aidés," *Le Monde,* 29 October 2005, 1, 6.

79. Lucie Robequain, "A 7,5 percent, le taux de chômage revient à son niveau de 1983," *Les Echos,* 7 March 2008, 5.

80. Interview, Selleret.

81. Interview, Eric Aubry, Conseiller Social, Cabinet du Premier Ministre, 10 June 2008.

82. Leila de Comarmond, "Représentativité: Le Medef cherche un accord avec la CFDT et la CGT," *Les Echos,* 9 April 2008, 3.

83. This scandal involved two key components. First, during mid- to late 2007, it was discovered that Denis Gautier-Sauvagnac, former head of the UIMM, had withdrawn more than €21 million in cash from secret accounts and directed much of it to unions to prevent labor disputes. Just as this shady practice was coming to light, it was discovered that the UIMM had paid Gautier-Sauvagnac €1.5 million to step down in November. The scandal was a major embarrassment for MEDEF and shifted the organization to a more moderate position by ending the dominance of its most aggressively neoliberal constituency. For details, see Guillaume Delacroix, "L'UIMM fait bloc face à la crise tout en calmant le jeu avec le Medef," *Les Echos,* 4 March 2008, 3; "Des comptes opaques au service de 'gens très honorables'," *Le Monde,* 24 July 2008, 3; Katrin Bennhold, "Golden Parachute Feeds French Ire over Lobbyist," *International Herald Tribune,* 4 March 2008, 12.

84. This change in strategy has apparently played well among workers, whose support for the CGT in the December 2008 *elections prud'hommales* increased by 1.6 percent, while the CFDT and FO lost support. These elections select councils responsible for resolving disputes between workers and employers and are widely seen as barometers of support for particular unions: interview, Xavier Lacoste, director-general, Altedia, and former Conseiller Social du Ministre de l'Economie et des Finances, 17 July 2008; Derek Perrotte, "Dans la foulée des élections prud'homales, les syndicats ont élevé leurs exigences," *Les Echos,* 26 December 2008, 2.

85. Lefebvre, "Représentativité," 4.

86. Interview, Pierre-Alain de Malleray, Conseiller, Ministère du Travail, des Relations Sociales et de la Solidarité, 1 July 2008.

87. Derek Perrotte and Lucie Robequain, "Négociation, temps de travail: Les nouvelles règles du jeu," *Les Echos,* 18 June 2008, 2.

88. Interview, Lacoste.

89. While the social partners manage social-security funds in both France and Germany, in the latter the state's signature has normally not been required for changes in policies such as unemployment insurance.

90. According to one observer linked to the government, the Schröder administration felt that the urgency of reform should not obscure the need to preserve social solidarity even if it chose to pursue this goal through market-like mechanisms. At the same time, the government realized that state intervention in the labor market would expose many problems, such as the unemployment "hidden" by BA training and job schemes: interview, Michael Alvarez, Heinrich Böll Stiftung, 20 October 2000.

91. Interview, Eden Andreas, Bundesanstalt für Arbeit, 18 April 2001.

92. OECD, *OECD Economic Surveys, 2000–2001: Germany* (Paris: OECD, 2001), 29. My calculations are from data in Stewart Wood, "Labour Market Regimes under Threat? Sources of Continuity in Germany, Britain, and Sweden," in *The New Politics of the Welfare State,* ed. Paul Pierson (Oxford: Oxford University Press, 2001), 384.

93. By 1999, the percentage of German private-sector jobs represented by services had risen to 60.2 percent of all employment, from 51.1 percent in 1989: OECD, *OECD in Figures,* 32; idem, *OECD Economic Surveys, 2000–2001: Germany,* 138.

94. Elisabeth Niejahr and Wolfgang Uchatius, "Schröder auf Jobsuche," *Die Zeit,* vol. 10, 1 March 2001, 18.

95. Herbert Kitschelt and Wolfgang Streeck, "From Stability to Stagnation: Germany at the Beginning of the Twenty-First Century," in *Germany: Beyond the Stable State,* ed. Herbert Kitschelt and Wolfgang Streeck (London: Frank Cass, 2004), 1–34.

96. Bundesanstalt für Arbeit, *Annual Report 1999* (Nuremberg: BA, 2000), 23; OECD, *OECD Economic Surveys, 2000–2001: Germany,* 37.

97. The law served as a model for exceptions to collective wage agreements to preserve jobs. The most notable of these deals was that of Volkswagen, in 1993, which subsequently served as a model for a similar 1994 deal across the metalworking sector: Stephen J. Silvia, "Political Adaptation to Growing Labor Market Segmentation," in *Negotiating the New Germany: Can Social Partnership Survive?* ed. Lowell Turner (Ithaca, N.Y.: Cornell University Press, 1997), 169–171.

98. Christopher Flockton, "Economic Management and the Challenge of Reunification," in *Developments in German Politics 2,* ed. Gordon Smith, William E. Paterson, and Stephen Padgett (London: Macmillan, 1996), 222–223. See also Wolfgang Streeck, "No

Longer the Century of Corporatism: Das Ende des 'Bündnisses für Arbeit'," Max-Planck-Institut für Gesellschaftsforschung Working Paper 03/04, May 2003, 5.

99. This account is supported by an expert who participated in the closed negotiations of the Bündnis: interview, 29 July 2007.

100. For a skeptical analysis of the Bündnis, see Wolfgang Streeck, "Industrial Relations: From State Weakness as Strength to State Weakness as Weakness: Welfare Corporatism and the Private Use of the Public Interest," in *Governance in Contemporary Germany: The Semisovereign State Revisited,* ed. Simon Green and William E. Paterson (Cambridge: Cambridge University Press, 2005), 138–164.

101. The Bündnis came under repeated attacks for failing to address the inflexibility of the German labor market. Some portrayed it as a cartel inherently incapable of addressing unemployment and claimed that the government cynically used it to create a veneer of social dialogue: see "Der Fehler ist System: Das Bündnis für Arbeit schafft keine Jobs," *Die Zeit,* vol. 10, 1 March 2001, 1.

102. Interview, Michael Vollert, Abteilung II Politik, Referent für Sozial- und Gesundheitspolitk, SPD Parteivorstand, 8 November 2000.

103. Konstantin von Hammerstein and Michael Sauga, "Das System ist faul," *Der Spiegel,* vol. 21, 21 May 2001, 96–97.

104. SPD and Bündnis 90/Die Grünen Bundestagsfraktionen, "Zur Reform der Arbeitsförderung: Eckpunkte der Fraktionen SPD und Bündnis 90/Die Grünen vom 3. Juli 2001 für ein Job-Aktivierien, Qualifizieren, Trainieren, Investieren, Vermitteln-Gesetz," July 2001.

105. Even among German liberals, there is little support for mass privatization of social and labor-market policies. At the same time, understandings of the Social Market Economy vary in the degree to which the system's market foundations or social components are emphasized. Some argue that Erhard's original conception assumed the existence of responsible social groups and that it had been corrupted by state dominance: interviews, Carl Graf Hohenthal, *Frankfurter Allgemeine Zeitung,* 13 October 2000, and Dr. Uwe Bentrup and Dr. Doerte Treuheit, Bundesministerium für Bildung und Forschung, 21 May 2001.

106. Bundesanstalt für Arbeit, "Ausbildung, Qualifizierung und Beschäftigung Jugendlicher," Informationen für die Beratungs- und Vermittlungsdieste der Bundesanstalt für Arbeit, 2/99, 13 January 1999, 69, 72.

107. Bundesagentur für Arbeit, *Arbeitsmarkt 2005: Amtliche Nachrichten der Bundesagentur für Arbeit* (Nuremberg: BA, 2006), 19, 24; Institut für Arbeitsmarkt- und Berufsforschung, Bundesagentur für Arbeit, "Jugendliche, die Schwächsten kamen seltener zum Zug," IAB Kurzbericht, no. 2 (Nuremberg: BA, 2007), 5.

108. For details, see Bundesanstalt für Arbeit, "Sofortprogramm zum Abbau der Jugendarbeitslosigkeit: Zwischenergebnisse aus der Begleitforschung," Informationen für die Beratungs- und Vermittlungsdieste der Bundesanstalt für Arbeit, 20/00, 17 May 2000.

109. Bundesanstalt für Arbeit, "JUMP: Das Sofortprogramm zum Abbau der Jugendarbeitslosigkeit," special issue of *Direkt: Fördern und Qualifizieren* 10 (April 2000): 2.

110. Bundesanstalt für Arbeit, "Ausbildung, Qualifizierung und Beschäftigung Jugendlicher," 69, 72; idem, *Arbeitsmarkt 2005,* 19, 24; Institut für Arbeitsmarkt—und Berufsforschung, Bundesagentur für Arbeit, "Jugendliche, Die Schwächsten kamen seltener zum Zug." The law was initially intended to last only twelve months but has been

extended each year by agreement between the BA and the government; for details, see Bundesanstalt für Arbeit, "Sofortprogramm zum Abbau der Jugendarbeitslosigkeit." Bundesanstalt für Arbeit, "JUMP," 2. According to the Labor Ministry, between 1998 and 2001, 406,000 people benefited from the program, obtaining either employment or apprenticeship or training slots: Bundesministerium für Arbeit und Sozialordnung, "Jump ist ein voller Erfolg," press release, 15 February 2002.

111. My calculations from data in BA, *Annual Report 1999* (Nuremberg: BA, 2000), 93. The 1995 figures are from Uwe Blien, Ulrich Walwei, and Heinz Werner, *Labour Market Policy in Germany,* IAB Labour Market Research Topics, no. 49 (Nuremberg: BA, 2002), 6

112. Niejahr and Uchatius, "Schröder auf Jobsuche," 18.

113. "101,2 Milliarden DM für die Bundesanstalt," *Frankfurter Allgemeine Zeitung,* 17 November 2000, 15.

114. The federal government is required by law to cover the BA's deficit. Traditionally an exceptional measure for difficult years, by the early 2000s this supplement had become an annual fixture due to the BA's continual shortfalls. Only in 2006 did declining unemployment rates result in a surplus. The 2002 figures are from Bundesanstalt für Arbeit, *2002 Annual Report* (Nuremberg: BA, 2003), 66.

115. Bundesanstalt für Arbeit, *Haushaltsplan, Haushaltsjahr 2001* (Nuremberg: BA, 2001), 9.

116. Wolfgang Streeck, "Endgame? The Fiscal Crisis of the German State," Max-Planck-Institut für Gesellschaftsforschung Discussion Paper 07/7 (Cologne: Max-Planck-Institut für Gesellschaftsforschung, 2007), 14.

117. OECD, *OECD Economic Surveys, 1998–1999: Germany* (Paris: OECD, 1999), 85, 177.

118. OECD, *OECD Economic Surveys, 2000–2001: Germany,* 69–70. Firms with fewer than fifteen employees were exempt.

119. In 1999, 19.5 percent of jobs were part time, compared with 14 percent in 1991: Bundesvereinigung der Deutschen Arbeitgeberverbände (BDA), *Geschäftsbericht 2000* (Berlin: BDA, 2000), 16.

120. Interviews, Jutte Kemme, Assessorin, Abteilung Soziale Sicherung; and Dr. Volker Hansen, Stellvertrender Abteilungsleiter, Abteilung Soziale Sicherung, 29 November 2000 and 25 May 2001.

121. "Im Streit um die Arbeitsmarktpolitik verhärten sich die Fronten," *Frankfurter Allgemeine Zeitung,* 7 August 2001, 15.

122. See "Bundesanstalt gerät immer stärker ins Kreuzfeuer der Kritik," *Frankfurter Allgemeine Zeitung,* 6 February 2002, 13; "Jagoda weist Rücktrittsforderungen zurück," *Frankfurter Allgemeine Zeitung,* 7 February 2002, 13.

123. Hartz Commission, "Moderne Dienstleistungen am Arbeitsmarkt: Vorschläge der Kommission zum Abbau der Arbeitslosigkeit und zur Umstrukturierung der Bundesanstalt für Arbeit," report, Berlin, August 2002. The thin character of the commission's tripartism could also be seen in the selection as its leader of Peter Hartz, the personnel director at Volkswagen and Schröder's former business associate, rather than the creation of a board of union representatives and employers, to direct its work.

124. "Schröders Agenda Zwanzig-Zehn: So will der Kanzler punkten," *Frankfurter Allgemeine Zeitung,* 15 March 2003, 11.

125. The laws also liberalized protections against layoffs in Germany's smallest firms and the country's strict shop-opening laws, reduced health-insurance contributions, and cut taxes. Many of the Agenda 2010 reforms initially had been proposed by the Hartz Commission and were later subsumed under the broader initiative.

126. The Hartz IV reform also resulted in a flood of court challenges, leading to a decision in early 2008 by the Federal Constitutional Court in Karlsruhe that the local labor offices, jointly administered by the BA and municipalities, had violated the *Grundgesetz*'s distribution of authority among levels of government and that eligibility restrictions for some groups had to be loosened: see "Der Nebel über Hartz IV lichtet sich: Bundesrichter haben viele Grundsatzentscheidungen zur Arbeitsmarktreform gefällt," *Frankfurter Allgemeine Zeitung,* 29 January 2008, 14.

127. The earlier reforms involved the introduction of a requirement that all unemployed people register with the BA or suffer a cut in jobless benefits; measures to promote self-employment; and a restructuring of the BA's offices to enable them to provide more personalized placement services. For a discussion, see "Allemagne: L'opposition impose à Schröder de sérieuses concessions sur le marché du travail," *Les Echos,* 16 December 2003, 5; "Von der Agenda 2010 bis zur Einigung im Vermittlungsausschuß," *Frankfurter Allgemeine Zeitung,* 16 December 2003, 3.

128. The Linke was founded in June 2007 as a union of the Linkspartei, composed of left-wing defectors from the SPD and members of the former East German Communist Party (the PDS), and the smaller, West German Arbeit und Soziale Gerechtigkeit—Die Wahlalternative (WASG). It is led by the renegade former social democrat Oskar Lafontaine and the former PDS head Lothar Bisky.

129. Interview, Peter Jülicher, Bundesministerium für Arbeit und Soziales, 19 June 2007.

130. The ongoing battle over the creation of a minimum wage is a case in point. Though the CDU blocked a unified statutory minimum wage, a compromise made in 2007 represents a significant intrusion of the state into the wage-setting process.

131. OECD, *OECD Employment Outlook,* 227.

132. Bundesministerium für Wirtschaft und Arbeit, "Arbeitslosigkeit sinkt stärker als in den vergangenen 15 Jahren—die neue Arbeitsmarktpolitik entfaltet ihre Wirkung," press release, 2 November 2005.

133. "Hinweise auf das Ende des Stellenabbaus," *Frankfurter Allgemeine Zeitung,* 30 June 2006, 14.

134. Bundesagentur für Arbeit, *Geschäftsbericht 2006* (Nuremberg: BA, 2007), attached tables; "Arbeitslosigkeit auf tiefstem Stand seit zwölf Jahren," *Frankfurter Allgemeine Zeitung,* 28 September 2007, 1.

135. Karl de Meyer, "En Allemagne, un nouveau recul du nombre de demandeurs d'emploi," *Les Echos,* 28 November 2008, 2.

136. The government also attempted to change German collective bargaining, notably through a 2000 reform of *Mitbestimmung,* or co-determination, long demanded by unions and fiercely resisted by employers. This law lowered from 300 to 200 the number of workers that a firm must have before workers there enjoy a statutory right to a works council. Although the government claimed that it was working to "adjust" co-determination to new economic realities—in particular, the rapid emergence of smaller firms in information technology that are almost entirely non-unionized—sources close to the negotiations between the government and unions characterized the measure as a sop to the unions for

their loss in pension reform: interviews, Axel Börsch-Supan, Fakultät für Volkswirtschaftslehre, University of Mannheim, 20 February 2001; Erich Standfest, Leiter der Abteilung Sozialpolitik, Bundesvorstand, Deutscher Gewerkschaftsbund, 7 February 2001; and Michael Dörnmann, Bundesministerium für Arbeit und Sozialordnung, 23 November 2000. For a discussion, see "Der Mitbestimmungspoker," *Die Zeit,* vol. 8, 15 February 2001, 3.

CHAPTER 6

1. In 1970, after more than a decade of rising benefits, total social contributions were a mere 10.2 percent of GDP in Germany and 13.1 percent in France, compared with 13.9 percent and 20 percent in 1989, respectively: Fritz W. Scharpf and Vivien A. Schmidt, "Statistical Appendix," in *Welfare and Work in the Open Economy, Volume 1: From Vulnerability to Competitiveness,* ed. Fritz W. Scharpf and Vivien A. Schmidt (Oxford: Oxford University Press, 2000), 363.

In all but four years between 1947 and 1963, the French *régime général,* the ensemble of funds that provides most social-insurance benefits, was either in balance or in surplus: Bruno Palier, *Gouverner la sécurité sociale: Les réformes du système français de protection sociale depuis 1945* (Paris: Presses Universitaires de France, 2002), 137.

2. For an overview of French and German welfare expansion during this period, see Jonah D. Levy, "France: Directing Adjustment?" in *Welfare and Work in the Open Economy, Volume 2: Diverse Responses to Common Challenges,* ed. Fritz W. Scharpf and Vivien A. Schmidt (Oxford: Oxford University Press, 2000); Christopher Flockton, "Economic Management and the Challenge of Reunification," in *Developments in German Politics 2,* ed. Gordon Smith, William E. Paterson, and Stephen Padgett (London: Macmillan, 1996).

3. Scharpf and Schmidt, "Statistical Appendix," 364.

4. Marc de Montalembert, ed., *La protection sociale en France,* 3rd ed. (Paris: La Documentation Française, 2001), 12; Pierre-Alain Greciano, *Les retraites en France: Quel avenir?* (Paris: La Documentation Française, 2002), 219.

5. Monika Queisser, *Pensions in Germany,* Policy Research Working Paper 1664, Financial Sector Development Department, World Bank, Washington, D.C., October 1996, 16.

6. Greciano, *Les retraites en France,* 98, 100, 219.

7. Organization for Economic Cooperation and Development, *OECD Economic Surveys 2000–2001: Germany* (Paris: OECD, 2001), 59.

8. OECD health data are cited in Patrick Hassenteufel, *Les médecins face à l'Etat: Une comparaison européenne* (Paris: Presses de la Fondation Nationale des Sciences Politiques, 1997). OECD pension data are drawn from John Myles and Paul Pierson, "Reforming Public Pensions," paper presented at the New Politics of the Welfare State conference, Center for European Studies, Harvard University, Cambridge, Mass., 5–7 December 1997.

9. Pensions and health care account for the largest share of social spending in France and Germany. In 2000, for example, French health care and pensions accounted for 78.2 percent of all social expenditures. In Germany in 1998, the figure was 67.3 percent. My calculations are based on OECD data in de Montalembert, *La protection sociale en France,* 64.

10. Bruno Palier places particular emphasis on this logic as one of the sources of difficulty in reforming the French welfare state: Palier, *Gouverner la sécurité sociale,* 196–201.

11. These risks were particularly salient in France, where memories of the near-revolution of May 1968 were still fresh. During the 1970s, fears of social unrest informed a series of policies designed to pacify disgruntled groups. For a discussion, see Jonah D. Levy, *Tocqueville's Revenge: State, Society, and Economy in Contemporary France* (Cambridge, Mass.: Harvard University Press, 1999), 39–43; John T. S. Keeler, "Corporatist Decentralization and Commercial Modernization in France: The Royer Law's Impact on Shopkeepers, Supermarkets, and the State," in *Socialism, the State, and Public Policy in France,* ed. Philip Cerny and Martin Schain (London: Frances Pinter, 1985). For a detailed discussion of the events of May 1968, see Chris Howell, *Regulating Labor: The State and Industrial Relations Reform in Postwar France* (Princeton, N.J.: Princeton University Press, 1992), chap. 3.

12. For example, in 1991 French Prime Minister Michel Rocard published a study of the French pension system containing proposals for reform. This study would become a reference point for reform under subsequent governments: Michel Rocard, *Livre blanc sur les retraites: Garantir dans l'équité les retraites de demain* (Paris: La Documentation Française, 1991).

13. Like Bruno Palier, I argue that French social-protection reform has been shaped in important ways by relationships among the state and social partners. However, I adopt a broader view of the social partners' influence, which Palier sees as deriving primarily from their administrative power over social-insurance funds: see Bruno Palier, "The Necessity for French Governments to Negotiate Welfare State Reforms with the Social Partners," paper presented at the Thirteenth Conference of Europeanists, Palmer House, Chicago, 14–16 March 2002.

14. Thierry Bréhier et al., "Un entretien avec Edouard Balladur," *Le Monde,* 18 May 1993, 1, 8–10.

15. Agence France-Presse wire service, 17 May 1993.

16. These conventions are generally binding on all physicians, even if only one medical union accepts them.

17. Mireille Elbaum, *Economie politique de la protection sociale* (Paris: Presses Universitaires de France, 2008), 75.

18. As with pensions, certain groups, such as farmers, miners, and the merchant marine, have independent funds, for which the CNAMTS plays the lead role in negotiations: see David Wilsford, "Reforming French Health Care Policy," in *Chirac's Challenge: Liberalization, Europeanization, and Malaise in France,* ed. John T. S. Keeler and Martin A. Schain (New York: St. Martin's Press, 1996), 234.

19. David Wilsford, "The Continuity of Crisis: Patterns of Health Care Policymaking in France, 1978–1988," in *The French Welfare State: Surviving Social and Ideological Change,* ed. John S. Ambler (New York: New York University Press, 1991), 105–107. In contrast to its indirect management of the ambulatory sector, state control over the hospital system has tended to make it a conspicuous target for cost control.

In January 1995, the 20.1 percent of French hospital beds in private, for-profit establishments and 5.1 percent of those in private, nonprofit institutions were not subject to *budgets globaux.* An additional 10.4 percent were in privately owned, nonprofit hospitals that participated in the public hospital system and thus were subject to the *budgets.* The reform of 24 April 1996 introduced "regional quantitative objectives" for private institutions participating in the public system: Marie-Thérèse Join-Lambert et al., *Politiques sociales,* 2nd ed. (Paris: Presses de Sciences Po et Dalloz, 1997), 528–533.

20. The divergent logics of the liberal ambulatory and state-run hospital sectors reflect the same hybrid between Bismarckian and Beveridgean paradigms characteristic of the French welfare state: Béatrice Majnoni d'Initignano, *La protection sociale* (Paris: Fallois, 1993), 24–30, 186.

21. Hassenteufel, *Les médecins face à l'Etat,* 261–262.

22. As an additional concession to doctors, Veil announced the cancellation of the previous government's proposal to tighten the regulation of doctors' retirement contributions.

23. MG France initially refused to accept the 1993 convention, which placed a disproportionately heavy burden on generalists, and signed on only in January 1995 with the express aim of working to undermine specialists' control: Hassenteufel, *Les médecins face à l'Etat,* 311–312.

24. During the 1980s, the annual rate of growth of the French population older than sixty increased to 1.65 percent, up from .05 percent during the previous decade and compared with a growth rate for the entire population of .05 percent: Rocard, *Livre blanc,* 45, 180.

25. Join-Lambert et al., *Politiques sociales,* 458–465; Gilles Huteau and Éric Le Bont, *Sécurité sociale et politiques sociales,* 2nd ed. (Paris: Armand Colin, 1997), 279–281.

26. At the time, complementary pensions represented between 28 percent and 45 percent of total coverage for each beneficiary. Since *cadres* receive *two* complementary pensions, one from ARRCO and a second from AGIRC, their benefits on average were 50–90 percent higher than those of non-*cadres.* State workers who were part of a *régime spécial* enjoyed even more generous coverage (as well as earlier retirement ages) and therefore had little incentive to join a complementary fund: See Majnoni d'Initignano, *La protection sociale,* 90; Emmanuel Reynaud and Giovanni Tamburi, *Les retraites en France: Le rôle des régimes complémentaires* (Paris: La Documentation Française, 1994), 32, 34, 36–37.

27. Majnoni d'Initignano, *La protection sociale,* 92.

28. See Huteau and Le Bont, *Sécurité sociale et politiques sociales,* 13; Join-Lambert et al., *Politiques sociales,* 455–456.

29. Unlike the 1995 *remboursement de la dette sociale* (RDS), proceeds from the increased CSG (about FFr 50 billion per year) were earmarked for the newly created *fonds de solidarité vieillesse*: Giuliano Bonoli, "Pension Politics in France: Patterns of Co-operation and Conflict in Two Recent Reforms," *West European Politics* 20, no. 4 (October 1997): 118.

30. "La déclaration de politique générale du gouvernement d'Edouard Balladur," pt. 2, *Le Monde,* 10 April 1993, 3–8.

31. Jean-Michel Normand, "Selon un projet préparé par le gouvernement, la durée de cotisation des retraites serait progressivement allongée: Dans les pas de Michel Rocard," *Le Monde,* 8 May 1993, 1, 15; idem, "Les réactions et le plan de M. Balladur: Le programme de redressement économique et social: Dans les syndicats," *Le Monde,* 12 May 1993, 18.

32. Normand, "Selon un projet"; emphasis added.

33. Jean-Michel Normand, "Retraites, SMIC, assurance-maladie: Le gouvernement accentue les mesures de rigueur," *Le Monde,* 22 June 1993, 22.

34. Although Bonoli is right to note this concession, he overestimates its importance to the exclusion of other important factors: Bonoli, "Pension Politics in France," 118–119.

35. Agence France-Presse observed that "the French are, contrary to the fears of the government, clearly convinced by the idea that [increased financial obligations are] the price to pay in order to get out of the infernal recession-unemployment spiral. The 'Balladur tone' clearly has much to do with this. Its very courteous firmness, its avoidance of provocation, and its ability to calm emotional debates is remarkable. More importantly, it is reassuring": Agence France-Presse wire service, 2 September 1993.

36. As of November 1995, the projected 1995 budget deficit was FFr 322 billion, with the social-security deficit an additional FFr 64 billion: see "Crying Out for Reform," in "No Escape? A Survey of France," *Economist,* 25 November–1 December 1995, 7.

37. Hervé Maisonneuve and Joël Ménard, "The Juppé Plan," *Lancet,* vol. 349, 15 March 1997, 792–793.

38. Michel Noblecourt, "Comment Alain Juppé, en voulant réformer la Sécurité sociale et les retraites, déclencha le mouvement de l'automne 1995," *Le Monde,* 17 May 1997, 10–11.

39. As one of Chirac's closest social-affairs advisers bluntly put it: "You believe that you can buy time by employing the element of surprise—it will be your undoing. Years spent engaging in debate are not years wasted but time gained." Jean-Pierre Denis, Chirac's adjunct secretary-general, merely responded, perhaps with unconscious irony, "We don't have the time": ibid.

40. The rhetoric of this battle became quite acerbic. Marc Blondel, leader of the FO, suggested that Notat consider a change of career, since her behavior resembled more closely that of a government minister than that of a major union leader.

41. Although the CFDT saw the strikes as a threat to social stability, the CGT and the FO were more worried about the symbolic abrogation of a promise to workers.

42. In the fourth week of the strike, estimates of the number of protestors ranged from 600,000 (according to the police) to more than 2 million (according to the unions).

43. "M. Juppé: La France n'a le choix qu'entre le changement ou le déclin," *Le Monde,* 7 December 1995, 8–9.

44. Quoted in "Revue de presse," *Le Monde,* 20 December 1995, 13; the back-translation into English is mine.

45. According to one poll, 54 percent of the population both supported the strike and felt that the *substance* of Juppé's pension reforms was legitimate, confirming that sympathy for the strike reflected hostility toward Juppé as much as a judgment of his reforms' merits: Robert Diard Pascale, "La grève générale de la fonction publique menace de paralyser le pays," *Le Monde,* 24 November 1995, 8.

46. Hassenteufel, *Les médecins face à l'état,* 341.

47. Ibid., 344–345. These penalties, which were to have been imposed on the profession as a whole, would be imposed only on individual physicians.

48. The most important were the Charpin Report in 1999 and a follow-up report published in 2002 by the Conseil d'Orientation des Retraites: Jean-Michel Charpin, *L'avenir de nos retraites,* Rapport au Premier Ministre (Paris: La Documentation Française, 1999); idem, *Retraites: Renouveler le contrat social entre les générations* (Paris: La Documentation Française, 2002).

49. Interviews, Anne-Marie Brocas, Conseil d'Orientation des Retraites, 22 April 2002, and Stéphane Lefoll, director of the Cabinet of the First Secretary, Parti Socialiste, 11 April 2002.

50. Palier, *Gouverner la sécurité sociale,* 250–251.

51. Dominique Seux, "Retraites: Le pouvoir fait bloc avant la manifestation de mardi," *Les Echos,* 9 May 2003, 2.

52. Raffarin's approach, however, was a bit firmer than Balladur's. At the height of union protests in early May, he declared, "We will listen to all unions who exhibit a constructive attitude, until the last moment. But let there be no misunderstanding. The government will consult, but then it will decide. In other words, it will govern": see "Retraites: Le gouvernement décidé à aller jusqu'au bout," *Les Echos,* electronic ed., 6 May 2003. Raffarin's one significant concession was to allow workers who began their careers at sixteen or younger to retire after forty years of contributions, regardless of their age.

53. Etienne Lefebvre, "Seuls les députés UMP ont approuvé la réforme de l'assurance-maladie," *Les Echos,* 21 July 2004, 3.

54. For details, see Elbaum, *Economie politique de la protection sociale,* 116–120.

55. Interview, François-Xavier Selleret, Conseiller auprès du Ministre, Ministère du Travail, des Relations Sociales et de la Solidarité, 16 July 2008.

56. A poll in September 2007 found that seven out of ten supported the government's reform, in stark contrast to 1995. At the same time, the same percentage of those surveyed saw the reform as "risky" and urged the government to negotiate. Known for following poll numbers with an almost American obsession, Sarkozy's subsequent strategy suggested that he was also doing so in this case: see Cecile Cornudet, "Régimes spéciaux: Les Français souhaitent que l'exécutif mette les formes," *Les Echos,* 18 September 2007, 5.

57. Etienne Lefebvre, "Régimes spéciaux: Bertrand met fin aux 'retraites couperet'," *Les Echos,* 3 October 2007, 4.

58. Etienne Lefebvre, "Les principes généraux de la réforme ne bougeront plus," *Les Echos,* 13 November 2007, 4.

59. Lucile Chevallard and Leila de Comarmond, "Régimes spéciaux: L'exceptionnelle mobilisation conduit le gouvernement à rediscuter," *Les Echos,* 19 October 2007, 2.

60. This negotiating posture on the part of the CGT reflects a broader strategic shift in the face of Sarkozy's election. Like the CFDT in the early 2000s, the CGT, under the charismatic and relatively moderate Bernard Thibault, has recognized that playing the government's game and negotiating stands to benefit it more in the current political and economic climate than would its traditional intransigence. In the words of one (center-right) official at the Labor Ministry, this reasoned approach means that "if he had to join a union today, it would be the CGT": interview (name withheld on request), 16 July 2008. Such accounts of the CGT's shift in strategy were confirmed in other interviews, with, among others, Xavier Lacoste, Directeur Général, Altedia, and former conseiller social du Ministre de l'Economie et des Finances, 17 July 2008; Véronique Cazals, Directeur de la Protection Sociale, MEDEF, 10 July 2008; and Alain Petitjean, CFDT, 1 July 2008.

61. By comparison, in 1996, between 55 percent and 60 percent of those polled saw the strike as legitimate: see "Sarkozy's Bad Week," *Economist,* 20–26 October 2007, 71; Cecile Cornudet, "Sarkozy conforté par l'opinion dans sa stratégie sur les régimes spéciaux," *Les Echos,* 13 November 2007, 2.

62. Dominique Seux, "Les paris de Nicolas Sarkozy et de Bernard Thibault," *Les Echos,* 15 November 2007, 14.

63. The reform's final details delayed the effective date for the increased contribution requirement until June and established a maximum two-and-a-half-year penalty for those retiring early who have forty years of contributions: Etienne Lefebvre, "Régimes spéciaux: La durée de cotisation va être portée à quarante et un ans d'ici à 2016," *Les Echos,* 26 December 2007, 3.

64. Jean-Francis Pécresse, "Régimes spéciaux: Nouvelle menace de grève, petite concession à l'étude," *Les Echos,* 31 October 2007, 3.

65. Since the early 2000s, a favored tactic of French governments has been to create standing organizations to study and issue recommendations for reform in particular policy areas and then to use such reports as part of the rationale for reform. This adds an air of empirical necessity, dispassionately concluded, to controversial reforms. The Conseil d'Orientation des Retraites has been publishing studies of the French pension system since the early 2000s, and data from its recent reports were incoporated into Sarkozy's proposals for reforming the *régimes spéciaux*: see Conseil d'Orientation des Retraites, "Retraites: 20 fiches d'actualisation pour le rendez-vous de 2008, Cinquième Rapport," 21 November 2007.

66. Even those proposals that have been passed into law have not succeeded in controlling exploding health expenditures, however. Having reached the alarming level of 9.9 percent of GDP in 1995, health expenditures continued to rise after a brief decline between 1996 and 1998. By 2005, they had increased to 10.4 percent of GDP: Huteau and Le Bont, *Sécurité sociale et politiques sociales,* 168, 172; Observatoire Français des Conjunctures Economiques, *L'économie française 2008* (Paris: La Découverte, 2007), 36.

67. Generalists, for example, are compensated at lower rates than specialists for identical services.

68. The Verband der Niedergelassenen Ärzte Deutschlands represents physicians excluded from the *Kassen.* Their political weakness has led them to support the SPD's model of a more centralized health system: Hassenteufel, *Les médecins face à l'état,* 141–143.

69. German health spending was relatively steady during the 1980s, fluctuating between a low of 7.91 percent of GDP in 1980 and a high of 8.46 percent in 1988: Markus Schneider, "Health Care Cost Containment in the Federal Republic of Germany," *Health Care Financing Review,* vol. 12, no. 3 (Spring 1991): 91.

70. By 1989, annual real growth in health expenditures had risen to 7.7 percent, the highest level since 1975, compared with an annual average of 2.6 percent since 1980. My calculations are from data in ibid., 94.

71. Cost concerns were sharpened by a jump in average health-contribution rates, set by the *Kassen,* from 11.5 percent to nearly 13 percent during the mid-1980s: Jeremy W. Hurst, "Reform of Health Care in Germany," *Health Care Financing Review,* vol. 12, no. 3 (Spring 1991): 80–81.

72. Schneider, "Health Care Cost Containment," 91. The reform also increased the daily hospital charge from DM 5 to DM 10 and raised contribution rates for pensioners and children.

73. A dramatic example of this failure was a 7 percent increase in pharmaceutical expenditures during the first nine months of 1990 alone.

74. In addition to introducing an additional 17 million people with no contribution record, reunification created an *initial* need of DM 20 billion for buildings and equipment

to equilibrate the Eastern and Western health infrastructures: see Hurst, "Reform of Health Care in Germany," 81.

75. John K. Iglehart, "Health Policy Report: Germany's Health Care System," pt. 1, *New England Journal of Medicine* 324, no. 7, 14 February 1991, 504.

76. "Austerity Measures Proposed for Health Care," *The Week in Germany,* German Information Center, 5 June 1992.

77. As early as June, the SPD's vice president in the Bundestag complained, "[The plan] guarantees increased revenue to doctors while taking money hand-over-fist from patients' pockets": quoted in Hassenteufel, *Les médecins face à l'état,* 323.

78. This concession had been worked out in advance to secure the SPD's support: ibid., 323.

79. Ibid., 335.

80. Götz Aly, "Ein Sittenwidriges Schneeballsystem," *Berliner Zeitung,* 2–3 December 2000, 4.

81. In the early 1990s, only 48.5 percent of private-sector workers enjoyed a supplementary pension: Lucy ApRoberts and Emmanuel Reynaud, *Les systèmes de retraite à l'étranger: Etats-Unis, Allemagne, Royaume-Uni* (Paris: Institut de Recherches Economiques et Sociales, 1992), 156.

82. Philip Manow and Eric Seils, "Adjusting Badly: The German Welfare State, Structural Change, and the Open Economy," in *Welfare and Work in the Open Economy, Volume 2: Diverse Responses to Common Challenges,* ed. Fritz W. Scharpf and Vivien A. Schmidt (Oxford: Oxford University Press, 2000), 292.

83. "Penury or Plenty?" in "All Our Tomorrows: A Survey of the Economics of Ageing," *Economist,* 27 January–2 February 1996, 9.

84. "The Chancellor's Old-Age Table Talk," *Economist,* 17–23 February 1996, 45.

85. This concession to the left was designed to compensate for the new penalty for early retirement. The formula allocated points for each year of contributions, fixing the ratio of a retiring worker's salary to the average net wage level. Although this modified formula altered some workers' benefits, the average replacement rate for a full forty-five-year career remained 70 percent. The measure also preserved the five-year-contribution requirement for partial vestment, which was low by international standards: see ApRoberts and Reynaud, *Les systèmes de retraite à l'étranger,* 169.

86. Ibid., 153.

87. John Myles and Paul Pierson, "The Comparative Political Economy of Pension Reform," in *The New Politics of the Welfare State,* ed. Paul Pierson (Oxford: Oxford University Press 2001), 309.

88. For a detailed discussion, see Karl Hinrichs, "Reforming the Public Pension Scheme in Germany: The End of Traditional Consensus?" manuscript, Zentrum für Sozialpolitik, Universität Bremen, Arbeitspapier 11/98, 1998, 20–27.

89. Only laws that directly affect the *Länder* are subject to the Bundesrat's approval.

90. Christoph Pauly, Christian Reiermann, and Michael Sauga, "Riesters Reformruine," *Der Spiegel,* vol. 7, 12 February 2001, 90.

91. The 64 percent figure is deceptive, since it represents only the benefits of an "average" worker having contributed for forty-five years. Most workers' benefits would actually be lower.

92. Bundesministerium für Arbeit und Sozialordnung, "Die Rentenreform 2000: Ein mutiger Schritt zu mehr Sicherheit," Bonn, BMA, August 2000.

93. SPD and Bündnis 90/Die Grünen Bundestagsfraktionen, "Entwurf eines Gesetzes zur Reform der gesetzlichen Rentenversicherung und zur Förderung eines kapitalgedeckten Altersvorsorgevermögens," 14 November 2000, 4. This increased federal share was in addition to the provisions of the 1999 *Ökosteuer,* or environmental tax, which replaced .8 percent of annual pension contributions with federal tax monies.

94. Interview, Ludger Loop, Gesellschaft für Innovation, Beratung und Service, IG Metall, 13 March 2001.

95. "Schröder bleibt bei der Rentenreform hart: 'Wir werden es machen. Basta,'" *Frankfurter Allgemeine Zeitung,* 6 November 2000, 1.

96. "Unmut über Riester in der SPD-Fraktion," *Frankfurter Allgemeine Zeitung,* 9 November 2000, 8; Bundesverband der Deutschen Industrie, "Zwei Jahre Rot–Grüne Bundesregierung: Wirtschaftspolitische Zwischenbilanz für die 14. Legislaturperiode gemessen am Regierungsprogramm und den Vorschlägen des BDI," Berlin, BDI, September 2000, 10.

97. Schröder's approach typically involved including a small number of experts and responsible ministers in discussions and only later informing the rest of the government and party. For a discussion, see "Der Kanzler sagt 'Basta' und alle gehorchen," *Frankfurter Allgemeine Zeitung,* 11 November 2000, 1.

98. One CDU member admitted privately that his party had no coherent positions on social-policy reform: interview, member of CDU/CSU Arbeitsgruppe Arbeit und Soziales, 15 March 2001.

99. "Das Wort vom zweiten Mißgriff wird der CDU-Generalsekretär so leicht nicht los," *Frankfurter Allgemeine Zeitung,* 25 January 2001, 3.

100. Despite claims of highly placed CDU experts that the government's reform had merely incorporated CDU ideas, neither the substance of the reform (e.g., the abandonment of the *Ausgleichsfaktor* and the private accounts), nor the CDU/CSU's vigorous contestation of the measure supports this assertion. The opposition was so eager to profit from the politically charged atmosphere surrounding the reform that its "true" priorities for this policy area quickly ceased to be relevant. The characterizations are drawn from interviews with Thomas Koch, Member, Department of Arbeit und Soziales, Gesundheit, Familie, Senioren, Frauen und Jugend, CSU Landesgruppe, 22 March 2001, and Dr. Christoph Wilk, Office of Mitglied des Deutschen Bundestages Horst Seehofer, CDU/CSU Fraktion im Deutschen Bundestag, 19 March 2001.

101. Much has been made of the Bundesrat's ability to block legislation. As the 2000 pension reform demonstrates, however, the government's control over the ways in which laws are drafted and gray areas in the German Constitution provide flexibility in determining which laws will be subject to the upper house's approval.

102. Interview, Susanne Stumpenhusen, ÖTV, 16 February 2001.

103. "Riester spricht von der 'größten Sozialreform der Nachkriegszeit'," *Frankfurter Allgemeine Zeitung,* 27 January 2001, 1.

104. "Union erklärt Rentenkonsensgespräche für beendet," *Frankfurter Allgemeine Zeitung,* 30 September 2001, 1.

105. In the complex German tax system, the federal government and the *Länder* share revenues from a variety of sources. The additional federal money was required because the *Länder* were already suffering decreased revenues as a result of the govern-

ment's 2000 tax reform. This DM 1 billion supplement was added to other subsidies to the pension system, which by 2001 had risen sharply to an annual DM 114 billion.

106. The government had secured Bundesrat approval for the tax reform by granting federal money for infrastructure projects, including the construction of a new soccer stadium, to *Länder* whose votes were needed.

107. These debates centered on whether to subsidize workers whose retirement savings are in the form of real-estate holdings and the tax treatment of the supplemental private accounts created by Riester's 2001 pension reform.

108. This party incorporated the Partei des Demokratischen Sozialismus (PDS), the successor to the East German Communist Party, and members of the left wing of the SPD who left the party in response to the government's labor-market reforms and cuts in unemployment insurance.

109. The unions objected to the increase in the retirement age and the requirement that workers contribute for forty-five years to receive full benefits. They contended that high rates of unemployment and low job security mean that many workers will fail to fulfill this requirement: "Rente mit 67? Nein Danke!" press release, IG Metall, 12 December 2006.

110. One SPD official claimed that the increase in the retirement age, and the heavy-handed way in which it was undertaken, was worse for party morale and for relations between the party's leadership and its left wing and the unions than even Hartz IV: interview, 24 July 2007.

111. In May 2003, the commission also proposed a series of further pension reforms, including a gradual increase in the retirement age from sixty-five to sixty-seven between 2003 and 2011, limits on early-retirement benefits, and a gradual reduction in replacement rates: see Kerstin Schwenn, "Nur eine Minderheit der Beschäftigten arbeitet bis zum Alter von 65 Jahren," *Frankfurter Allgemeine Zeitung,* 5 May 2003, 15.

112. Vincent De Féligonde, "Allemagne: Consensus politique sur une vaste réforme du financement de la santé," *Les Echos,* 22 July 2003, 6.

CHAPTER 7

1. Steen Mangen, "German Welfare and Social Citizenship," in *Developments in German Politics* 2, ed. Gordon Smith, William E. Paterson, and Stephen Padgett (Durham, N.C.: Duke University Press, 1996), 264–265.

2. Jonas Pontusson, *Inequality and Prosperity: Social Europe versus Liberal America* (Ithaca, N.Y.: Cornell University Press, 2005), 40. As a ratio between segments of income across a population, a Gini coefficient must vary between 0 and 1. It is common practice, however, to report the figures as numbers between 0 and 100.

3. Isabella Mares, *Taxation, Wage Bargaining, and Unemployment* (Cambridge: Cambridge University Press, 2006), 171; Pontusson, *Inequality and Prosperity,* 45.

4. Tony Atkinson, Michel Glaude, and Lucile Olier, eds., *Inégalités économiques,* Rapport du Conseil d'Analyse Economique (Paris: La Documentation Française, 2001), 329.

5. Bruno Palier, *Gouverner la sécurité sociale: Les réformes du système français de protection sociale depuis 1945* (Paris: Presses Universitaires de France, 2002), 283–287.

6. The post-1973 increase in French unemployment and widespread layoffs brought an end to the implicit postwar guarantee of lifetime employment. As a result, the state

became a sort of arbiter between workers and firms, leading to a series of efforts (such as the administrative authorization for layoffs) to protect workers from economic vulnerability: interview, Frédéric Bruggeman, Syndex, 15 February 2002.

7. The fact that this benefit was created so long before other antipoverty programs reflected the urgency of the problem of old-age poverty in the immediate postwar era. In 1958 and 1959, the benefits of nearly 59 percent of those who enjoyed a basic pension under the auspices of the *régime général* were low enough to entitle them to the new means-tested program: Marie-Thérèse Join-Lambert et al., *Politiques sociales,* 2nd ed. (Paris: Presses de Sciences Po et Dalloz, 1997), 459.

8. In 1980, the government also created a widow's benefit, the *allocation d'assurance-veuvage.*

9. The bulk of such benefits were created by Mitterrand's government after the repudiation of dirigisme. Before 1983, economic redistribution was generally seen as a desirable effect of activist industrial policies rather than as a goal to be pursued through separate policy instruments.

10. Cited in Palier, *Gouverner la sécurité sociale,* 300; my translation.

11. Gilles Huteau and Éric Le Bont, *Sécurité sociale et politiques sociales,* 2nd ed. (Paris: Armand Colin, 1997), 380.

12. Marc de Montalembert, ed., *La protection sociale en France,* 4th ed. (Paris: La Documentation Française, 2004), 182. By 2008, the benefit had increased to €447.91 for a single person and €671.87 for a couple: Mireille Elbaum, *Economie politique de la protection sociale* (Paris: Presses Universitaires de France, 2008), 127.

13. These job-placement services included offers of public-sector jobs and internships in the private sector: Join-Lambert et al., *Politiques sociales,* 632–633.

14. As Jonah Levy points out, the RMI also represented a continuation of the conversion of family benefits, paid to parents irrespective of income, into means-tested antipoverty benefits, which focus on workers at lower income levels. This trend began under the Socialists in the early 1980s: Jonah D. Levy, "Vice into Virtue? Progressive Politics and Welfare Reform in Continental Europe," *Politics and Society* 27, no. 2 (June 1999): 248–249.

15. The term was introduced into common parlance by René Lenoir in *Les exclus: Un français sur dix* (Paris: Seuil, 1974).

16. Jonah D. Levy, "France: Directing Adjustment?" in *Welfare and Work in the Open Economy, Volume 2: Diverse Responses to Common Challenges,* ed. Fritz W. Scharpf and Vivien A. Schmidt (Oxford: Oxford University Press, 2000), 328. The unemployment data are drawn from Fritz W. Scharpf and Vivien A. Schmidt, "Statistical Appendix," in *Welfare and Work in the Open Economy, Volume 1: From Vulnerability to Competitiveness,* ed. Fritz W. Scharpf and Vivien A. Schmidt (Oxford: Oxford University Press, 2000), 341.

17. Cited in Palier, *Gouverner la sécurité sociale,* 284.

18. For example, in Dreux, a small town about forty miles east of Paris whose economy had been devastated by a series of factory closings in the 1970s and 1980s and where a large number of immigrants, mostly from North Africa, coexisted with unemployed whites, the Front National garnered between 15 percent and 18 percent of the vote in a series of local and national elections in the 1980s. For a discussion, see Françoise Gaspard, *A Small City in France,* trans. Arthur Goldhammer (Cambridge, Mass.: Harvard University Press, 1995).

19. Levy, "France: Directing Adjustment?" 328.

20. Palier, *Gouverner la sécurité sociale,* 300; de Montalembert, *La protection sociale en France,* 163.

21. In 1970, the SMIC replaced the *salaire minimum interprofessionnel garanti* (SMIG), established in 1950. The name change reflected the shift to the current system of indexation, conceived as a response to the SMIG's failure to keep pace with aggregate increases in purchasing power across the French economy. For a discussion, see Join-Lambert et al., *Politiques sociales,* 148.

22. Marc de Montalembert, ed., *La protection sociale en France,* 3rd ed. (Paris: La Documentation Française, 2001), 25. The SMIC is indexed to prices and must be raised when the increase in the aggregate price index exceeds 2 percent relative to the point at which the value of the SMIC was last set. In 2008, the SMIC was €8.71 per hour, or €1321.02 per month. The data are drawn from the Institut National de la Statistique et des Études Économiques (INSEE) website, available online at http://www.insee.fr/fr/themes/tableau.asp?ref_id=NATnon04145&reg_id=0 (accessed 7 August 2008).

23. The government had initially attempted to increase the incomes of low-wage workers by exempting them from the CSG. This measure, however, was annulled by the Constitutional Council, which declared that the proposal violated the principle of equality before the tax laws. The *prime* risked no such violation, since it was a tax credit rather than a tax exemption: "Que faire pour les bas salaires?" *Le Monde,* 10 January 2001, 1, 6.

24. Elbaum, *Economie politique de la protection sociale,* 284.

25. Palier, *Gouverner la sécurité sociale,* 317.

26. See "La droite s'abstient sur la 'prime pour l'emploi' votée par la gauche," *Le Monde,* 8 February 2001, 7.

27. A report by INSEE in March 2001 demonstrated that the incidence of poverty had not declined since 1996, despite the relatively favorable economic climate of the late 1990s. According to the report, more than 4 million French residents were living in poverty, including a disproportionate number of immigrants and the young: see "Quatre millions de pauvres en France," *Le Monde,* 23 March 2001, 1, 6.

28. Although the benefit is adjusted according to a household's income, even those with incomes above an established ceiling are entitled to a reduced payment.

29. De Montalembert, *La protection sociale en France,* 4th ed., 181.

30. "'L'année utile' d'Elisabeth Guigou commence par les personnes âgées," *Le Monde,* 18 April 2001, 7.

31. Palier, *Gouverner la sécurité sociale,* 252.

32. Elbaum, *Economie politique de la protection sociale,* 121.

33. Ibid., 253.

34. Interview, Jean-Marie Spaeth, president, CNAMTS, 6 February 2002. More dispassionate observers pointed out that public opinion broadly supports such initiatives, despite lip service paid to the idea that concertation among the social partners should be the primary engine of social policy.

35. A member of Parliament from the Union pour la Démocratie Française (UDF), expressing concerns shared by broad segments of the political opposition, complained about the government's "authoritarian" approach to health policy, going as far as to claim that "social partnership in health policy is dead": interview, Jean-Luc Préel, UDF, Député de la Vendée, Assemblée Nationale, 5 March 2002. In mid-2001, the policy already had 6.5 million beneficiaries, representing 8.8 percent of the French population: Palier, *Gouverner la sécurité sociale,* 252.

36. Jean-Francis Pécresse, "A l'Assemblée, François Fillon obtient de la majorité la création d'un RMA a minima," *Les Echos,* 24 November 2003, 3.

37. Emmanuelle Heidsieck, "L'Etat s'en prend aux plus fragilisés," *Le Monde Initiatives* (October 2003): 2.

38. Dominique Seux, "Chômeurs en fin de droits: Fillon assume sa réforme mais prévoit un léger assouplissement," *Les Echos,* 31 December 2003, 3. Those recipients whose rights are terminated had to rely on the RMI, whose administration was devolved to the departments in November 2003.

39. Leïla de Comarmond, "La rémunération des smicards augmentera de 1,6 percent à 5,3 percent selon les cas au 1er juillet," *Les Echos,* 24 June 2003, 3.

40. Initially €2.5 billion per year, cost estimates had risen by 2003 to an annual €3.7 billion: see "Allocation d'autonomie: L'Etat s'endette sans résoudre le problème du financement," *Les Echos,* 14 March 2003, 2.

41. Elbaum, *Economie politique de la protection sociale,* 128–129.

42. Derek Perrotte, "Le gouvernement précise le fonctionnement du RSA mais reste flou sur son financement," *Les Echos,* 10 July 2008, 4.

43. In December 2008, Parliament instituted a one-time payment of €200 for low-income households, the so-called *prime de solidarité active,* to provide support in the wake of the ongoing international economic crisis as they await the final implementation of the RSA: Vincent Collen, "La 'prime de solidarité active' bénéficiera à 3,8 millions de ménages," *Les Echos,* 5 December 2008, 5.

44. In a 1999 poll, 69.6 percent expressed "support" or "sympathy" with protests in defense of "social rights," including incomes policies as well as a broad array of other social programs. This figure is even more remarkable when one recalls that fewer than 10 percent of French workers are union members: Anne Muxel, ed., *Les Français et la politique,* Series Problèmes et politiques sociaux, no. 865 (Paris: La Documentation Française, 2001), 73.

45. The effects of these policies on income inequality have been significant. Despite the advent of mass unemployment, income inequality remained stable, with the aggregate Gini coefficient (measured in percentage rather than decimal terms) increasing from 27.75 percent in 1984 to 28.56 percent in 1994, and this before the major antipoverty reforms undertaken by Jospin. Furthermore, the contribution of all antipoverty programs to reductions in income inequality grew, from –0.58 percent to –1.56 percent over the same period. Between 1989 and 2000, the French Gini coefficient declined from .287 to .278, and the relative poverty rate declined by more than 40 percent. The data are from Atkinson et al., *Inégalités économiques,* 320; Luxembourg Income Study (LIS) Key Figures, available online at http://www.lisproject.org/keyfigures.htm (accessed 7 August 2008).

46. Mangen, "German Welfare and Social Citizenship," 265; Peter J. Katzenstein, *Policy and Politics in West Germany: The Growth of a Semi-Sovereign State* (Philadelphia: Temple University Press, 1987), 178.

47. This "subsidiarity principle" is informed by the central assumptions of Christian Democracy, according to which "each private, semiprivate, or semipublic association or institution of society performs indispensable moral, social, and economic tasks. In principle, government should be disinclined to take over responsibility for these tasks": Kees van Kersbergen, "Contemporary Christian Democracy and the Demise of the Politics of Mediation," in *Continuity and Change in Contemporary Capitalism,* ed. Herbert Kitschelt et al. (Cambridge: Cambridge University Press, 1999), 353. See also Kees van Kersbergen,

Social Capitalism: A Study of Christian Democracy and the Welfare State (London: Routledge, 1995). Wilhelm Breuer and Dietrich Engels, "Basic Information and Data on Social Assistance in Germany," paper prepared for the Federal Ministry of Health, ISG Sozialforschung und Gesellschaftspolitik, Cologne, 1999, 2–3. The law provided for counseling and in-kind assistance as well as monetary benefits.

48. BSHG, art. 3, para. 1, cited in Breuer and Engels, "Basic Information and Data on Social Assistance in Germany," 3.

49. The German tax system is Byzantine, consisting of an extensive network of municipal, *Länder,* and federal levies and an equally complex system of revenue sharing (*Finanzausgleich*) among the *Länder.* For a detailed discussion, see Bundesministerium der Finanzen, "Bund-Länder Finanzbeziehungen auf der Grundlage der geltenden Finanzverfassungsordnung," Berlin, Bundesministerium der Finanzen, October 2003.

50. Since the 1980s, the *Länder* and municipalities have suffered from large and mounting deficits. Taken together, the annual deficits of all *Länder,* including the municipalities, increased from €19.1 million in 1991 to €27.4 million in 2001. Aggregate debts (including municipalities) grew from €241.4 billion to €440.3 billion over the same period. Some *Länder,* such as Berlin and Niedersachsen, have suffered disproportionately: ibid., 29–31.

51. In 1999, the basic standard rate ranged from a low of DM 522 (€266.89) per month in Thüringen and Mecklenburg-Vorpommern to a high of DM 548 (€280.19) per month in Hessen and Baden-Württemberg: Breuer and Engels, "Basic Information and Data on Social Assistance in Germany," 4.

52. Ibid., 18.

53. If one defines 1995 price levels as 100, the index of the real value of the standard rate shrank from 102.9 in 1992 to 102.7 in 1997 after increasing by nearly 3 percent in the period 1991–1992: data from ibid., 22.

54. A study conducted by the Hans-Böckler Stiftung and the German Parity Welfare Union in 2000 concluded that 9.1 percent of Germans lived under the poverty level (defined as 50 percent or less of the average per capita income level)—8.7 percent in the West and 10.7 percent in the East: "Jeder elfte lebt unter der Armutsgrenze," *Frankfurter Allgemeine Zeitung,* 5 October 2000, 18.

55. In 1981, 2.6 percent of the total population earned less than 40 percent, 5.3 percent less than 50 percent, and 10.6 percent less than 60 percent of the median income. By 2000, these figures had risen to 4.9 percent, 8.3 percent, and 13.1 percent, respectively: data from Atkinson et al., *Inégalités économiques,* 229; Luxembourg Income Survey, "Relative Poverty Rates for the Total Population, Children and the Elderly," table, available online at www.lisproject.org/keyfigures/povertytable.htm (accessed 13 April 2009). Over the same period, poverty rates for children increased even more rapidly than those for the population as a whole.

56. This stagnation of benefits was also partly attributable to actions taken by the municipalities themselves, which twice blocked federal initiatives to increase the consumption basket: Katzenstein, *Policy and Politics,* 185.

57. Karl de Meyer, "L'Allemagne se découvre 22 percent de travailleurs pauvres," *Les Echos,* 21 April 2008, 7.

58. Although the federal government lacks formal competence to devise social-assistance policies, its financial contributions to the *Länder* in other domains give it

significant potential leverage over politics on the *Land* level. The fact that it has failed to use such indirect influence (in contrast to its dealings with the *Länder* in the 2000 pension reform, discussed in Chapter 6) reflects both the low priority assigned to antipoverty measures and, more recently, the increasing federal emphasis on reducing unemployment as the chief means of improving economic welfare.

As described in Chapter 4, a variety of income-support schemes were introduced in Eastern Germany following reunification, such as a minimum pension benefit. Because such policies were part of the expansion of welfare policies in support of reunification and were limited to Eastern Germany, however, I discuss them separately.

59. In 2001, about 1.9 million people were receiving some sort of benefit under the program: "Richter urteilen über Pflegeversicherung," *Frankfurter Allgemeine Zeitung*, 3 April 2001, 19.

60. Mangen, "German Welfare and Social Citizenship," 262–263. Initial estimates put the savings to the municipalities at DM 5 billion per year.

61. Breuer and Engels, "Basic Information and Data on Social Assistance in Germany," 19, 32.

62. Wilfried Herz, "Karlsruhe korrigiert die Pflegeversicherung zu Recht," *Die Zeit*, vol. 15, 12 April 2001, 1.

63. Borrowing the second part of the formulation used by Bill Clinton during his pursuit of American welfare reform ("Welfare is a second chance, not a way of life"), Koch entitled his manifesto, published in the *Frankfurter Allgemeine Zeitung*, "Sozialhilfe ist kein Lebensstil," 22 August 2001. Koch lauded the "Wisconsin model" and proclaimed that, if such a policy were adopted by all German *Länder*, the number of social-assistance recipients would be halved.

64. One CDU/CSU social-policy expert on Seehofer's staff identified the major problem with *Sozialhilfe* as the fact that the right to benefits is independent of "effort" rather than its lack of generosity or the system's shaky financial situation: interview, Dr. Christoph Wilk, CDU/CSU Fraktion im Bundestag, 19 March 2001.

65. In 2001, the Red–Green coalition passed the so-called BAFÖG, or Federal Assistance Training Act, which provides a mixture of grants and loans to students enrolled in universities. Both the Schröder administration and the current grand coalition have regularly increased the subsidy, most recently in 2007. For details, see Federal Ministry for Education and Research webpage, available online at http://www.das-neue-bafoeg.de.

66. The data are drawn from Luxembourg Income Study (LIS) Key Figures, available online at http://www.lisproject.org/keyfigures.htm (accessed 13 April 2009).

67. Organization for Economic Cooperation and Development (OECD), *Society at a Glance: OECD Social Indicators* (Paris: OECD, 2005), 53.

68. "Class Concerns," *Economist*, 11–17 November 2006, 60.

69. For details, see "Kein gesetzlicher Mindestlohn: Tarifliche und gesetzliche Untergrenzen in allen Branchen," *Frankfurter Allgemeine Zeitung*, 20 June 2007, 2.

70. According to officials in the Labor Ministry, declining membership and the challenging economic climate have weakened unions' negotiating position and provided them with incentives to accept the minimum-wage law as a boost to their members' incomes, despite the undermining of *Tarifautonomie*. Here, too, the state is stepping in to broker deals that the social partners are either unwilling or unable to accomplish: interview, Dr. Günther Horzetzky, Bundesministerium für Arbeit und Soziales, 23 July 2007.

71. In November 2007, the SPD and CDU agreed to extend the duration of eligibility for unemployment insurance for workers older than fifty. Partially reversing the Hartz IV reform's limitation of eligibility for unemployment insurance to a year, the new measure extends eligibility to fifteen months for workers age fifty to fifty-five, eighteen months for those age fifty-six to fifty-eight, and two full years for those older than fifty-eight: Patrice Drouin, "Baisse des cotisations chômage et accord sur l'indemnisation des plus de 50 ans," *Les Echos,* 14 November 2007, 9.

CONCLUSION

1. Gøsta Esping-Andersen, *The Three Worlds of Welfare Capitalism* (Princeton, N.J.: Princeton University Press, 1990).

2. See, e.g., Bernhard Ebbinghaus and Philip Manow, eds., *Comparing Welfare Capitalism: Social Policy and Political Economy in Europe, Japan and the USA* (London: Routledge, 2001).

3. Peter Gourevitch, *Politics in Hard Times: Comparative Responses to International Economic Crises* (Ithaca, N.Y.: Cornell University Press, 1986), 17.

4. The term is Peter Katzenstein's, from *Policy and Politics in West Germany: The Growth of a Semi-Sovereign State* (Philadelphia: Temple University Press, 1987).

5. For excellent analyses of the varied character of new forms of state intervention, see the chapters in Jonah D. Levy, ed., *The State after Statism: New State Activities in the Age of Liberalization* (Cambridge, Mass.: Harvard University Press, 2006).

6. See, e.g., Ebbinghaus and Manow, *Comparing Welfare Capitalism.* For less explicit but important moves toward such an integrated approach, see Wolfgang Streeck and Kozo Yamamura, "Introduction: Convergence or Diversity? Stability and Change in German and Japanese Capitalism," in *The End of Diversity? Prospects for German and Japanese Capitalism,* ed. Wolfgang Streeck and Kozo Yamamura (Ithaca, N.Y.: Cornell University Press, 2003).

7. Philip Manow, "Welfare State Building and Coordinated Capitalism in Japan and Germany," in *The Origins of Nonliberal Capitalism: Germany and Japan in Comparison,* ed. Wolfgang Streeck and Kozo Yamamura (Ithaca, N.Y.: Cornell University Press, 2001), 96. Although Manow cites work by some contributors to the *Varieties of Capitalism* volume as exceptions to this pattern, those studies limit their focus to social policies, such as vocational training systems and unemployment insurance, that directly shape incentives faced by firms, rather than considering the overall structure of social protection and its relationship to the organization of the economy. See Isabela Mares, "Firms and the Welfare State: When, Why, and How Does Social Policy Matter to Employers?" and Margarita Estevez-Abe, Torben Iversen, and David Soskice, "Social Protection and the Formation of Skills: A Reinterpretation of the Welfare State," in *Varieties of Capitalism: The Institutional Foundations of Comparative Advantage,* ed. Peter A. Hall and David Soskice (Oxford: Oxford University Press, 2001).

8. One of the central reasons for this limitation is the approach's "extremely thin notion of politics and state action" and "a latent functionalism in which capitalist political economies and the social relations that undergird them are fundamentally nonconflictual": Chris Howell, "Varieties of Capitalism: And Then There Was One?" *Comparative Politics* 36, no. 1 (October 2003): 110. A recent follow-up volume to *Varieties of Capitalism*

employs a more complex typology that includes "statist" and "compensating state" categories but does little to alter the presumption of self-reinforcing policy and institutional patterns in each of the four categories. Consequently, it fails to correct for the approach's underestimation of the degree to which political economies are capable of change or the role of politics and the state in mediating it: Bob Hancké, Martin Rhodes, and Mark Thatcher, eds., *Beyond Varieties of Capitalism: Conflict, Contradictions, and Complementarities in the European Economy* (Oxford: Oxford University Press, 2007).

9. Mark Blyth, *Great Transformations: Economic Ideas and Institutional Change in the Twentieth Century* (Cambridge: Cambridge University Press, 2002), 11.

Index